D1014874

BLOOM'S

HOW TO WRITE ABOUT

Emily Dickinson

ANNA PRIDDY

Introduction by Harold Bloom

BLOOM'S
LITERARY CRITICISM
An imprint of Infobase Publishing

Bloom's How to Write about Emily Dickinson

Copyright © 2008 by Anna Priddy

Bloom's Literary Criticism
An imprint of Infobase Publishing
132 West 31st Street
New York NY 10001

Library of Congress Cataloging-in-Publication Data
Priddy, Anna.
    Bloom's how to write about Emily Dickinson / Anna Priddy; introduction by Harold Bloom.
        p. cm.
    Includes bibliographical references and index.
    ISBN 978-0-7910-9492-1 (alk. paper)
    1. Dickinson, Emily, 1830–1886—Criticism and interpretation. 2. Criticism—Authorship. 3. Report writing. I. Bloom, Harold. II. Title. III. Title: How to write about Emily Dickinson.
    PS1541.Z5P75 2008
    811'.4—dc22   2006100573

Text design by Annie O'Donnell
Cover design by Ben Peterson

Printed in the United States of America

Bang FOF 10 9 8 7 6 5 4 3 2 1

CONTENTS

Series Introduction v

Volume Introduction vi

How to Write a Good Essay 1

How to Write about Emily Dickinson 41

#67—"Success is counted sweetest" 61

#214—"I taste a liquor never brewed" 72

#258—"There's a certain Slant of light" 79

#280—"I felt a Funeral, in my Brain" 90

#288—"I'm Nobody! Who are you?" 103

#303—"The Soul selects her own Society" 111

#324—"Some keep the Sabbath going to Church" 121

#341—"After great pain, a formal feeling comes" 127

#435—"Much Madness is divinest Sense" 139

#441—"This is my letter to the World" 145

#448—"This was a Poet—It is That" 156

#465—"I heard a Fly buzz—when I died" 162

#569—"I reckon—when I count at all" 177

#585—"I like to see it lap the Miles" 183

#613—"They shut me up in Prose" 195

#657—"I dwell in Possibility" 203

#712—"Because I could not stop for Death"   214

#754—"My Life had stood—a Loaded Gun"   230

#1129—"Tell all the Truth but tell it slant"   240

#1732—"My life closed twice before its close"   250

Index   256

SERIES
INTRODUCTION

BLOOM's How to Write about Literature series is designed to inspire students to write fine essays on great writers and their works. Each volume in the series begins with an introduction by Harold Bloom, meditating on the challenges and rewards of writing about the volume's subject author. The first chapter then provides detailed instructions on how to write a good essay, including how to find a thesis; how to develop an outline; how to write a good introduction, body text, and conclusions; how to cite sources; and more. The second chapter provides a brief overview of the issues involved in writing about the subject author and then a number of suggestions for paper topics, with accompanying strategies for addressing each topic. Succeeding chapters cover the author's major works.

The paper topics suggested within this book are open-ended, and the brief strategies provided are designed to give students a push forward on the writing process rather than a roadmap to success. The aim of the book is to pose questions, not answer them. Many different kinds of papers could result from each topic. As always, the success of each paper will depend completely on the writer's skill and imagination.

HOW TO WRITE ABOUT EMILY DICKINSON: INTRODUCTION

by Harold Bloom

1

AFTER FIFTY-THREE consecutive years of teaching at Yale, writing more than thirty books and about a thousand introductions, essays, and reviews, and having read incessantly morn through night for nearly three-quarters of a century, I came to realize that teaching, writing, and reading are, for me, three words for the same activity. The ancients regarded what we call rhetoric, psychology, and cosmology as three names for the one entity. Rhetoric is the art of persuasion and defense, while psychology is our ongoing quest for identity, and cosmology our projection of ourselves into the heavens.

Emily Dickinson and William Blake seem to me the two poets in Anglo-American tradition who revive in themselves something of William Shakespeare's highly original cognitive power. Like Shakespeare, Dickinson and Blake thought everything through again for themselves, almost as if there had been no philosophers before them. The quarrel between poetry and philosophy is very old, going back to the Pre-Socratics, the Hebrew prophets, the forest sages of early India, and the masters of the Tao who may have preceded Confucius. Plato, philosopher and poet, cast out all external poets, and after a lifetime of internal struggle exiled the poet within himself in his harsh, late treatise, the

Laws. Dickinson, like Shakespeare, was no problem-solver, while the apocalyptic Blake took on the prophetic burden of the Valley of Vision. Emily Dickinson is not quite the very greatest of American poets, but she is only a step or two behind our father, the old man Walt Whitman, who has affected all the world beyond the United States, as well as altering his and our nation. Dickinson asserted that she declined to read Whitman, presumably because he was indecorous, yet I suspect that her irony was in play, as she always was darkly playful, and I sometimes detect a glint and glimmer of Walt in the recluse of Amherst.

2

Writing about Emily Dickinson tends not to engage her agile believings and disbelievings, her deliberate evasions of our prosy explanation. Did she ever carnally embrace her unstable sister-in-law Sue? I doubt it, but scarcely believe it matters in apprehending the elusive Miss Dickinson of Amherst. Did she embrace Christ? I more than doubt it, though she saw in him a paradigm for her own sufferings, which were mostly in the realm of what Freud was to term "Mourning and Melancholia." The Viennese prophet's grand metaphor, "the work of mourning," could be an apt title for Dickinson's *Complete Poems*, now wonderfully available to us, though she published fewer than a handful of lyrics during her own life, and those anonymously. Mostly they were taken for Ralph Waldo Emerson's, which may have wryly both aroused and annoyed her.

She is very difficult to write about (or read deeply, or teach well) because she is vastly more intelligent than her critics (myself included). Shakespeare *contains* us; he is so universal and so comprehensive that sometimes I believe that I, and all my friends and enemies, are merely thoughts in his mind. Dickinson's circumference, though always expandable at her will, is more modest. She puts only a part of each of us upon her stage. Her concern is with her losses, to death and to erotic absence, and to our own vastations in those realms.

Shakespeare is always up ahead of us, as Walt Whitman attempted to be. Dickinson, unnervingly, is exactly where we are, in the unlived life or the life no longer fully lived. Her proximity governs and makes problematical the enterprise of writing useful criticism of her many hundreds of strong poems. To compose good criticism of any among them, we need to read her closely, bringing to the enterprise our own minds at their keenest and most alert. Rather than continue to state the challenge to all her readers, for whom she becomes a teacher of how to think, I will proceed with an instance. Where there is so much wealth for choice, a kind of arbitrariness had to be indulged, so that I will choose one of her poems that means most to me, but my selection is sanctioned by the justified renown this lyric enjoys.

I generally begin a sequence of classes on Dickinson with "Because I could not stop for Death—", partly because I believe it is widely and deeply misread by many, mostly through carelessness:

> Because I could not stop for Death—
> He kindly stopped for me—
> The Carriage held but just Ourselves—
> And Immortality.
>
> We slowly drove—He knew no haste
> And I had put away
> My labor, and my leisure too,
> For his Civility—
>
> We passed the School, where children strove
> At Recess—in the Ring—
> We passed the Fields of Gazing Grain—
> We passed the Setting Sun—
>
> Or rather—He passed Us—
> The Dews grew quivering and Chill—
> For only Gossamer, my Gown—
> My Tippet—only Tulle—
>
> We paused before a House that seemed—
> A Swelling of the Ground—
> The Roof was scarcely visible—
> The Cornice—in the Ground—

Since then—'tis Centuries—and yet
Feels shorter than the Day
I first surmised the Horses' Heads
Were toward eternity—

Miss Dickinson, daughter of Amherst's leading citizen—lawyer, poli-
tician, educational founder—cannot "call" upon her Amherst neighbor,
Gentleman Death, by stopping her carriage to pick him up for a courtship-
drive. Social convention is rigorously and properly preserved: Death follows
decorum by his "civility." Doubtless cards were exchanged; she was invited
and accepted a particular time on an agreed-upon day, but only to be taken
for an outing, not to die in any sense, whether literal or sexual. That is why
the Carriage also conveys the chaperone or duenna, Immortality, in addition to Death and the Lady. Note also that there is no coachman. Death, as
driver, must concentrate on the road and not on the virgin at his side.

At first, the pace is stately and slow, as is suitable, and so stays within
mundane limits: schoolchildren competing at recess games, and then
the grain fields beyond. The initial odd touch is the Pathetic Fallacy of
the Gazing Grain, which prepares us for the sudden movement of the
poem beyond *social* convention. The courtly drive turns into an abduction by a demon lover: "We passed the Setting Sun—." Dressed probably
in her Sunday best, Dickinson feels the evening Chill, and yet expresses
no alarm at what must be a speeding-up, since the Setting Sun passes Us.
After that, the poem is all questions, each unanswerable. Is her uncon-
cern the presence of Immortality? Hardly, since that mere chaperone has
no power to avert a kidnapping.

The penultimate stanza is generally misread, rather hastily, as the
description of a burial mound, yet the structure depicted belongs more
to the realm of faerie or mythology than to a Poe-like gothic. With the
final quatrain, the imperturbable victim of being carried off still displays
no anxiety or, indeed, explicit affect of any kind whatsoever. Centuries
have gone by, and yet Miss Dickinson's perspectivism remains dominant.
The centuries seem shorter than the particular day of surmise that Eternity was the journey's destination.

Emily Dickinson's ironies, like Shakespeare's or Chaucer's, are too
large to be seen by us, to borrow a fine observation from G. K. Chesterton.

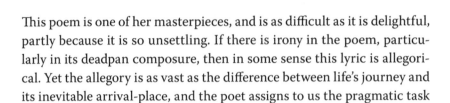

This poem is one of her masterpieces, and is as difficult as it is delightful, partly because it is so unsettling. If there is irony in the poem, particularly in its deadpan composure, then in some sense this lyric is allegorical. Yet the allegory is as vast as the difference between life's journey and its inevitable arrival-place, and the poet assigns to us the pragmatic task of determining that difference.

HOW TO WRITE
A GOOD ESSAY

W HILE THERE are many ways to write about literature, most assignments for high school and college English classes call for analytical papers. In these assignments, you are presenting your interpretation of a text to your reader. Your objective is to interpret the text's meaning in order to enhance your reader's understanding and enjoyment of the work. Without exception, strong papers about the meaning of a literary work are built upon a careful, close reading of the text or texts. Careful, analytical reading should always be the first step in your writing process. This volume provides models of such close, analytical reading, and these should help you develop your own skills as a reader and as a writer.

As the examples throughout this book demonstrate, attentive reading entails thinking about and evaluating the formal (textual) aspects of the author's works: theme, character, form, and language. In addition, when writing about a work, many readers choose to move beyond the text itself to consider the work's cultural context. In these instances, writers might explore the historical circumstances of the time period in which the work was written. Alternatively, they might examine the philosophies and ideas that a work addresses. Even in cases where writers explore a work's cultural context, though, papers must still address the more formal aspects of the work itself. A good interpretative essay that evaluates Charles Dickens's use of the philosophy of utilitarianism in his novel *Hard Times*, for example, cannot adequately address the author's treatment of the philosophy without firmly grounding this discussion in the book itself. In other words, any analytical paper about a text, even

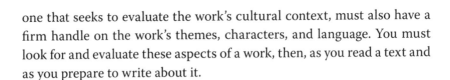

one that seeks to evaluate the work's cultural context, must also have a firm handle on the work's themes, characters, and language. You must look for and evaluate these aspects of a work, then, as you read a text and as you prepare to write about it.

WRITING ABOUT THEMES

Literary themes are more than just topics or subjects treated in a work; they are attitudes or points about these topics that often serve to structure other elements in a work. Writing about themes therefore requires that you not just identify a topic that a literary work addresses but also discuss what that work says about that topic. For example, if you were writing about the culture of the American South in William Faulkner's famous story "A Rose for Emily," you would need to discuss what Faulkner says, argues, or implies about that culture and its passing.

When you prepare to write about thematic concerns in a work of literature, you will probably discover that, like most works of literature, your text touches upon other themes in addition to its central theme. These secondary themes also provide rich ground for paper topics. A thematic paper on "A Rose for Emily" might consider gender or race in the story. While neither of these could be said to be the central theme of the story, they are clearly related to the passing of the "old South" and could provide plenty of good material for papers.

As you prepare to write about themes in literature, you might find a number of strategies helpful. After you identify a theme or themes in the story, you should begin by evaluating how other elements of the story—such as character, point of view, imagery, and symbolism—help to develop the theme. You might ask yourself what your own responses are to the author's treatment of the subject matter. Do not neglect the obvious, either: What expectations does the title set up? How does the title help develop thematic concerns? Clearly, the title "A Rose for Emily" says something about the narrator's attitude toward the title character, Emily Grierson, and all she represents.

WRITING ABOUT CHARACTER

Generally, characters are essential components of fiction and drama. (This is not always the case, though; Ray Bradbury's "August 2026: There

Will Come Soft Rains" is technically a story without characters, at least any human characters.) Often, you can discuss character in poetry, as in T. S. Eliot's "The Love Song of J. Alfred Prufrock" or Robert Browning's "My Last Duchess." Many writers find that analyzing character is one of the most interesting and engaging ways to work with a piece of literature and to shape a paper. After all, characters generally are human, and we all know something about being human and living in the world. While it is always important to remember that these figures are not real people but creations of the writer's imagination, it can be fruitful to begin evaluating them as you might evaluate a real person. Often you can start with your own response to a character. Did you like or dislike the character? Did you empathize with the character? Why or why not?

Keep in mind, though, that emotional responses like these are just starting places. In order to truly explore and evaluate literary characters, you need to return to the formal aspects of the text and evaluate how the author has drawn these characters. The 20th-century writer E. M. Forster coined the terms *flat* and *round* characters. Flat characters are static, one-dimensional characters who frequently represent a particular concept or idea. In contrast, round characters are fully drawn and much more realistic characters who frequently change and develop over the course of a work. Are the characters you are studying flat or round? What elements of the characters lead you to this conclusion? Why might the author have drawn characters like this? How does their development affect the meaning of the work? Similarly, you should explore the techniques the author uses to develop characters. Do we hear a character's own words, or do we hear only other characters' assessments of him or her? Or, does the author use an omniscient or limited omniscient narrator (one who knows and sees all) to allow us access to the workings of the characters' minds? If so, how does that help develop the characterization? Often, you can even evaluate the narrator as a character. How trustworthy are the opinions and assessments of the narrator? You should also think about characters' names. Do they mean anything? If you encounter a hero named Sophia or Sophie, you should probably think about her wisdom (or lack thereof) since *Sophia* means "wisdom" in Greek. Similarly, since the name *Sylvia* is derived from the word *sylvan*, meaning "of the wood," you might want to evaluate that character's relationship with nature. Once again, you might look to the title of the work. Does Herman Melville's "Bartleby, the Scrivener" signal anything about Bartleby himself? Is Bartleby adequately defined by his job as scrivener? Is this part of Melville's point? Pursuing questions like these can help you develop thorough papers about characters from psychological, sociological, or more formalistic perspectives.

WRITING ABOUT FORM AND GENRE

Genre, a word derived from French, means "type" or "class." Literary genres are distinctive classes or categories of literary composition. On the most general level, literary works can be divided into the genres of drama, poetry, fiction, and essays, yet within those genres there are classifications that are also referred to as genres. Tragedy and comedy, for example, are genres of drama. Epic, lyric, and pastoral are genres of poetry.

Form, on the other hand, generally refers to the shape or structure of a work. There are many clearly defined forms of poetry that follow specific patterns of meter, rhyme, and stanza. Sonnets, for example, are poems that follow a fixed form of 14 lines. Sonnets generally follow one of two basic sonnet forms, each with its own distinct rhyme scheme. Haiku is another example of poetic form, traditionally consisting of three unrhymed lines of five, seven, and five syllables.

While you might think that writing about form or genre might leave little room for argument, many of these forms and genres are very fluid. Remember that literature is evolving and ever changing, and so are its forms. As you study poetry, you may find that poets, especially more modern poets, play with traditional poetic forms, bringing about new effects. Similarly, dramatic tragedy was once quite narrowly defined, but over the centuries playwrights have broadened and challenged traditional definitions, changing the shape of tragedy. When Arthur Miller wrote *Death of a Salesman,* many critics challenged the idea that tragic drama could encompass a common man like Willy Loman.

Evaluating how a work of literature fits into or challenges the boundaries of its form or genre can provide you with fruitful avenues of investigation. You might find it helpful to ask why the work does or does not fit into traditional categories. Why might Miller have thought it fitting to write a tragedy of the common man? Similarly, you might compare the content or theme of a work with its form. How well do they work together? Many of Emily Dickinson's poems, for instance, follow the meter of traditional hymns. While some of her poems seem to express traditional religious doctrines, many seem to challenge or strain against traditional conceptions of God and theology. What is the effect, then, of her use of traditional hymn meter?

WRITING ABOUT LANGUAGE, SYMBOLS, AND IMAGERY

No matter what the genre, writers use words as their most basic tool. Language is the most fundamental building block of literature. It is essential that you pay careful attention to the author's language and word choice as you read, reread, and analyze a text. Imagery is language that appeals to the senses. Most commonly, imagery appeals to the sense of vision, creating a mental picture, but authors also use language that appeals to other senses. Images can be literal or figurative. Literal images use sensory language to describe an actual thing. In the broadest terms, figurative language uses one thing to speak about something else. For example, if I call my boss a snake, I am not saying that he is literally a reptile. Instead, I am using figurative language to communicate my opinions about him. Since we think of snakes as sneaky, slimy, and sinister, I am using the concrete image of a snake to communicate these abstract opinions and impressions.

The two most common figures of speech are similes and metaphors. Both are comparisons between two apparently dissimilar things. Similes are explicit comparisons using the words *like* or *as;* metaphors are implicit comparisons. To return to the previous example, if I say, "My boss, Bob, was waiting for me when I showed up to work five minutes late today—the snake!" I have constructed a metaphor.

Writing about his experiences fighting in World War I, Wilfred Owen begins his poem "Dulce et decorum est," with a string of similes: "Bent double, like old beggars under sacks, / Knock-kneed, coughing like hags, we cursed through sludge." Owen's goal was to undercut clichéd notions that war and dying in battle were glorious. Certainly, comparing soldiers to coughing hags and to beggars underscores his point.

"Fog," a short poem by Carl Sandburg, provides a clear example of a metaphor. Sandburg's poem reads:

The fog comes
on little cat feet.

It sits looking
over harbor and city
on silent haunches
and then moves on.

Notice how effectively Sandburg conveys surprising impressions of the fog by comparing two seemingly disparate things—the fog and a cat.

Symbols, by contrast, are things that stand for, or represent, other things. Often they represent something intangible, such as concepts or ideas. In everyday life we use and understand symbols easily. Babies at christenings and brides at weddings wear white to represent purity. Think, too, of a dollar bill. The paper itself has no value in and of itself. Instead, that paper bill is a symbol of something else, the precious metal in a nation's coffers. Symbols in literature work similarly. Authors use symbols to evoke more than a simple, straightforward, literal meaning. Characters, objects, and places can all function as symbols. Famous literary examples of symbols include Moby-Dick, the white whale of Herman Melville's novel, and the scarlet *A* of Nathaniel Hawthorne's *The Scarlet Letter.* As both of these symbols suggest, a literary symbol cannot be adequately defined or explained by any one meaning. Hester Prynne's Puritan community clearly intends her scarlet *A* as a symbol of her adultery, but as the novel progresses, even her own community reads the letter as representing not just "adultery," but "able," "angel," and a host of other meanings.

Writing about imagery and symbols requires close attention to the author's language. To prepare a paper on symbolism or imagery in a work, identify and trace the images and symbols and then try to draw some conclusions about how they function. Ask yourself how any symbols or images help contribute to the themes or meanings of the work. What connotations do they carry? How do they affect your reception of the work? Do they shed light on characters or settings? A strong paper on imagery or symbolism will thoroughly consider the use of figures in the text and will try to reach some conclusions about how or why the author uses them.

WRITING ABOUT HISTORY AND CONTEXT

As noted above, it is possible to write an analytical paper that also considers the work's context. After all, the text was not created in a vacuum. The author lived and wrote in a specific time period and in a specific cultural context and, like all of us, was shaped by that environment. Learning more about the historical and cultural circumstances that surround the author and the work can help illuminate a text and provide you with productive material for a paper. Remember, though, that when you write analytical papers, you should use the context to illuminate the text. Do not lose sight of your goal—to interpret the meaning of the literary work. Use historical or philosophical research as a tool to develop your textual evaluation.

Thoughtful readers often consider how history and culture affected the author's choice and treatment of his or her subject matter. Investigations into the history and context of a work could examine the work's relation to specific historical events, such as the Salem witch trials in 17th-century Massachusetts or the Restoration of Charles to the British throne in 1660. Bear in mind that historical context is not limited to politics and world events. While knowing about the Vietnam War is certainly helpful in interpreting much of Tim O'Brien's fiction, and some knowledge of the French Revolution clearly illuminates the dynamics of Charles Dickens's *A Tale of Two Cities,* historical context also entails the fabric of daily life. Examining a text in light of gender roles, race relations, class boundaries, or working conditions can give rise to thoughtful and compelling papers. Exploring the conditions of the working class in 19th-century England, for example, can provide a particularly effective avenue for writing about Dickens's *Hard Times.*

You can begin thinking about these issues by asking broad questions at first. What do you know about the time period and about the author? What does the editorial apparatus in your text tell you? These might be starting places. Similarly, when specific historical events or dynamics are particularly important to understanding a work but might be somewhat obscure to modern readers, textbooks usually provide notes to explain historical background. These are a good place to start. With this information, ask yourself how these historical facts and circumstances might have affected the author, the presentation of theme, and the presentation of character. How does knowing more about the work's specific historical context illuminate the work? To take a well-known example, understanding the complex attitudes toward slavery during the time Mark Twain wrote *Adventures of Huckleberry Finn* should help you begin to examine issues of race in the text. Additionally, you might compare these attitudes to those of the time in which the novel was set. How might this comparison affect your interpretation of a work written after the abolition of slavery but set before the Civil War?

WRITING ABOUT PHILOSOPHY AND IDEAS

Philosophical concerns are closely related to both historical context and thematic issues. Like historical investigation, philosophical research can provide a useful tool as you analyze a text. For example, an investigation into the working class in Dickens's England might lead you to a topic on the philosophical doctrine of utilitarianism in *Hard Times*. Many other works explore philosophies and ideas quite explicitly. Mary Shelley's famous novel *Frankenstein,* for example, explores John Locke's tabula rasa theory of human knowledge as she portrays the intellectual and emotional development of Victor Frankenstein's creature. As this example indicates, philosophical issues are somewhat more abstract than investigations of theme or historical context. Some other examples of philosophical issues include human free will, the formation of human identity, the nature of sin, or questions of ethics.

Writing about philosophy and ideas might require some outside research, but usually the notes or other material in your text will provide you with basic information, and often footnotes and bibliographies suggest places you can go to read further about the subject. If you have identified a philosophical theme that runs through a text, you might ask yourself how the author develops this theme. Look at character development and the interactions of characters, for example. Similarly, you might examine whether the narrative voice in a work of fiction addresses the philosophical concerns of the text.

WRITING COMPARISON AND CONTRAST ESSAYS

Finally, you might find that comparing and contrasting the works or techniques of an author provide a useful tool for literary analysis. A comparison and contrast essay might compare two characters or themes in a single work, or it might compare the author's treatment of a theme in two works. It might also contrast methods of character development or analyze an author's differing treatment of a philosophical concern in two works. Writing comparison and contrast essays, though, requires some special consideration. While they generally provide you with plenty of material to use, they also come with a built-in trap: the laundry list. These papers often become mere lists of connections between the works. As this chapter will discuss, a strong thesis must make an assertion that you want to prove or validate. A strong comparison and contrast thesis, then, needs to comment on the significance of the similarities and the differences you observe. It is not enough merely to assert that the works contain similarities and differences. You might, for example, assert why the similarities and differences are important and explain how they illuminate the works' treatment of theme. Note that a thesis should not be a statement of the obvious. A comparison and contrast paper that focuses only on very obvious similarities or differences does little to illuminate the connections between the works. Often, an effective method of shaping a strong thesis and argument is to begin your paper by noting the similarities between the works but then to develop a thesis that asserts how these apparently similar elements are different. If, for example, you observe that Emily Dickinson wrote a number of poems about spiders, you might analyze how she uses spider imagery differently in two poems. Similarly, many scholars have noted that Hawthorne created many "mad scientist" characters, men who are so devoted to their science or their art that they lose perspective on all else. A good thesis comparing two of these characters—Aylmer of "The Birth-mark" and Dr. Rappaccini of "Rappaccini's Daughter," for example—might initially identify both characters as examples of Hawthorne's mad scientist type but then argue that their motivations for scientific experimentation differ. If you strive to analyze the similarities or differences, discuss significances, and move beyond the obvious, your paper should move beyond the laundry list trap.

PREPARING TO WRITE

Armed with a clear sense of your task—illuminating the text—and with an understanding of theme, character, language, history, and philosophy, you are ready to approach the writing process. Good writing is grounded in good reading, and close reading takes time, attention, and more than one reading of your text. Read for comprehension first. As you go back and review the work, mark the text to chart the details of the work as well as your reactions. Highlight important passages, repeated words, and image patterns. "Converse" with the text through marginal notes. Mark turns in the plot, ask questions, and make observations about characters, themes, and language. If you are reading from a book that does not belong to you, keep a record of your reactions in a journal or notebook. If you have read a work of literature carefully, paying attention to both the text and the context of the work, you have a leg up on the writing process. Admittedly, at this point, your ideas are probably very broad and undefined, but you have taken an important first step toward writing a strong paper.

Your next step is to focus, to take a broad, perhaps fuzzy topic and define it more clearly. Even a topic provided by your instructor will need to be focused appropriately. Remember that good writers make the topic their own. There are a number of strategies—often called "invention"— that you can use to develop your own focus. In one such strategy, *freewriting*, you spend 10 minutes or so just writing about your topic without referring back to the text or your notes. Write whatever comes to mind; the important thing is that you just keep writing. Often this process allows you to develop fresh ideas or approaches to your subject matter. You could also try *brainstorming*. Write down your topic and then list all the related points or ideas you can think of. Include questions, comments, words, important passages or events, and anything else that comes to mind. Let one idea lead to another. In the related technique of *clustering*, or *mapping*, write your topic on a sheet of paper and write related ideas around it. Then list related subpoints under each of these main ideas. Many people then draw arrows to show connections between points. This technique helps you narrow your topic and can also help you organize your ideas. Similarly, asking journalistic questions—Who? What? Where? When? Why? and How?—can develop ideas for topic development.

Thesis Statement

Once you have developed a focused topic, you can begin to think about your thesis statement, the main point or purpose of your paper. It is imperative that you craft a strong thesis; otherwise, your paper will likely be little more than random, disorganized observations about the text. Think of your thesis statement as a kind of road map for your paper. It tells your reader where you are going and how you are going to get there.

To craft a good thesis, you must keep a number of things in mind. First, as the title of this subsection indicates, your paper's thesis should be a statement, an assertion about the text that you want to prove or validate. Beginning writers often formulate a question that they attempt to use as a thesis. For example, a writer exploring Dickinson's poem #709— "Publication—is the Auction" might ask, What does this poem tell us about Dickinson's attitude toward the publication of her own work? While a question like this is a good strategy to use in the invention process to help narrow your topic and find your thesis, it cannot serve as the thesis statement because it does not tell your reader what you want to assert about Emily Dickinson's poem. You might shape this question into a thesis by instead proposing an answer to that question: For Dickinson, the publication of her poems equates in her mind with the selling of her very self. It is clear that in Emily Dickinson's poem #709—"Publication—is the Auction," not publishing becomes a method of self-protection. Notice that this thesis provides an initial plan or structure for the rest of the paper, and notice, too, that the thesis statement does not necessarily have to fit into one sentence.

Second, remember that a good thesis makes an assertion that you need to support. In other words, a good thesis does not state the obvious. If you tried to formulate a thesis about "Publication—is the Auction" by simply saying, Emily Dickinson believed publication to be an auction of the mind, you've done nothing but state the obvious. Since the poem's first two lines say "Publication—is the Auction / of the Mind of Man," there would be no point in spending three to five pages to support that assertion. You might try to develop a thesis from that point by asking yourself some further questions: What does it mean to auction the mind? Does the poem seem to indicate that to publish is always a negative thing? Does it explicitly condemn those who publish? How does the poem reflect upon Dickinson's own reluctance to publish? Such a line of questioning might lead you to a more viable thesis, like the one in the preceding paragraph.

As the comparison with the road map also suggests, your thesis should appear near the beginning of the paper. In relatively short papers (three to six pages) the thesis almost always appears in the first paragraph. Some writers fall into the trap of saving their thesis for the end, trying to provide a surprise or a big moment of revelation, as if to say, "TA-DA! I've just proved that Hawthorne uses color in 'Young Goodman Brown' to reflect his belief that humans are neither evil nor pure, but a mixture of both." Placing a thesis at the end of an essay can seriously mar the essay's effectiveness. If you fail to define your essay's point and purpose clearly at the beginning, your reader will find it difficult to assess the clarity of your argument and understand the points you are making. When your argument comes as a surprise at the end, you force your reader to reread your essay in order to assess its logic and effectiveness.

Finally, you should avoid using the first person ("I") as you present your thesis. Though it is not strictly wrong to write in the first person, it is difficult to do so gracefully. While writing in the first person, beginning writers often fall into the trap of writing self-reflexive prose (writing about their paper in their paper). Often this leads to the most dreaded of opening lines: "In this paper, I am going to discuss . . ." Not only does this voice make for very awkward prose; it frequently allows writers to boldly announce a topic while completely avoiding a thesis statement. An example might be a paper that begins as follows: "Publication—is the Auction," one of Emily Dickinson's more popular poems, discusses how publication is equivalent to selling the mind. In this paper, I am going to discuss the significance of publishing in this poem and in Dickinson's life. The author of this paper has done little more than announce a topic for the paper (the significance of publishing). While the last sentence might be intended as a thesis, the writer fails to present an opinion about the significance of publishing in the poem. To improve this "thesis," the writer would need to back up a couple of steps. First, the announced topic of the paper is too broad; literary scholars have discussed Dickinson's attitudes toward publication for more than a hundred years without yielding any one, definitive interpretation. The writer should first consider some of the many ideas related to publication presented in the text. From here, the author could select the idea that seems most appealing and then begin to craft a specific thesis. A writer who chooses to explore the relationship between publication and God might, for example, craft a thesis that reads, `Emily Dickinson reveals her belief that poetry is a gift from God in "Publication—is the Auction."`

Outline

While developing a strong, thoughtful thesis early in your writing process should help focus your paper, outlining provides an essential tool for logically shaping that paper. A good outline helps you see—and develop—the relationships among the points in your argument and assures you that your paper flows logically and coherently. Outlining not only helps place your points in a logical order but also helps you subordinate supporting points, weed out any irrelevant points, and decide if there are any necessary points that are missing from your argument. Most of us are familiar with formal outlines that use numerical and letter designations for each point. However, there are different types of outlines; you may find that an informal outline is a more useful tool for you. What is important is that you spend the time to develop some sort of outline—formal or informal.

An outline is a tool to help you shape and write a strong paper. If you do not spend sufficient time planning your supporting points and shaping the arrangement of those points, you will most likely construct a vague, unfocused outline that provides little, if any, help with the writing of the paper. Consider the following example.

`Thesis: Emily Dickinson reveals her belief that poetry is a gift from God in "Publication—is the Auction."`

`I. Introduction and Thesis`

`II. References to God`
    `A. The White Creator`
    `B. Him`
    `C. Royal Air`
    `D. Heavenly Grace`

```
III. Dickinson's Publication History

IV. Justifications
    A. Poverty

V. Negative Images of Publication

VI. Conclusion
    A. Poetry is a gift from God
```

This outline has a number of flaws. First, the major topics labeled with the Roman numerals are not arranged in a logical order. If the paper's aim is to show that Dickinson's poem reveals the belief that poetry is a gift from God, a more likely arrangement would be to move linearly through the poem, discussing the images of poetry as God given as they appear. Similarly, the thesis makes no reference to Dickinson's publication history or to the possible justifications for publishing, yet the writer includes each of them as major sections of this outline. Both of these topics may well have a place in this paper, but the writer fails to provide detail about their place in the argument. Third, the writer includes the "Royal Air" and "Heavenly Grace" among the lettered items in section II. Letters A and B refer directly to God; "Royal Air" and "Heavenly Grace" both refer to poetry and do not belong in this list. One could argue that these refer to poetry in terms of its being godlike and God given, but this would not make it a direct reference to God. A fourth problem is the inclusion of a letter A in sections IV and VI. An outline should not include an A without a B, a 1 without a 2, and so forth. The final problem with this outline is the overall lack of detail. None of the sections provides much information about the content of the argument, and it seems likely that the writer has not given sufficient thought to the content of the paper.

A better start to this outline might be the following:

```
Thesis: Emily Dickinson reveals her belief that poetry
is a gift from God in "Publication—is the Auction."

    I. Introduction and Thesis
```

```
II. Stanza 2
    A. Reference to God: White Creator
    B. Reference to Poetry: Our Snow

III. Stanza 3
    A. Reference to God: Him
    B. Reference to Poetry: Royal Air

IV. Results of Publication
    A. The selling of the mind
    B. The sullying of the self
    C. The diminishment of the Human Spirit

 V. Conclusion
```

This new outline would prove much more helpful when it came to write the paper.

An outline like the latter could be shaped into an even more useful tool if the writer fleshed out the argument by providing specific examples from the text to support each point. Once you have listed your main point and your supporting ideas, develop this raw material by listing related supporting ideas and material under each of those main headings. From there, arrange the material in subsections, and order the material logically.

For example, you might begin with one of the theses cited above: For Dickinson, the publication of her poems equates in her mind with the selling of her very self. In Emily Dickinson's #709—"Publication—is the Auction," not publishing becomes a method of self-protection. As noted above, this thesis already gives you the beginning of an organization: Start supporting the thesis by showing how publication is linked to the selling of the self. You might begin your outline, then, with three topic headings: (1) publication as disgrace, (2) owning her self, and (3) divided attitude toward the world. Under each of those headings you could list ideas that support the particular point. Be sure to include references to parts of the text that help build your case. An informal outline might look like this:

Thesis: For Dickinson, the publication of her poems equates in her mind with the selling of her very self. In Emily Dickinson's #709—"Publication—is the Auction," not publishing becomes a method of self-protection.

1: Publication as disgrace
- "Auction / Of the Mind of Man"
- "so foul a thing"
- In other poems she talks about the pitfalls of fame
  - Poem #1659 compares it to an unwholesome meal
  - Poem #1763 compares it to a bee: "Fame is a bee / It has a song— / It has a sting— / Ah, too, it has a wing"

2: Owning her self
- The idea that publication is like an auction implies that not publishing is like owning
  - Paula Bennett: "In her art she was master of herself."
- But this leads to questions of what it means to own oneself and who the self is, as well
  - Richard Sewall believes her various signatures show a confusion about naming herself

3: Divided attitude toward the world
- Publication may have been desired, but only on her own terms
  - She wrote to Higginson: "Two editors of journals came to my father's house this winter, and asked me for my mind, and when I asked them 'why' they said I was penurious, and they would use it for the world" (Letters, 405).

- Dickinson, though, was concerned with other worlds besides the one the editors named
  - Worlds within herself: "I feel the presence of that within me, unseen, yet indescribably mighty, that can comprehend worlds & systems of worlds & yet cannot comprehend itself" (*Letters*, 241).
  - "Publication is the Auction" talks about the world of the creator, seemingly a Christian afterlife
- But she must have been conflicted
  - Sewall quotes Mrs. Ford on her belief that Dickinson actually did desire renown
- Of course, the presence of the poems belies some of this
  - "This is my letter to the World"

Conclusion:
- "Publication is the Auction" disparages publishing, though Dickinson was likely conflicted about it
- One mark of her power as a poet is her desire to be in control of her own work

You would set about writing a formal outline with a similar process, though in the final stages you would label the headings differently. A formal outline for a paper that argues the thesis about "Publication—is the Auction" cited above—Emily Dickinson reveals her belief that poetry is a gift from God in "Publication—is the Auction"—might look like this:

Thesis: Emily Dickinson reveals her belief that poetry is a gift from God in "Publication—is the Auction."

I. Introduction and thesis

    II. References to God as the giver of poetry
       A. Stanza 2: "the White Creator"
       B. Stanza 3: "Him"
          1. "Thought belong to Him who gave it"
          2. Cannot "Sell the Royal Air"
       C. Stanza 4: Poetry is "Heavenly Grace"

   III. The results of publication are all negative
       A. It is like an "auction" to the highest bidder, described as "foul" and dirty
       B. Moreover, it compromises the one who would be involved in an act like publication
          1. Images of sullying
             a. "so foul a thing"
             b. Would rather die still being "White"—a symbol for purity
          2. Price is a disgrace, as is merchandising one's self
          3. A bit like prostitution?
       C. Could publishing ever be justified? Perhaps by poverty, but the speaker would rather be poor

    IV. Conclusion:
       A. Because poetry comes from God, the poet has no right to sell what does not properly belong to him
       B. The "Human Spirit," too, comes from God
       C. Poetry is an outcry of the "Human Spirit" and thus is a sacred act

As in the previous example, the thesis provided the seeds of a structure, and the writer was careful to arrange the supporting points in a logical manner, showing the relationships among the ideas in the paper.

Body Paragraphs

Once your outline is complete, you can begin drafting your paper. Paragraphs, units of related sentences, are the building blocks of a good paper, and as you draft you should keep in mind both the function and the qualities of good paragraphs. Paragraphs help you chart and control the shape and content of your essay, and they help the reader see your organization and your logic. You should begin a new paragraph whenever you move from one major point to another. In longer, more complex essays, you might use a group of related paragraphs to support major points. Remember that in addition to being adequately developed, a good paragraph is both unified and coherent.

Unified Paragraphs

Each paragraph must be centralized around one idea or point, and a unified paragraph carefully focuses on and develops this central idea without including extraneous ideas or tangents. For beginning writers, the best way to ensure that you are constructing unified paragraphs is to include a topic sentence in each paragraph. This topic sentence should convey the main point of the paragraph, and every sentence in the paragraph should relate to that topic sentence. Any sentence that strays from the central topic does not belong in the paragraph and needs to be revised or deleted.

Consider the following paragraph about Emily Dickinson's poems, publishing, and fame. Notice how the paragraph veers away from the main point, that Dickinson had a variety of reasons for not pursuing publication.

Publication represents a sullying in this case, a disgrace to what is divine in nature. It is not only divinity contained therein, however, but also the human spirit. Purity of spirit and of motive alone is not what keeps Dickinson from pursuing publication and the fame that might accompany it. In poems like #1659, she compares fame to an overly rich and ultimately unwholesome meal. As so often in Dickinson's poems, the birds are possessed of a knowledge that human beings do not have. Those birds are a stand-in for the poet, their song and her song, even

their "ironic caw," much her own. Poem #1763 seems to
speak more to a fear that fame would be transitory. "Fame
is a bee. / It has a song— / It has a sting— / Ah, too,
it has a wing," she wrote, and one senses emotions here
running somewhere between longing and fear. At times in
Emily Dickinson's poems, the sender of the message seems
to become confused with the receiver of the message, as
in this one: "I aimed my Pebble—but Myself / Was all the
one that fell— / Was it Goliah—was too large—/ Or was
myself—too small?" (#540).

Although the paragraph begins solidly, if a bit slowly, and the third sentence provides the central theme, the author soon goes on a tangent. If the purpose of the paragraph is to demonstrate Dickinson's negative view of fame, the sentences about the sender and her message are tangential here. They may find a place later in the paper, but they should be deleted from this paragraph.

Coherent Paragraphs
In addition to shaping unified paragraphs, you must also craft coherent paragraphs, paragraphs that develop their points logically with sentences that flow smoothly into one another. Coherence depends on the order of your sentences, but it is not strictly the order of the sentences that is important to paragraph coherence. You also need to craft your prose to help the reader see the relationship among the sentences.

Consider the following paragraph about Dickinson's avoidance of publication. Notice how the writer uses the same ideas as the paragraph above, while removing all tangential material, yet fails to help the reader see the relationships among the points.

Publication represents a sullying in this case, a
disgrace to what is divine in nature. It is not only
divinity contained therein, however, but also the human
spirit. Purity of spirit and of motive alone is not
what keeps Dickinson from pursuing publication and the
fame that might accompany it. In poems like #1659,
she compares fame to an overly rich and ultimately

unwholesome meal. As so often in Dickinson's poems, the birds are possessed of a knowledge that human beings do not have. Those birds are a stand-in for the poet, their song and her song, even their "ironic caw," much her own. Poem #1763 seems to speak more to a fear that fame would be transitory. "Fame is a bee. / It has a song— / It has a sting— / Ah, too, it has a wing," she wrote, and one senses emotions here running somewhere between longing and fear.

This paragraph demonstrates that unity alone does not guarantee paragraph effectiveness. The argument is hard to follow because the author fails both to show connections between the sentences and to indicate how they work to support the overall point.

A number of techniques are available to aid paragraph coherence. Careful use of transitional words and phrases is essential. You can use transitional flags to introduce an example or an illustration (*for example, for instance*), to amplify a point or add another phase of the same idea (*additionally, furthermore, next, similarly, finally, then*), to indicate a conclusion or result (*therefore, as a result, thus, in other words*), to signal a contrast or a qualification (*on the other hand, nevertheless, despite this, on the contrary, still, however, conversely*), to signal a comparison (*likewise, in comparison, similarly*), and to indicate a movement in time (*afterward, earlier, eventually, finally, later, subsequently, until*).

In addition to transitional flags, careful use of pronouns aids coherence and flow. If you were writing about *The Wizard of Oz*, you would not want to keep repeating the phrase *the witch* or the name *Dorothy*. Careful substitution of the pronoun *she* in these instances can aid coherence. A word of warning, though: When you substitute pronouns for proper names, always be sure that your pronoun reference is clear. In a paragraph that discusses both Dorothy and the witch, substituting *she* could lead to confusion. Make sure that it is clear to whom the pronoun refers. Generally, the pronoun refers to the last proper noun you have used.

While repeating the same name over and over again can lead to awkward, boring prose, it is possible to use repetition to help your paragraph's coherence. Careful repetition of important words or phrases can lend coherence to your paragraph by reminding readers of your key points. Admittedly, it takes some practice to use this technique effectively. You may find that reading your prose aloud can help you develop an ear for effective use of repetition.

To see how helpful transitional aids are, compare the paragraph below to the preceding paragraph about Dickinson's reluctance to publish. Notice how the author works with the same ideas and quotations but shapes them into a much more coherent paragraph whose point is clearer and easier to follow.

> When Dickinson writes in #709—"Publication—is the Auction" that it is better to avoid "so foul a thing" (4) and instead go "White—Unto the White Creator" (7), she compares her writing to "Snow" (8). She lets the reader know that publication represents a sullying of the "snow," a disgrace to what is divine and God given (from the "White Creator," who is himself pure). It is not only divinity contained in the poems, she argues, but also the "Human Spirit" (15). Although these are compelling reasons to guard against any adulteration of her work, these are not the only reasons Dickinson gives for not pursuing publication and the fame that (she feared?) might follow. In #1659—"Fame is a fickle food," she compares fame to an overly rich and ultimately unwholesome meal. Here, as often in Dickinson's poems, the birds are possessed of a knowledge that human beings do not have. The birds look at the "crumbs" of fame and "Flap past it to the / Farmer's Corn— / Men eat of it and die" (8-10). Those birds are a stand-in for the poet, their song and her song, even their "ironic caw," much her own. But "Fame is a fickle food" also speaks to a fear that fame would be transitory if it came at all. In poem #1763, quoted here in its entirety, she states succinctly: "Fame is a bee. / It has a song— / It has a sting— / Ah, too, it has a wing." It seems her emotions here are moving somewhere between longing and fear.

Similarly, the following paragraph from a paper on Dickinson's early belief that her ability to write poems was a gift from God demonstrates both unity and coherence. In it, the author argues that Dickinson had a sense from a very early age, documented in the poems, that she would be a poet.

Slowly emerging in the poems, however, is an assertion of something far greater. In Dickinson's #454, "It was given to me by the Gods— / When I was a little Girl—," one finds the clear recognition on the part of the poet that she has been the recipient of a rare gift. The poem hints at what has sometimes been characterized as the arrogance of Dickinson: "Rich! 'Twas Myself—was rich— / To take the name of Gold— / And Gold to own—in solid Bars— / The Difference—made me bold—." Her recognition that in taking "the name" she becomes the owner of the object shows an early awareness of the power of language as her instrument. The recognition comes to her while still a student and even then is hidden from the others, who talk, while she knows. Dickinson believed she was called to poetry. Divinity in the form of gods, or God, or the immortal dead recognized her gifts, even if no one else did.

Introductions

Introductions present particular challenges for writers. Generally, your introduction should do two things: capture your reader's attention and explain the main point of your essay. In other words, while your introduction should contain your thesis, it needs to do a bit more work than that. You are likely to find that starting that first paragraph is one of the most difficult parts of the paper. It is hard to face that blank page or screen, and as a result, many beginning writers, in desperation to start somewhere, start with overly broad, general statements. While it is often a good strategy to start with more general subject matter and narrow your focus, do not begin with broad, sweeping statements such as All over the world, poets talk about their "gift," or, Throughout time, poetry has been related to the divine. Such sentences are nothing but empty filler. They begin to fill the blank page, but they do nothing to advance your argument. Instead, you might try to gain your readers' interest. Some writers like to begin with a pertinent quotation or with a relevant question. Or, you might begin with an introduction of the topic you will discuss. If you are writing about Dickinson's belief in the religious nature of poetry, for instance, you might begin by talking about this identification being present throughout Western culture. Another common trap to avoid is depending on your title to introduce the author and the text you are writing about. Always include the work's author and title in your opening paragraph.

Compare the effectiveness of the following introductions.

Throughout time, poetry has been related to the divine. Think about stories of classical times and the muses. Dickinson's poems often talk about poetry as a gift from God.

Since at least the time of the mythical Orpheus, whose mother was Calliope, the muse of epic poetry, and who was given the lyre by the god Apollo, poetry has been considered divine inspiration, god given. It is so closely allied with praise that the word can substitute for prayer. As Emily Dickinson wrote to her cousins upon the death of their father: "Let Emily sing for you because she cannot pray" (*Letters*, 421). With her letter, she encloses a poem, the equivalent of the prayer she cannot make, though God has given her this other means of communication. In Dickinson's poems, particularly "Publication—is the Auction," she reveals the belief that those poems are a gift from God.

The first introduction begins with a vague, overly broad sentence; cites unclear, undeveloped examples; and then moves abruptly to the thesis. Notice, too, how a reader deprived of the paper's title does not know the poem that the paper will analyze. The second introduction works with the same material and thesis but provides more detail and is conse-quently much more interesting. It begins by discussing a cultural myth regarding the origin of poetry, gives specific examples, and then speaks briefly about Dickinson's beliefs. The paragraph ends with the thesis, which includes both the author and the title of the work to be discussed.

The paragraph below provides another example of an opening strat-egy. It begins by introducing the author and the text it will analyze, and then it moves on by briefly introducing relevant details of the story in order to set up its thesis.

One question that confounds readers of Emily Dickinson's poetry is why she was so reluctant to have her work known in her lifetime. Not even her family knew, until after her death, the extent of Dickinson's writing, that she had left behind 1,775 poems. "Publication—is the Auction," poem #709, provides some insight into Dickinson's thinking. She compares publication to an "Auction / Of the Mind of Man" (1–2), and not even poverty truly justifies it. To sell what has been given you and is only yours while you are on earth is like reducing the "Human Spirit / To Disgrace of Price" (15–16). In this poem, Dickinson equates the publication of poems to the selling of her self. Not publishing, then, is a form of self-preservation.

Conclusions

Conclusions present another series of challenges for writers. No doubt you have heard the old adage about writing papers: "Tell us what you are going to say, say it, and then tell us what you've said." While this formula does not necessarily result in bad papers, it does not necessar-ily result in good ones, either. It will almost certainly result in boring papers (especially boring conclusions). If you have done a good job estab-lishing your points in the body of the paper, the reader already knows and understands your argument. There is no need to merely reiterate. Do not just summarize your main points in your conclusion. Such a bor-ing and mechanical conclusion does nothing to advance your argument or interest your reader. Consider the following conclusion to the paper about God in "Publication—is the Auction."

> In conclusion, Dickinson believes that God gave her the ability to write poems. In stanzas two and three she refers to God symbolically. She also calls her poems "Heavenly Grace" (14). It is obvious that she gives the credit for her poems to God.

Besides starting with a mechanical and obvious transitional device, this conclusion does little more than summarize the main points of the outline (and it does not even touch on all of them). It is incomplete and uninteresting.

Instead, your conclusion should add something to your paper. A good tactic is to build upon the points you have been arguing. Asking "why?" often helps you draw further conclusions. For example, in the paper on "Publication—is the Auction," you might speculate or explain why this picture of poetry as "God given" is important to understanding Dickinson. Since scholars often discuss this poem as a key to understanding her reluctance to publish, you could discuss the significance of religion in that decision. Another method of successfully concluding a paper is to speculate on other directions in which to take your topic by tying it into larger issues. You might do this by envisioning your paper as just one section of a larger paper. Having established your points in this paper, how would you build upon this argument? Where would you go next? In the following conclusion to the paper on God and "Publication—is the Auction," the author reiterates some of the main points of the paper but does so in order to amplify the discussion of the poem's theological message.

> "Publication—is the Auction" reveals that Emily Dickinson believed that the ability to write was a sacred ability, entrusted to only a few and given by God. If the poet is only the messenger and it is God who speaks through her, then the glory is his. To appear before him without having taken precious care of his gift would find her shamed and compromised. Although Dickinson's reluctance

to publish has been attributed to shyness or neuroses, "Publication—is the Auction" offers a more compelling explanation.

Similarly, in the following conclusion to the paper on "Publication—is the Auction," the author draws a conclusion that Dickinson's reluctance to publish was self-protective and characteristic of a writer who wanted to be in complete control of her work. The author incorporates references to Dickinson's own words, taken both from a letter and from another poem, to make this point. The paragraph incorporates critics who speak to Dickinson's originality and power.

The movement toward the successful realization of the poet is for Dickinson an uncommonly bold one. Haughtily, she proclaims her own power: "Rich! 'Twas Myself—was rich— / To take the name of Gold— / And Gold to own—in solid Bars— / The Difference—made me bold— (#454). Outside the poems, Dickinson was equally unrelenting, remarking that "the heart wants what it wants, or else it does not care" (*Letters* 405). This is why it is odd to find a critic who would imagine that Dickinson "possessed power in abundance but she confined it to the speaker of her verse" (Bennett 43), so clearly does her power exhibit itself in all she does. Her originality caused William Dean Howells to welcome Dickinson as a "distinctive addition to the literature of the world" (Benfey, "Mystery of Dickinson" 40). Emily Dickinson would not sell the substance of herself, her words. To her, her gift was greater than gold. When the world was ready for Dickinson the poet, it found her.

Citations and Formatting
Using Primary Sources
As the examples included in this chapter indicate, strong papers on literary texts incorporate quotations from the text in order to support their points. It is not enough for you to assert your interpretation without providing

support or evidence from the text. Without well-chosen quotations to support your argument you are, in effect, saying to the reader, "Take my word for it." It is important to use quotations thoughtfully and selectively. Remember that the paper presents your argument, so choose quotations that support your assertions. Do not let the author's voice overwhelm your own. With that caution in mind, there are some guidelines you should follow to ensure that you use quotations clearly and effectively.

Integrate Quotations:

Quotations should always be integrated into your own prose. Do not just drop them into your paper without introduction or comment. Otherwise, it is unlikely that your reader will see their function. You can integrate textual support easily and clearly with identifying tags, short phrases that identify the speaker. For example:

> As Dickinson wrote to Samuel Bowles, "If it were not
> that I could write you, you could not go away; therefore
> pen and ink are very excellent things."

While this tag appears before the quotation, you can also use tags after or in the middle of the quoted text, as the following examples demonstrate:

> "Pardon my sanity, Mrs. Holland, in a world insane, and
> love me if you will, for I had rather be loved than
> to be called a king in earth, or a lord in Heaven,"
> Dickinson continued.
>   "It is finished," wrote Emily Dickinson, "can never
> be said of us."

You can also use a colon to formally introduce a quotation:

> Instead of joining the company, Dickinson sent out
> a flower accompanied by a note that said simply: "I,
> Jesus, send mine angel."

When you quote brief sections of poems (three lines or fewer), use slash marks to indicate the line breaks in the poem:

As the poem ends, Dickinson speaks of the power of the imagination: "The revery alone will do, / If bees are few."

Longer quotations (more than four lines of prose or three lines of poetry) should be set off from the rest of your paper in a block quotation. Double-space before you begin the passage, indent it 10 spaces from your left-hand margin, and double-space the passage itself. Because the indentation signals the inclusion of a quotation, do not use quotation marks around the cited passage. Use a colon to introduce the passage:

Emily Dickinson wrote to Mrs. Holland in 1856:

> If roses had not faded, and frosts had never come, and one had not fallen here or there whom I could not waken, there were no need of other Heaven than the one below—and if God had been here this summer, and seen the things I have seen—I guess He would think His Paradise superfluous.

Dickinson expresses a belief that heaven cannot much rival Amherst.

The whole of Dickinson's poem speaks of the imagination:

> To make a prairie it takes a clover and one bee,
> One clover, and a bee,
> And revery.
> The revery alone will do,
> If bees are few.

Clearly, she argues for the creative power of the mind.

It is also important to interpret quotations after you introduce them and explain how they help advance your point. You cannot assume that your reader will interpret the quotations the same way that you do.

Quote Accurately:

Always quote accurately. Anything within quotations marks must be the author's exact words. There are, however, some rules to follow if you need to modify the quotation to fit into your prose.

1. Use brackets to indicate any material that might have been added to the author's exact wording. For example, if you need to add any words to the quotation or alter it grammatically to allow it to fit into your prose, indicate your changes in brackets:

```
Dickinson   tells   Higginson   that   she   read
"Prescott's 'Circumstance', but it followed [her]
in the dark, so [she] avoided it."
```

2. Conversely, if you choose to omit any words from the quotation, use ellipses (three spaced periods) to indicate missing words or phrases:

```
Here is another view of those noisy frogs: The
frogs sing sweet today . . . how nice to be a
frog!"
```

3. If you delete a sentence or more, use the ellipsis after a period:

```
She wrote to Higginson: "I smile when you suggest
I delay 'to publish.'. . . My barefoot rank is
better."
```

4. If you omit a line or more of poetry, or more than one paragraph of prose, use a single line of spaced periods to indicate the omission:

```
To make a prairie it takes a clover and
    one bee,
. . . . . . . . . . . . . . . . . .
And revery.
The revery alone will do,
If bees are few.
```

Punctuate Properly:

Punctuation of quotations often causes more trouble than it should. Once again, you just need to keep these simple rules in mind.

1. Periods and commas should be placed inside quotation marks, even if they are not part of the original quotation:

   > Instead of joining the company, Dickinson sent out a flower accompanied by a note that said simply: "I, Jesus, send mine angel."

   The only exception to this rule is when the quotation is followed by a parenthetical reference. In this case, the period or comma goes after the citation (more on these later in this chapter):

   > Instead of joining the company, Dickinson sent out a flower accompanied by a note that said simply: "I, Jesus, send mine angel" (272).

2. Other marks of punctuation—colons, semicolons, question marks, and exclamation points—go outside the quotation marks unless they are part of the original quotation:

   > Why does Dickinson tell Higginson that she "never had a Mother"?

   > Dickinson asks, "Did I sing—too loud?"

Documenting Primary Sources

Unless you are instructed otherwise, you should provide sufficient information for your reader to locate material you quote. Generally, literature papers follow the rules set forth by the Modern Language Association (MLA). These can be found in the *MLA Handbook for Writers of Research Papers* (sixth edition). You should be able to find this book in the reference section of your library. Additionally, its rules for citing both primary and secondary sources are widely available from reputable online sources. One of these is the Online Writing Lab (OWL) at Purdue University. OWL's guide to MLA style is available at http://owl.english.

purdue.edu/owl/resource/557/01/. The Modern Language Association also offers answers to frequently asked questions about MLA style on this helpful Web page: http://www.mla.org/style_faq. Generally, when you are citing from literary works in papers, you should keep a few guidelines in mind.

Parenthetical Citations:

MLA asks for parenthetical references in your text after quotations. When you are working with prose (short stories, novels, or essays) include page numbers in the parentheses:

> Instead of joining the company, Dickinson sent out a flower accompanied by a note that said simply: "I, Jesus, send mine angel" (272).

When you are quoting poetry, include line numbers:

> Dickinson's speaker tells of the arrival of a fly: "There interposed a Fly— / With Blue—uncertain stumbling Buzz— / Between the light—and Me" (12-14).

Works Cited Page:

These parenthetical citations are linked to a separate works cited page at the end of the paper. The works cited page lists works alphabetically by the authors' last name. The above quote from Dickinson is in the Sewall biography, which would have this citation:

> Sewall, Richard. *The Life of Emily Dickinson*. 2 vols. New York: Farrar, Straus & Giroux, 1974.

The *MLA Handbook* includes a full listing of sample entries, as do many of the online explanations of MLA style.

Documenting Secondary Sources

To ensure that your paper is built entirely upon your own ideas and analysis, instructors often ask that you write interpretative papers without any outside research. If, on the other hand, your paper requires research, you must document any secondary sources you use. You need to document direct quotations, summaries or paraphrases of others' ideas, and factual information that is not common knowledge. Follow the guidelines above for quoting primary sources when you use direct quotations from secondary sources. Keep in mind that MLA style also includes specific guidelines for citing electronic sources. OWL's Web site provides a good summary: http://owl.english.purdue. edu/owl/resource/557/09/.

Parenthetical Citations:

As with the documentation of primary sources, described above, MLA guidelines require in-text parenthetical references to your secondary sources. Unlike the research papers you might write for a history class, literary research papers following MLA style do not use footnotes as a means of documenting sources. Instead, after a quotation, you should cite the author's last name and the page number:

> "In her art she was master of herself, whatever that self was, however aggressive, unwomanly, or even inhuman society might judge it to be" (Bennett 7).

If you include the name of the author in your prose, then you would include only the page number in your citation. For example:

> According to Paula Bennett, "In her art she was master of herself, whatever that self was, however aggressive, unwomanly, or even inhuman society might judge it to be" (7).

If you are including more than one work by the same author, the parenthetical citation should include a shortened yet identifiable version of the title in order to indicate which of the author's works you cite. For example:

> Christopher Benfey notes that William Dean Howells called her a "distinctive addition to the literature of the world" ("Mystery of Dickinson" 40).

Similarly, and just as important, if you summarize or paraphrase the particular ideas of your source, you must provide documentation:

> Christopher Benfey believes it was poet Adrienne Rich's
> work that touched off the current trend of feminist
> readings of Dickinson ("Dickinson and the American
> South" 44).

Works Cited Page:

Like the primary sources discussed above, the parenthetical references to secondary sources are keyed to a separate works cited page at the end of your paper. Following is an example of a works cited page that uses the examples cited above. Note that when two or more works by the same author are listed, you should use three hyphens followed by a period in the subsequent entries. You can find a complete list of sample entries in the *MLA Handbook* or from a reputable online summary of MLA style.

WORKS CITED

Benfey, Christopher. "Emily Dickinson and the American South." *The Cambridge Companion to Emily Dickinson*. Ed. Wendy Martin. Cambridge: Cambridge UP, 2002. 30–50.
———. "The Mystery of Emily Dickinson." *The New York Review of Books* 44.6 (8 April 1999): 39–44.
Bennett, Paula. *My Life a Loaded Gun: Female Creativity and Feminist Poetics*. Boston: Beacon Press, 1986.

Plagiarism

Failure to document carefully and thoroughly can leave you open to charges of stealing the ideas of others, which is known as plagiarism, and this is a very serious matter. Remember that it is important to use quotation marks when you use language used by your source, even if you use just one or two words. For example, if you wrote, in her art Dickinson was master of herself, you would be guilty of plagiarism, since you used Bennett's distinct language without acknowledging her as the source. Instead, you should write: "In her art she was master of herself" (Bennett 7). In this case, you have properly credited Bennett.

Similarly, neither summarizing the ideas of an author nor changing or omitting just a few words means that you can omit a citation. Richard Sewall's biography of Emily Dickinson contains the following quoted reminiscence from Dickinson's friend Mrs. Ford:

> I think in spite of her seclusion, she was longing for poetic sympathy and renown, and that some of her later habits of life originated in this suppressed and ungratified desire of distinction. She wore white, she shut herself away from her race as a mark of her separation from the mass of minds. I only wish the interest and delight her poems have aroused could have come early enough in her career to have kept her social and communicative, and at one with her friends (Sewall 378).

Below are two examples of passages plagiarized from Mrs. Ford's quote:

> She secluded herself because of an ungratified desire for fame. She dressed unusually and became reclusive. If she had been able to fully realize herself as a poet she would not have needed to do so.

> She did want to be famous, or she would not have begun to live as she did later. She wore white and shut herself away. If she had gotten attention for her poems, she would not have become a recluse (Sewall 378).

While the first passage does not use Mrs. Ford's exact language, it does contain the same ideas without citing her or Sewall's work. Since these are Mrs. Ford's ideas alone, this constitutes plagiarism. The second passage has shortened what Mrs. Ford said, changed some wording, and included a citation, but some of the phrasing is still Ford's. The first passage could be fixed with a parenthetical citation. Because some of the wording in the second passage remains the same, though, it would require the use of quotation marks, in addition to a parenthetical citation.

The passage below represents an honestly and adequately documented use of the original passage:

> Her friend Mrs. Ford suggested that if Dickinson had been able to fully realize herself as a poet, her life would have been lived differently. Mrs. Ford said, "She wore white, she shut herself away from her race as a mark of her separation from the mass of minds." Had she known the appreciation her work would bring, she would not have done so (Sewall 378).

This passage acknowledges that the ideas appear in Sewall's book and that they come from Mrs. Ford, while appropriately using quotations to indicate Ford's precise language.

While it is not necessary to document well-known facts, often referred to as "common knowledge," any ideas or language that you take from someone else must be properly documented. Common knowledge generally includes the birth and death dates of authors or other well-documented facts of their lives. An often-cited guideline is that if you can find the information in three sources, it is common knowledge. Despite this guideline, it is, admittedly, often difficult to know if the facts you uncover are common knowledge or not. When in doubt, document your source.

Sample Essay

Hadley Kronick
Mr. Alexander
English 160
May 23, 2007

EMILY DICKINSON AND PUBLICATION AS "AUCTION"

One question that confounds readers of Emily Dickinson's poetry is why she was so reluctant to have her work known in her lifetime. Not even her family knew, until after her death, the extent of Dickinson's writing, that she had left behind 1,775 poems. "Publication—is the Auction," poem #709, provides some insight into Dickinson's thinking. She compares publication to an "Auction / Of the Mind of Man" (1-2), and not even poverty truly justifies it. To sell what has been given you and is only yours while you are on Earth is like reducing the "Human Spirit / To Disgrace of Price" (15-16). In this poem, Dickinson equates the publication of poems to the selling of her self. Not publishing, then, is a form of self-preservation.

When Dickinson writes in #709—"Publication—is the Auction" that it is better to avoid "so foul a thing" (4) and instead go "White—Unto the White Creator" (7), she compares her writing to "Snow" (8). She lets the reader know that publication represents a sullying of the "Snow," a disgrace to what is divine and God-given (from the "White Creator," who is himself pure). It is not only divinity contained in the poems, she argues, but also the "Human Spirit" (15). Although these are compelling reasons to guard against any adulteration of her work, these are not the only reasons Dickinson gives for not pursuing publication and the fame that (she feared?) might follow. In #1659—"Fame is a fickle food," she compares fame to an overly rich and ultimately unwholesome meal. Here, as often in Dickinson's poems, the birds are possessed of a knowledge that human beings do not have. The birds look at the "crumbs" of fame and "Flap past it to the / Farmer's Corn— / Men eat of it and die" (8-10). Those birds are a stand-in for the poet, their song and her song, even their "ironic caw," much her own. But "Fame is a fickle food" also speaks to a fear that fame would be transitory if it came at all. In poem #1763, quoted immediately below in its entirety, she states succinctly: "Fame is a bee. / It has a song— / It has a sting— / Ah, too, it has a wing." It seems her emotions here are moving somewhere between longing and fear.

The possession of the voice, her own voice, was at least in part what caused Dickinson so much difficulty when faced with the prospect of actually publishing her work. Ownership of her work, and by extension herself, was supremely important to her, as Paula Bennett has recognized: "In her art she was master of herself, whatever that self was, however aggressive, unwomanly, or even inhuman society might judge it to be" (7). How best to be the owner of her work was a concern and a question that vexed her. In Richard Sewall's biography, he lists in a footnote several variants of Dickinson's signature, including Emily E. Dickinson, Emilie Dickinson, E. D., Dickinson, and sometimes merely the word *Amherst* (380). What these most suggest is someone practicing his or her autograph for the purpose of providing an autograph.

And so the pull between publication (and the fame she seemed to believe would come with it) and the realization of her work on her own terms remained a preoccupation. As she recounted to T. W. Higginson (Dickinson's friend and adviser, he was the editor of the *Atlantic Monthly*), there were the occasional calls from editors who wished to publish her work. She wrote and told him: "Two editors of journals came to my father's house this winter, and asked me for my mind, and when I asked them 'why' they said I was penurious, and they would use it for the world" (405). The "world" that the editors would use it for, however, was not the world that most concerned Dickinson. The ambition in her to go beyond the concerns of this world, to even, perhaps, achieve a fame beyond this world, is but one of the more fascinating aspects of her. The power of this woman, whose life appears so circumscribed, who could say, "I feel the presence of that within me, unseen, yet indescribably mighty, that can comprehend worlds & systems of worlds & yet cannot comprehend itself" (241), is to be wondered at.

Questions about her intent and her feelings regarding publication have persisted since the time Dickinson both sent her poems to Higginson and also turned those two editors away. Her decision struck even those who knew her as inexplicable. As Dickinson's friend Mrs. Ford wrote to Mabel Todd while Todd was at work on the editing of one of the later posthumous volumes:

> I think in spite of her seclusion, she was longing for poetic sympathy and renown, and that some of her later habits of life originated in this suppressed and ungratified desire of distinction. She wore white, she shut herself away from her race as a mark of her separation from the mass of minds. I only wish the interest and delight her poems have aroused could have come early enough in her career to have kept her social and communicative, and at one with her friends (Sewall 378).

Dickinson's wishes regarding her work are still not entirely clear. Yet, careful study of Dickinson and the temperament that comes through in her poems and her letters makes it hard not to trust her, whatever her motives might have been. It would be mere conjecture to consider what her reaction might be to her standing in American letters today, but her poems speak of fame as an inevitability.

The movement toward the successful realization of the poet is for Dickinson an uncommonly bold one. Haughtily, she proclaims her own power: "Rich! 'Twas Myself—was rich— / To take the name of Gold— / And Gold to own—in solid Bars— / The Difference—made me bold— (#454). Outside the poems, Dickinson was equally unrelenting, remarking that "the heart wants what it wants, or else it does not care" (*Letters* 405). This is why it is odd to find a critic who would imagine that Dickinson "possessed power in abundance but she

confined it to the speaker of her verse" (Bennett 43),
so clearly does her power exhibit itself in all she
does. Her originality caused William Dean Howells to
welcome Dickinson as a "distinctive addition to the
literature of the world" (Benfey 40). Emily Dickinson
would not sell the substance of herself, her words. To
her, her gift was greater than gold. When the world was
ready for Dickinson the poet, it found her.

WORKS CITED

Benfey, Christopher. "The Mystery of Emily Dickinson."
  The New York Review of Books 44.6 (8 April 1999):
  39–44.

Bennett, Paula. *My Life a Loaded Gun: Female Creativity
  and Feminist Poetics*. Boston: Beacon Press, 1986.

Dickinson, Emily. *The Letters of Emily Dickinson*. Ed.
  Thomas H. Johnson and Theodora Ward. Cambridge, MA:
  Harvard UP, 1955.

——. *The Poems of Emily Dickinson*. Ed. Thomas H. Johnson.
  3 vols. Boston: Little, Brown, 1960.

Sewall, Richard. *The Life of Emily Dickinson*. 2 vols.
  New York: Farrar, Straus & Giroux, 1974.

HOW TO WRITE ABOUT
EMILY DICKINSON

AN OVERVIEW

ONE OF the difficulties in writing about Emily Dickinson's poems is the temptation to write about Dickinson instead of her writing. As a character, Dickinson fascinates her readers. She also invites an odd familiarity. Even seasoned critics are guilty of referring to her as "Emily." Take care that you do not. As with any writer, if you do not use the entire name, simply refer to him or her by last name. You should be aware that Dickinson herself wrote to the transcendentalist Thomas Wentworth Higginson, "When I state myself, as the Representative of the Verse, it does not mean—me—but a supposed person" (*Letters* 412). You would not want to confuse Dickinson with the speaker of the poems. But we also would not say that the poet can divorce herself from all of her experience, and a biographical inquiry can be quite interesting and illuminating. A teacher may assign you to write about Dickinson's life, or a brief discussion of her background might find a place in a longer paper.

Dickinson was born in Amherst, Massachusetts, on December 10, 1830. She was her parents' middle child; her brother, Austin (1829–95), preceded her, and she had a younger sister, Lavinia (1833–99), called "Vinnie." Although Dickinson has been often portrayed as a recluse and someone therefore out of touch with the concerns of her society, this is far from the truth. Dickinson came from a socially prominent family. The Dickinsons were among the first families and founders of the town of Amherst and Amherst College. Dickinson traveled through the eastern states and spent some time in Washington, D.C., when her father served

41

in the House of Representatives from 1853 to 1854. Still, her home, called the Homestead, and her family formed the core of her life.

Her youth was unremarkable. She loved her family and her friends exceedingly. She excelled at her studies, particularly botany. She enjoyed all the pursuits common to a girl of her class at the time. The sense that she was to be a poet was perhaps with her from her early girlhood, however. She speaks in letters of a sense of possibility. Her early letters also reveal a theatric way with language and a tendency toward questioning that was to mark all of her life.

Her education placed her among the more educated women of her time. As a youth, she attended Amherst Academy. At 17, she matriculated at the Mount Holyoke Female Seminary (now Mount Holyoke College), for what was to be a two-year program of study. She stayed for only one academic year. Though it was not unusual for students to depart after one year, Dickinson's reasons for returning home have been much speculated about. The clearest reason seems to have been homesickness. Although Mount Holyoke is only 10 miles from Amherst, at the time, this distance was enough to make travel difficult. She only visited the Homestead at holidays. For someone as passionately attached to her home as Dickinson was, it was emotionally difficult to be so removed.

After the completion of her year at Mount Holyoke, she spent her 20s at home, again pursuing the normal activities of any young woman. In addition to tending to her family and the Homestead, she hosted parties and reading circles. Her circle of correspondents grew.

The years of 1861 and 1862 marked a turn in Dickinson's life. These were also the years of her greatest creativity. There is a great deal of evidence to support the belief that Dickinson underwent some grave emotional or psychological trauma at this time that somehow opened the floodgates of her poetry. The exact nature of that trauma is unknown. She wrote to Higginson about it, saying only, "I had a terror—since September—I could tell to none—and so I sing as the Boy does by the Burying Ground—because I am afraid" (*Letters* 404). She had already begun to turn more inward, but now her seclusion was near complete. She spent much of her time in her room. She rarely left her house or garden. Even to cross to Austin Dickinson's home, only a few feet away from her own, was something she rarely did.

This is particularly noteworthy because one of the most important relationships in Dickinson's life was with Susan Gilbert Dickinson, early friend to Emily Dickinson and later Austin Dickinson's wife. Like Emily Dickinson, Susan Gilbert was well read and interested in literature, and in their early years, their friendship was exceptionally close. Many of Dickinson's poems were written for or about "Sister Sue," as Dickinson sometimes referred to her. There has been some conjecture that this relationship was intimate and that Dickinson's disappointments in love stem from latent lesbian desires toward her sister-in-law and perhaps the disappointment of Gilbert's marrying her brother. The evidence of this is scant and no more than the evidence that Dickinson's great love was one of the important men in her life, perhaps the minister Charles Wadsworth or the newspaper publisher Samuel Bowles. Time showed Dickinson and Gilbert to be very different people, and eventually the friendship took place only in correspondence. Sue and Austin Dickinson's marriage was notoriously unhappy, and perhaps this contributed to the breakdown of relations between the sisters-in-law. Still, the relationship has been a focal point for critics. Susan Gilbert Dickinson was one of Emily Dickinson's earliest and most trusted readers. Emily Dickinson sent her more than 300 of her poems. After Emily Dickinson's death, Sue became one of her editors and an authority on her sister-in-law. If you were to write about their relationship, you could consider them in terms of the intimate friendships conducted by girls in 19th-century America, family dynamics, homoerotic desire, or writer and editor, among other topics.

Dickinson began to conduct more of her relationships (outside those with her immediate family) by correspondence. Some of those who came to know her later in her life never actually met with her face to face. She dressed almost entirely in white and became known as an eccentric. One of her endearing habits was to lower a basket of her baked goods from her bedroom window as schoolchildren passed on their way home.

Despite her seclusion, she was in correspondence with many of the prominent intellectuals of her time, including Bowles, editor of the *Springfield Republican,* and Higginson, editor of the *Atlantic Monthly.* Many of her poems were included in letters or were mailed as messages. She wrote, particularly, in times of illness, death, or other hardship. Her letters make wonderful reading because you see the mind of the poet at work in her prose. If nothing else, you may wish to take a look at Dickinson's *Master Letters*, written in the years just prior to 1862. Dickinson's passion for the one she called "Master" is painfully evident in them. You may wish to consider what critics and biographers have said about Dickinson's relationship with "Master," whose identity remains one of the great literary mysteries. Dickinson's letters to this person are emotionally raw and painful. It is unclear whether they were ever sent.

The most often surmised reason for Dickinson's retirement from the world is a disappointment in love. This may be so, but Dickinson was also predisposed to this sort of life. She achieved happiness in it. The poems show someone who knew what it was to feel romantic passion. She had flirtations in her youth. Her *Master Letters* show that she suffered in love as a young woman. She was involved with Judge Otis Phillips Lord, a friend of her father's, in the years leading to his death in 1884. Dickinson died on May 15, 1886, of what was then called Bright's disease, an illness of the kidneys.

After Dickinson's death, her sister found drawers full of several hundred poems. Some were bundled in hand-sewn volumes that came to be known as Dickinson's fascicles. Though her family was aware that she wrote (seven of her poems appeared in print during her lifetime), they had no idea that she had written this much or this seriously. Lavinia Dickinson wished to see the poems through to publication. Inadvertently, her efforts caused a battle that was to last nearly a century. She gave some of the poems to Sue Dickinson, her brother's wife, who had literary leanings of her own. Disappointed that Sue Dickinson was not moving as quickly with the project as she would have liked, Lavinia Dickinson gave another group of poems to another literary woman she knew, Mabel Loomis Todd. But, as Todd was Austin Dickinson's mistress, the two editors had nothing but enmity for each other. (The story of the love affair between Austin Dickinson and Mabel Loomis Todd is recounted in Polly Longsworth's *Austin and Mabel: The Amherst Affair and Love Letters of Austin Dickinson and Mabel Loomis Todd*.) In 1890, Todd and Higginson published the first collection of approximately 100 Dickinson poems. The two editors normalized spelling and punctuation and attempted to "normalize" Dickinson's verse. They also gave her poems titles, something Dickinson did not do. This changing of the poet by her editors was to happen so often that it is still possible to pick up a book of Dickinson's work and find something other than what she intended. One possible writing assignment stemming from this is to compare Dickinson's originals with the versions of her poems that were changed by others.

In 1945, Millicent Todd Bingham, Mabel Loomis Todd's daughter, released 600 more of the poems that were in her family's possession. Meanwhile, between 1914 and 1973, Martha Dickinson Bianchi, Austin and Sue Dickinson's daughter, brought out eight volumes of her aunt's verse. The definitive edition of Dickinson's poems was not released until 1955, when Thomas H. Johnson's edition was published by Harvard University Press. He returned the poems to the form of the poet's original manuscripts. In his edition, the poems are numbered in an attempt to build a chronology. Today, Dickinson's poems are often titled by Johnson's number along with the poem's first line.

One useful line of inquiry when writing about almost any writer is to consider his or her literary influences. In her letters, Dickinson left some record of her reading. The preservation of the Dickinson Homestead allowed for a record of the Dickinson library. A description of that library can be found in Richard Sewall's biography. It may not surprise you to learn that Dickinson was exceedingly well read, though you may be surprised to learn that she was rather catholic in her tastes. She read the popular works of her day, romances and fictions, periodicals, and newspapers. She read William Shakespeare and the Bible but also such contemporaries as Nathaniel Hawthorne, Ralph Waldo Emerson, Henry Wadsworth Longfellow, and Henry David Thoreau. Among her favorite writers were George Eliot, George Sand, and Elizabeth Barrett Browning.

If you wish to consider Dickinson in the context of history, you will find ample material for discussion, but she is not easily pinned down. In spite of her living through some of her country's most formative events, she seems both of her time and removed from it. Some of her verse is startlingly contemporary, yet you will see in Dickinson traces of a true New England sensibility. Her religious thought was grounded in Calvinist teaching. Some of her poems reflect the influence of transcendentalism. One of the misperceptions about Dickinson that can be refuted by considering the conditions in which she lived is that she was obsessed by death. On the contrary, she was simply surrounded by it. The country was in a civil war. Mortality due to childbirth and illness was extremely high. Furthermore, the Dickinson Homestead bordered a graveyard. Death was an integral part of life.

Most of her poems are poems of the interior, poems that seem to speak to the emotional condition of the poet or the poem's speaker. Her punctuation, you'll notice right away, is one of the clearest identifiers of a Dickinson poem. Like her poems, her letters also commonly employ the dash as their principle mark of punctuation. Why she chose to punctuate in this manner has been much debated, and the earliest editions of her work regularized the punctuation and the capitalization. However, most agree that something is lost from the poems if the poet's original is tampered with.

Often, Dickinson's meaning may be initially obscure. You may find that only in repeated readings will the meaning of the poem begin to yield itself. She never wrote a long poem. So, although you might be initially gratified to note that a poem contains only, say, eight lines, those eight lines may require just as much thought and time on the part of the reader as any longer work of literature might. The poems will ask you to slow down and pay close attention to the diction, or the word choice, of the poet. A dictionary will prove a good companion.

It is tempting to let Dickinson speak for herself, for it is a delight when she does. Here is the description she sent to Higginson when he requested a portrait: "I had no portrait, now, but am small, like the Wren; and my Hair is bold like the Chestnut Bur; and my eyes, like the Sherry in the Glass, that the Guest leaves. Would this do just as well?" (*Letters* 411). One well-known quotation from Dickinson on her definition of poetry comes from Higginson's account of their first meeting: "If I read a book and it makes my whole body so cold no fire can ever warm me, I know that is poetry. If I feel physically as if the top of my head were taken off, I know that is poetry. These are the only ways I know it. Is there any other way?" (*Letters* 474). Her letters are always worthwhile. But you should consider that her brother and sister felt that Dickinson assumed a persona in her poems that was not in keeping with the sister they knew. Since the letters are wonderfully in keeping with what readers expect from Dickinson the poet, it is possible that she was aware of herself as a literary figure when composing them.

The letters and the poems are the first place to go to begin to dispel the misperceptions that have gathered around Emily Dickinson. You will not find in them a mad poet or a frail eccentric. But these perceptions persist, so it is worthwhile to consider why. Her life was perhaps unorthodox. She was certainly original. She was a poet. And her originality of voice and vision has, for the most part, been now recognized as character and conviction. She knew what she was about.

TOPICS AND STRATEGIES

The sample topics provided below will give you some ideas to consider as you approach an essay about Emily Dickinson's work. Although many of the following topics will include some suggested poems that are later discussed in depth in this book, most of these topics can be applied to any number of Dickinson's poems. After you have decided what poems you will be discussing, you will be able to arrive at your own thesis. But again, you will find some possibilities discussed below.

Themes

There are nearly as many themes in Dickinson's work as there are poems. Following are but four important ones. Dickinson regularly returns to the idea of home in her work. Although her characterization of home is almost unfailingly positive, home does take on a variety of forms and meanings. For the most part, Dickinson tends to favor "home" above any other place, including heaven. In one letter, she wrote, "Home—is the definition of God" (Sewall 270).

Loss is a theme important to all people, and Dickinson's poems about this topic hold universal relevance. Dickinson seemed to consider loss a painful but expected part of living. Being alive necessitated it. The most final loss is likely death, but her poems look at all sorts of loss, including those in battles, or between friends and lovers.

Isolation is another common theme in Dickinson. In addition to isolation, you might examine related concepts, such as seclusion, imprisonment, solitude, and loneliness. Like loss, isolation is often portrayed as a positive in Dickinson's poems. It serves to set the speaker apart from other people, proving that she is special, even exalted. The isolation can be spiritual, physical, or psychological.

Dickinson is often characterized as a poet in love with death. Death is one of her most prevalent themes. Her poems tend to consider what

death is. What is its nature? How are we to understand it? What will it be like when it comes?

Sample Topics:

1. **Home:** What is the importance of home in Emily Dickinson's work?

Some poems you might consider on this subject are "Some kept the Sabbath going to Church," "They shut me up in Prose," "I dwell in Possibility," and "I taste a liquor never brewed." You might wish to argue that in her work there is "no place like home," simply tracing the image throughout a number of poems to arrive at some idea of how exalted the place is in her poetry.

2. **Loss:** How do Emily Dickinson's poems confront the idea of loss?

You might want to read "Success is counted sweetest," "After great pain, a formal feeling comes," and "My life closed twice before its close." Does Dickinson offer the reader some help in dealing with loss? What is it like to lose? Is it possible to be victorious in it?

3. **Isolation:** How is isolation depicted in Dickinson's poems?

You might consider "There's a certain Slant of light," "I felt a Funeral, in my Brain," "I'm Nobody! Who are you?" and "Much Madness is divinest Sense." Dickinson isolated herself from other people. Did she see this as a virtue or a failing, or both? Is there a difference between physical and psychological isolation?

4. **Death:** Is Dickinson a poet of death?

Poems in this book on the subject of death include "Success is counted sweetest," "I felt a Funeral, in my Brain," "I heard a Fly buzz—when I died," and "Because I could not stop for Death." She wrote many more, although she is hardly macabre. Death

is a universal subject. Do her poems at all enlarge our understanding of it, or do they simply reveal another person's questions about death?

History and Context

One way to approach your discussion of Emily Dickinson is to consider her
place in 19th-century America. On the subject of death, you may recognize that mortality rates were much higher than they are today. The role of
women was far different. Her work captures some of her place and time.

Her most prolific period coincided with the Civil War, though few
would characterize Dickinson as a war poet. There are no poems that
address the war specifically, but there are many that consider violence
and warfare in a general fashion, as there are many on the subject of
death. One of the few poems she allowed to be published was "Success is
counted sweetest," and that was published in the *Brooklyn Daily Union,*
a publication that diverted funds to the war effort.

Keeping in mind the caution that poetry should not be read as
strictly biography, it is at times impossible to get away from the poet's
biography. In some of Dickinson's poems, the "I" is very clearly Dickinson, despite claims to the contrary. However, you cannot take this at
face value. And the poems would not be as valuable to readers if they
were only about the poet. There must be something beyond that. But an
interesting paper can be made that knowingly looks at a work in light of
the biography.

One curious fact about Dickinson is that her poems were published
in the 20th century. It was then that she came to have the standing she
still enjoys today. In some ways, Dickinson appears to be more of a 20th-
century poet than a 19th-century poet. Some of her poems seem particularly modern in concern and in execution.

Sample Topics:

1. **The 19th century:** How can you argue that Emily Dickinson is
   a 19th-century poet?

   You might wish to consider "Success is counted sweetest," "Some
   kept the Sabbath going to Church," "I heard a Fly buzz—when I
   died," and "Because I could not stop for Death." You might argue

that Dickinson's work proves her to be a poet of her time and place, uniquely American, uniquely 19th century.

2. **The Civil War:** Can Emily Dickinson be called a poet of the Civil War?

You might wish to consider "Success is counted sweetest," "I like to see it lap the Miles," and "My life had stood—a Loaded Gun." These poems speak to the violence and progress of this time. Do you find in them any national concerns, or are their concerns all personal?

3. **Biographical contexts:** Do Dickinson's poems help you to understand her life?

"My life had stood—a Loaded Gun," "My life closed twice before its close," and "This is my letter to the World" are but a few of Dickinson's poems that could be read in light of her biography. You might argue that a poem only reveals so much about its writer. You might also wish to provide your audience with knowledge about the poet from biographical sources.

4. **The 20th century:** Can you argue that Emily Dickinson is a 20th-century poet?

Some poems that could be discussed on the topic of the 20th century are "My life had stood—a Loaded Gun," "Tell all the Truth but tell it slant," "After great pain, a formal feeling comes," and "There's a certain Slant of light." Dickinson has been embraced as a feminist, a curiously 20th-century way of reading her work. Some might call her a modernist. Others argue that she would not have enjoyed the acclaim she has received had she been published in her lifetime.

Philosophy and Ideas

Religion is a common theme in Dickinson's poems, as is any number of questions regarding faith. Often she draws a contrast between organized religion and private faith. Individual faith is depicted as more deeply felt and perhaps more true. Many of Dickinson's poems are so questioning that they border on the blasphemous.

Dickinson is often characterized as a nature poet. Certainly the love of the natural world figures prominently in her work. But in the poem "I reckon—when I count at all," she places poets ahead of both nature and heaven. Still, her poems tend to take great joy in nature and feature some of the most original depictions of the natural world and its inhabitants.

Poetry was the question that concerned Dickinson above most others. What is poetry? How does it affect us? What is life without it? How is the poet to live? These are just a few of the questions addressed in her poems. Sometimes she writes of how poetry exalts us. Sometimes poetry seems a substitute for more conventional religious belief.

Dickinson has been embraced as a feminist poet. What does she have to say on what has elsewhere been termed the *woman question?* Unlike many of her contemporaries, Dickinson seems unafraid to be frankly passionate, violent, or "unwomanly." Many of the choices she made, her seclusion, her unwed state, her unwillingness to publish, have been offered as evidence of a character that was not of her time, essentially a more modern sensibility.

Sample Topics:

1. **Faith:** What do Dickinson's poems say about faith?

   "The Soul selects her own Society," "Some keep the Sabbath going to Church," "Much Madness is divinest Sense," and "I heard a Fly buzz—when I died" could all be discussed in terms of faith. Do you see Dickinson as a religious poet? If so, how would you characterize the religion of the poems? What does she seem to distrust about organized worship?

2. **Nature:** Would you characterize Emily Dickinson as a "nature poet"?

   Some poems you might consider on this subject are "Some kept the Sabbath going to Church," "This is my letter to the World,"

"I reckon—when I count at all," and "I taste a liquor never brewed." Does she often suggest that nature is superior to the made world? How does nature disappoint? Does it ever fail? Is nature her primary concern in these poems, or does nature suggest or symbolize something else?

3. **Poetry:** Does Dickinson's work amount to a philosophy of poetry?

On this topic you might discuss "This is my letter to the World," "This was a Poet—It is That," "I reckon—when I count at all," "They shut me up in Prose," and "I dwell in Possibility." What are Dickinson's beliefs about poetry? What does it "do" for her?

4. **Women:** What does Emily Dickinson have to say on the subject of women?

Some poems you may wish to consider are "Tell all the Truth but tell it slant," "My Life had stood—a Loaded Gun," "They shut me up in Prose," and "I'm Nobody! Who are you?" Do you find evidence in her poems of a feminist sensibility? Do you think she would have embraced current views of womanhood?

Form and Genre

The following topics are general and broad. They can be applied to any poems in Dickinson's canon. You might also choose to examine them very broadly, first doing background reading on the terms themselves before considering Dickinson's work.

Sample Topics:

1. **The lyric:** How is Dickinson a lyric poet?

Dickinson is generally considered to mark the beginning of a lyric tradition in America. After doing some background reading on the subject of the lyric, you might wish to argue for or against this title. How are her poems conventional lyrics? Are there any that do not fit this definition? How does she deviate from European lyric tradition to create something new and American?

2. **Common meter:** What can be said about Dickinson's reliance on and use of common, or hymn, meter?

An overwhelming majority of Dickinson's poems are in common meter. How is it different from the form of the ballad? How does this metrical pattern function to create music? Why did Dickinson choose to work in it so often? How does she change it from its traditional religious function? These are but a few questions you might address in a paper on this topic.

3. **The fascicles:** What do the fascicles reveal about the poet or her work?

Many of Dickinson's poems were found in volumes put together and hand sewn by the poet. You may wish to look at copies of these "fascicles." From them it is possible to conjecture about many things, such as why the poet arranged the poems as she did. For instance, do you sense any narrative in the books that Dickinson made? Did she make them for herself or for an audience? What do the fascicles reveal about her disinclination to publish?

4. **Punctuation:** Does Dickinson's unorthodox system of punctuation tell us anything about the poet or her work?

This has been a subject of interest to a number of scholars. Dickinson's punctuation is unusual and idiosyncratic. She relies heavily on the dash and very rarely employs the period. To some, this gives the work a sense of urgency and open-endedness. For others, accustomed to more conventional grammar, it can be frustrating. Her early editors considered it an error and corrected it. Why do you think she makes the decisions she does? What effect do you find it has on the poems?

Symbols, Imagery, and Language

The bird is a conventional stand-in for the poet throughout all poetry, and this is also true in Dickinson's work. Often in Dickinson's poems, the birds are possessed of a knowledge that human beings do not have. Think about the ideas and emotions we associate with birds and then ask yourself how Dickinson's birds meet or fail to meet our expectations. Poem #130—"These are the days when Birds come back" could be discussed in terms of religious imagery or the images of the seasons.

Another image and symbol in Dickinson's work is light and other images of seeing. If you chose to look at this image through a number of her poems, you might find yourself wondering what the importance of light is to Dickinson. Basically, is there a meaning that the poet attaches to this that is greater or other than the meanings we conventionally assign to it? Alongside this, you might also want to look at the color white. We know that Dickinson, after she became a recluse, exclusively wore white, but no one knows why. Did the color have symbolic value to her? You might look at poems such as "Publication is the Auction" or #365—"Dare you see a Soul *at the White Heat?*" to try to answer that question.

References to "little girls" are almost considered insulting when the subject is a grown woman, but in Dickinson's poems you will find references to this small person. A particularly interesting poem on this subject is Dickinson's #454, which includes the lines "It was given to me by the Gods— / When I was a little Girl." Other poems seem to contrast the power of the adult woman with the powerlessness of the child. Strangely, Dickinson also wrote a number of poems in which the speaker talks of being a boy.

Circumference is a key word and idea in Dickinson's work, as are its variants. In "Tell all the Truth but tell it slant," Dickinson writes that "Success in Circuit lies," and *circuit* becomes synonymous with circumference. In a letter to Higginson dated July 2, 1862, Dickinson famously wrote, "My Business is Circumference." By reading Dickinson's various references to this word, you may be able to arrive at some approximation of her definition of it. She was always, it seems, concerned with the idea of circumference.

Sample Topics:

    1. **Birds:** What does Dickinson's use of the bird as a symbol reveal about the poet or her work?

    In addition to those poems discussed above, you may wish to read "Some keep the Sabbath going to Church" or "This was a Poet—It is That." You can also consult a concordance to find other mentions of birds throughout her work. Does Dickinson seem to envy the bird its song and its freedom?

    2. **Light:** What meaning does Dickinson assign to light and its variants?

    If you wished to consider this question, you might look at such poems as "I taste a liquor never brewed," "There's a certain Slant of light," "I reckon—when I count at all," and "Tell all the Truth but tell it slant." And these are simply the ones discussed at length in this book. There are many other Dickinson poems that contain imagery relating to light and seeing.

    3. **The little girl:** What role does the little girl play in Dickinson's work?

    In addition to the poems discussed above and others you might locate with the help of a concordance, you might find yourself wishing to discuss "They shut me up in Prose," "This is my letter to the World," and "I'm Nobody! Who are you?" "They shut me up in Prose" speaks literally of the time when the poem's speaker was a little girl. The other two poems seem to echo the feeling of being silenced. Does reading Dickinson's work and considering her portrayal of the girl child make her seem any more or less a feminist?

    4. **Circumference:** What does this word mean in Dickinson's lexicon?

Some poems you may wish to consult for an essay on this topic include "Tell all the Truth but tell it slant," "I dwell in Possibility," "I reckon—when I count at all," and "This was a poet—It is That." Dickinson's use of the word *circumference* is an example of how a poet can take a quotidian sort of word and cause the reader to consider its implications until the word seems to encompass vast realms of meaning.

Compare and Contrast

You will notice that the following topics do not have suggested poems mentioned. This is because any of these topics could be applied to nearly any of the poems. If you have a choice in what you write about, choose those poems that seem to have the most to say to you.

Sample Topics:

1. **Self-portrait:** Do Dickinson's poems create a portrait of their writer?

   Dickinson declined to send Higginson a portrait of herself, though she sent him poems. How can the poems be said to stand in the place of a portrait? If you were asked to characterize Dickinson using her poems as a guide, what could you say about the person?

2. **Definition of poetry:** Can you find a definition of poetry in Dickinson's work?

   Poetry is difficult to define. Some of Dickinson's poems seem to attempt to. Looking at the poems, can you elucidate a definition of poetry? How close is it to Dickinson's own? Do any of her poems make you feel "the top of your head" was taken off?

3. **Didacticism:** Would you consider Dickinson a didactic writer? That is, does she seem to want to teach her readers?

   Some of her poems have been taken as lessons on how to write poetry. Others have been read in times of mourning or loss by those who would hope to find a way to recover. Do

you believe Dickinson's poems teach anything? Was she trying to teach?

4. **Other writers:** How does Dickinson compare to other writers?
What influence has she had on other writers?

This is a very broad topic. Perhaps in your reading you have
noticed other writers that Dickinson bears an affinity to. You
might contrast her with other women writers, either of her time
or later. Adrienne Rich is a 20th-century poet who has thought
deeply about Emily Dickinson. You might look to other poets'
poems about Dickinson. Billy Collins has an interesting one.
She is often placed next to Walt Whitman and Ralph Waldo
Emerson, among her contemporaries.

Bibliography and Online Resources

Anderson, Charles. *Emily Dickinson's Poetry: Stairway of Surprise*. New York:
Holt, Rinehart, & Winston, 1960.

Aviram, Amittai. *Telling Rhythm: Body and Meaning in Poetry*. Ann Arbor: U
of Michigan P, 1994.

The Belle of Amherst. Dir. Charles S. Dubin. Perf. Julie Harris. 1976. Kino Video,
2004.

Benfey, Christopher. "Emily Dickinson and the American South." *The Cambridge Companion to Emily Dickinson*. Ed. Wendy Martin. Cambridge:
Cambridge UP, 2002. 30–50.

———. *Emily Dickinson and the Problem of Others*. Amherst: U of Massachusetts P, 1984.

———. *Emily Dickinson: Lives of a Poet*. New York: George Braziller, 1986.

———. "The Mystery of Emily Dickinson." *The New York Review of Books* 44.6
(8 Apr. 1999): 39–44.

Bennett, Paula. *Emily Dickinson: Woman Poet*. Iowa City: Iowa UP, 1991.

———. *My Life a Loaded Gun: Dickinson, Plath, Rich, and Female Creativity*.
Chicago: U of Illinois P, 1990.

Bianchi, Martha Dickinson. *Emily Dickinson Face to Face*. Boston: Houghton
Mifflin, 1932.

Boswell, Jeanetta. *Emily Dickinson: A Bibliography of Secondary Sources, with
Selective Annotations, 1890 through 1897*. Jefferson, NC: McFarland & Co.,
1989.

Budick, E. Miller. *Emily Dickinson and the Life of Language*. Baton Rouge: Louisiana State UP, 1985.

Cameron, Sharon. *"Et in Arcadia Ego:* Representation, Death, and the Problem of Boundary in Emily Dickinson." *American Woman Poets: 1650–1950*. Ed. Harold Bloom. Philadelphia: Chelsea House, 2002. 45–86.

———. *Lyric Time: Dickinson and the Limits of Genre*. Baltimore: Johns Hopkins UP, 1979.

Campbell, Donna. "Emily Dickinson." *Washington State University*. 30 Oct. 2006. 10 Aug. 2006. <http://www.wsu.edu/~campbelld/amlit/dickinson.htm>.

Chase, Richard. *Emily Dickinson*. New York: Dell, 1965.

Cody, John. *After Great Pain: The Inner Life of Emily Dickinson*. Cambridge, MA: Harvard UP, 1971.

Crumbley, Paul. "Emily Dickinson's Life." *Modern American Poetry*. 1995. 27 Apr. 2006. <http://www.english.uiuc.edu/maps/poets/a_f/dickinson/bio.htm>.

Dickinson Electronic Archives. 1994. Martha Nell Smith. 10 Aug. 2006. <http://www.emilydickinson.org/writings_menu.html>.

Donoghue, Denis. "Emily Dickinson." *Six American Poets from Emily Dickinson to the Present*. Ed. Allen Tate. Minneapolis: U of Minnesota P, 1965. 9–44.

Doriani, Beth Maclay. *Emily Dickinson: Daughter of Prophecy*. Amherst: U of Massachusetts P, 1996.

"Emily Dickinson (1830–86)." *American Literature on the Web*. 28 Aug. 2000. 3 Aug. 2006. <http://www.nagasaki-gaigo.ac.jp/ishikawa/amlit/d/dickinson19re.htm>.

Farr, Judith, ed. *Emily Dickinson: A Collection of Critical Essays*. New York: Prentice Hall, 1996.

———. *The Passion of Emily Dickinson*. Cambridge, MA: Harvard UP, 1992.

Ford, Karen. *Gender and the Poetics of Excess: Moments of Brocade*. Oxford: UP of Mississippi, 1997.

Franklin, R. W., ed. *The Manuscript Books of Emily Dickinson*. 2 vols. Cambridge, MA: Harvard UP, 1981.

———. *The Master Letters of Emily Dickinson*. Amherst, MA: Amherst College Press, 1986.

———. *The Poems of Emily Dickinson: Reading Edition*. Cambridge, MA: Harvard UP, 1999.

———. *The Poems of Emily Dickinson: Variorum Edition.* 3 vols. Cambridge, MA: Harvard UP, 1998.

Gelpi, Albert. "Emily Dickinson and the Deerslayer: The Dilemma of the Woman Poet in America." *Shakespeare's Sisters: Feminist Essays on Women Poets.* Ed. Sandra M. Gilbert and Susan Gubar. Bloomington: Indiana UP, 1981. 122–134.

Gelpi, Albert J. *Emily Dickinson: The Mind of the Poet.* Cambridge, MA: Harvard UP, 1966.

Grabher, Gudrun, Roland Hagenbuchle, and Cristanne Miller, eds. *The Emily Dickinson Handbook.* Amherst: U of Massachusetts P, 1998.

Hecht, Anthony. "The Riddles of Emily Dickinson." *Obbligati: Essays on Criticism.* New York: Atheneum, 1986. 85–117.

Higginson, T. W., and Mabel Loomis Todd, eds. *Poems by Emily Dickinson.* Boston: Roberts Brothers, 1890.

———. *Poems by Emily Dickinson, Second Series.* Boston: Roberts Brothers, 1891.

———. *Poems by Emily Dickinson, Third Series.* Boston: Roberts Brothers, 1896.

Johnson, Thomas H., ed. *Complete Poems.* Boston: Little, Brown, 1960.

———. *The Poems of Emily Dickinson, including Variant Readings Critically Compared with All Known Manuscripts.* 3 vols. Cambridge, MA: Harvard UP, 1955.

———. *Selected Letters.* Cambridge, MA: Harvard UP, 1971.

Johnson, Thomas H., and Theodora Ward, eds. *Emily Dickinson: An Interpretive Biography.* Cambridge, MA: Harvard UP, 1955.

———. *The Letters of Emily Dickinson.* 3 vols. Cambridge, MA: Harvard UP, 1979.

Juhasz, Suzanne. *The Undiscovered Continent: Emily Dickinson and the Space of the Mind.* Bloomington: Indiana UP, 1983.

Longsworth, Polly. *Austin and Mabel: The Amherst Affair and Love Letters of Austin Dickinson and Mabel Loomis Todd.* Amherst: U of Massachusetts P, 1999.

Paglia, Camille. *Sexual Personae: Art and Decadence from Nefertiti to Emily Dickinson.* New York: Vintage, 1991.

Phillips, Elizabeth. *Emily Dickinson: Personae and Performance.* University Park: Pennsylvania State Press, 1988.

"Poet's Corner: Emily Dickinson." *Thomson Gale. Authors and Artists for Young Adults,* Vols. 7–26. Gale, 1992–99. 28 April 2006. <http://www.gale.com/free_resources/poets/bio/dickinson_e.htm>.

Pridmore, Jan. "Emily Dickinson (1830–1886): A Guide to Literary Criticism on the Internet for Emily Dickinson." *Literary History.* 27 Apr. 2006. <http://www.literaryhistory.com/19thC/DICKINSON_E.HTM>.

Reuben, Paul P. "Chapter 4: Emily Dickinson (1830–1886)." *PAL: Perspectives in American Literature—A Research and Reference Guide.* 13 Jan. 2006. 27 Apr. 2006 <http://www.csustan.edu/english/reuben/pal/chap4/dickinson.html>.

Rich, Adrienne. "Vesuvius at Home: The Power of Emily Dickinson." *On Lies, Secrets, and Silence: Selected Prose, 1966–1978.* New York: Norton, 1979. 157–183.

Rosenbaum, S. P. *A Concordance to the Poems of Emily Dickinson.* Ithaca, NY: Cornell UP, 1964.

Sewall, Richard B., ed. *Emily Dickinson: A Collection of Critical Essays.* Englewood Cliffs, NJ: Prentice-Hall, 1963.

———. *The Life of Emily Dickinson.* Cambridge, MA: Harvard UP, 1974.

Sielke, Sabine. "Emily Dickinson." *The Greenwood Encyclopedia of American Poets and Poetry.* Ed. Jeffery Gray. Vol. 2. Westport, CT: Greenwood Press, 2006. 387–392.

Stonum, Gary Lee. *The Dickinson Sublime.* Madison: U of Wisconsin P, 1990.

Tate, Allen. *Reactionary Essays on Poetry and Ideas.* New York: Scribner's Sons, 1936.

Weisbuch, Robert. *Emily Dickinson's Poetry.* Chicago: U of Chicago P, 1975.

Whicher, George F. *This Was a Poet: A Critical Biography of Emily Dickinson.* Ann Arbor: U of Michigan P, 1957.

Winters, Yvor. "Emily Dickinson and the Limits of Judgment." *In Defense of Reason.* 3rd ed. Denver: Swallow Press, 1987. 283–299.

Wolff, Cynthia Griffin. *Emily Dickinson.* New York: Knopf, 1986.

Wolosky, Shira. *Emily Dickinson: A Voice of War.* New Haven, CT: Yale UP, 1984.

#67—"SUCCESS IS COUNTED SWEETEST"

READING TO WRITE

"SUCCESS IS counted sweetest" is one of only seven poems published in Dickinson's lifetime. The poem is governed by paradox, beginning with the opening lines: "Success is counted sweetest / By those who ne'er succeed" (1–2). Its central theme could be said to be that it is only those who experience suffering who truly understand success. Or, to put it in other words, it is the lack of the thing we desire that teaches us its worth. One way to write about this poem is to consider how Dickinson dramatizes this situation with her example of the dying soldier.

You've likely heard the saying, "You never miss a drop of water until the well runs dry." Dickinson, far more poetically in poem #135—"Water, is taught by thirst," wrote:

> Water, is taught by thirst.
> Land—by the Oceans passed.
> Transport—by throe—
> Peace—by its battles told—
> Love, by Memorial Mold—
> Birds, by the Snow.

Both "Success is counted sweetest" and "Water, is taught by thirst" express a common theme of Dickinson's: Desire teaches the value of what we desire. The person who renounces what he or she desires, the person who does without, knows better the value of the desired object than the one who possesses it. In "Success is counted sweetest," it is only the dying, defeated soldier who truly understands the meaning of "Victory" (8). One way to approach "Success is counted sweetest" is to consider why, when the message is one that has grown almost to be a cliché, Dickinson's poems on this subject continue to be memorable. How does she convey her idea without allowing it to turn into cliché, even when she herself returned to the same idea numerous times?

You might want to concentrate on the metaphors in Dickinson's poem. One that gave her early editors pause is found in lines 3 and 4: "To comprehend a nectar / Requires sorest need." Although the meaning is clear enough, some readers may feel that to "comprehend a nectar" is too far fetched. Others, though, might find in a phrase such as this simply the unusual diction that marks Dickinson's work and that continues to surprise readers more than 100 years after it was written.

TOPICS AND STRATEGIES

This section of the chapter will seek to provide you with various approaches you might take in writing a paper about this poem. These ideas are by no means exhaustive and should be looked at as a starting point for your own investigation.

Themes

"Success is counted sweetest" is one of Dickinson's earliest poems in manuscript form, and in it, you will see themes that she returned to throughout her life. The first two lines of the poem are often taken out of context, as they seem to make a direct statement of the poem's "message": "Success is counted sweetest / By those who ne'er succeed" (1–2). However, if you take these lines too literally you might be left thinking this is a poem about never winning, when it is far more complicated. Better than excerpting the first two lines as a statement of this poem's theme would be to incorporate a consideration of how close the dying soldier has come to victory. He is close enough to hear the victory he cannot experience for himself. In Dickinson's poems, you will often find such a situation; as Moses being allowed to see the promised land though disallowed to enter, it is a form of victory to have come close.

It might also be possible to argue that Dickinson believes that losing is sometimes superior to winning. This idea is illustrated in many of her works where rewards and honors on Earth are shown to be empty in comparison to the rewards that will come in the afterlife or in heaven. Perhaps the soldier in "Success is counted sweetest" has won a moral victory simply by understanding victory's meaning.

A related theme can be found in the image of the vanquished and the victor in this poem. In stanza one Dickinson states, twice, the argument of the poem. Stanza two gives the reader an image of the victor, and stanza three provides the image of the vanquished. How would you compare the victor and the vanquished? We do not know the nature of their battle. Chiefly, their differences lie in their ability to perceive.

Dickinson could be called a poet of desire, as so many of her lyrics are on this theme. If you read even just a small selection of her poetry, you will find references to want, need, and desires, physical or spiritual, sometimes bordering on the macabre, as in #577 where she writes of her desire, seemingly, to possess her beloved's corpse: "If I may have it, when it's dead, / I'll be contented—so— / If just as soon as Breath is out / It shall belong to me" (1–4). "Success is counted sweetest" emphasizes the power of desire and equates desire with victory.

Sample Topics:

1. **Success:** What is Dickinson's attitude toward success, as represented in the poem "Success is counted sweetest"?

In this poem, the "loser" knows better the definition of victory than the "winners" do. If you were to take this poem as representative of Dickinson's attitude toward success, you might frame an argument that stated: Dickinson believed that success was not so much in winning as in knowing the value of victory.

2. **Superiority of failure:** Does "Success is counted sweetest" argue for the superiority of failure?

That failure is ennobling in "Success is counted sweetest" is one possible thesis statement. For evidence, you might discuss the connotations of such words as *sweetest* or *nectar*. Does it matter that the dying soldier can "tell" the definition of victory, as if speaking were somehow implied?

3. **Victor vs. vanquished:** What distinguishes the vanquished from the victor in "Success is counted sweetest"?

One possible thesis for an essay on this topic would be that it is perception that distinguishes the vanquished from the victor. The dying soldier understands "Victory" better than those "Who took the Flag" (6). He can "tell the definition," which implies an ability to speak. He can also tell it "clear," which implies an ability to see. The final stanza is about what the soldier can hear. Even if the sounds of victory are "forbidden" him, it seems he understands and hears them intuitively.

4. **Desire:** How does "Success is counted sweetest" show the importance Dickinson places on desire?

Dickinson writes that "To comprehend a nectar / Requires sorest need" (3–4). Presumably, the greater need leads to greater comprehension. And though the poem says that "Success is counted sweetest / By those who ne'er succeed," where *ne'er* is a contraction for *never,* there is a temptation to read the word as *near.* The dying soldier, after all, is still a soldier. He could not understand victory had he not desired it and strove to achieve it.

Philosophy and Ideas

The statement that opens this poem appears simple on the surface, but it hints at a greater psychological truth. Suffering ennobles the person who suffers. The person with the greatest "need" (4) has the deepest understanding. This idea is essential to many religions and belief systems and seems to be one that Dickinson embraced. The story of Christ offers an example of such suffering. A reading of "Success is counted sweetest" from a Christian perspective would perhaps see the "dying" soldier as victor, simply because he is passing into another realm. His earthly battles are over. He is passing to his eternal reward. The concerns of the world, such as warfare, are no longer his. Perhaps the sounds that "Burst agonized and clear" (12) upon the soldier's ear are heavenly music and not the sounds of the celebrating army. Think of the hymn "Onward, Christian Soldiers" written in 1865:

> At the sign of triumph Satan's host doth flee;
> on then, Christian soldiers, on to victory!
> Hell's foundations quiver at the shout of praise;
> brothers, lift your voices, loud your anthems raise.

In this hymn, the connection between warfare and Christianity is made explicit.

This poem seems to be one of the more masculine of Dickinson's works. The scene of the battlefield and the loneliness of the dying soldier contribute to this impression. The idea of home was important to her, and the sense is that this soldier is far from his home and its comforts. Perhaps there is some condemnation of the masculine pursuit of warfare, or of war in general. Emily Dickinson's brother, Austin Dickinson, paid another to go in his place when he was conscripted for the Civil War (to do so was not only allowed, it was a common practice among the upper classes, with apparently no shame attached). This poem is believed to have been written before the war, likely in 1859. But Dickinson's poems about violence and warfare do not shrink from descriptions of the bloodiness and the losses of battle.

Sample Topics:

1. **Suffering:** Do Dickinson's poems suggest that she prized suffering?

One possible thesis is that "Success is counted sweetest" shows the ennobling effect of suffering. You could discuss other poems, such as #241—"I like a look of agony," to further explore Dickinson's attitudes toward suffering.

2. **Religion:** Can "Success is counted sweetest" be read as a poem of religious belief?

In the Christian faith, death is less to be feared than welcomed. The soldier here, his battles over, meets his death as a victor.

Words such as *purple* and *Host* have religious connotations. As we find in 2 Chronicles in the Bible, "The battle [is] not yours, but God's" (20:15). An essay on this topic would continue to discuss any religious imagery in the poem.

3. **Masculinity:** Does "Success is counted sweetest" offer some insight into Dickinson's view of masculinity?

Many of Dickinson's poems seem to focus on concerns that were largely the province of women in 19th-century America, such as housekeeping. As a particularly masculine poem, does "Success is counted sweetest" tell you anything about Dickinson herself? To write an essay on this topic, you might want to look at some of her poems written from a male perspective.

4. **Futility of war:** Could this be called an antiwar poem?

Dickinson's poem "My portion is defeat—today," dated by editor Thomas H. Johnson to 1862, includes a graphic description of the waste of the battlefield. It could be referenced as evidence that when Dickinson writes of war, she takes the view of the losing soldier. An essay on this topic would likely make use of Shira Wolosky's book *Emily Dickinson: A Voice of War.*

Language, Symbols, and Imagery

Of all of Dickinson's poems, "Success is counted sweetest" is the most closely linked to the Civil War. However, the poem was clearly written before the war. Johnson gives its likely date of composition as 1859. But it is not only its subject matter that gives readers the impression that it was occasioned by the Civil War; its publication history also provides a link. The poem was first published anonymously in the *Brooklyn Daily Union* on April 27, 1864. The *Brooklyn Daily Union* worked closely with another publication, *Drum Beat,* which raised funds for the Civil War. Helen Hunt Jackson, a close friend of Dickinson's and a well-respected writer, later submitted it to *A Masque of Poets,* where it was printed in 1878 with the title "Success." *A Masque of Poets* was part of a series wherein all contributors appeared anonymously. Some of the series' popularity rested upon this guessing game, where the public attempted to guess who the anonymous writers were. "Success is counted sweetest" was widely believed to have been contributed by Ralph Waldo Emerson, so much so that when the poem was later reprinted in *Literary World* on December 10, 1878, it carried this head note: "If anything in the volume was contributed by Emerson, we should consider these lines upon 'Success' most probably his" (Pollak 331).

The battlefield is powerful as a subject, an image, and a metaphor. There is no reason to assume that the subject of this poem is warfare. On one level, the poem may be read as a straightforward look at clashing armies, but you should not neglect other possibilities. There is always a temptation to read a Dickinson poem as a veiled reflection on losing at romance, and this applies to "Success is counted sweetest." Perhaps some of the power and popularity of this poem is owed to the fact that its message can be applied to any situation where there are winners and losers.

The language of "Success is counted sweetest" is not difficult. Even syntactically, the poem is fairly clear. Part of what makes the language memorable is Dickinson's use of alliteration. The repetition of the "s" sound in the first line seems to give that line an authority, as if this was a truism passed down over time. Throughout the first stanza, the "s" sound and the "n" continue to be repeated. The words that are emboldened by the alliteration may be considered for their importance and for their added meaning. The word *nectar* is an unusual choice. What are the connotations of *nectar*? Have you heard the phrase "nectar of the gods"? Likely you have the sense that nectar is something rare and special. You can imagine other words that Dickinson might have used here, such as *water,* and why the one she chose is particularly apt. You may also wish to consider the words in this stanza that share with *nectar* the initial *n: ne'er* and *need.*

"Success is counted sweetest" is particularly good at engaging the senses of the reader. A paper could be written discussing how Dickinson achieved this. The word *purple* stands out in part because there is no alliteration for it in the poem. One of the connotations of purple is that it is the color of royalty or wealth. Another is that it is the color of blood. In the United States, the Purple Heart is the award given to soldiers in battle. The lines "To comprehend a nectar / Requires sorest need" speak to thirst and remind the reader of the dying soldier who cries out for water, or the person lost in the desert. The final stanza engages the sense of hearing. The dying soldier recognizes the "strains of triumph" (*strains* is another curious word choice), though he is unable to participate in them.

Sample Topics:

1. **War poem:** Why has the imagery of war captivated so many readers, and why does Dickinson's poem, written when the United States was not at war, seem so apt an expression of the war that was to come?

   You do not need to do historical research to construct an argument that Dickinson's poem, for instance, strikes a chord with many because it is from the perspective of the dying soldier. Another interesting approach to this poem would be to discuss why it was so widely attributed to Emerson. Is it surprising that "Success is counted sweetest" was written by a woman?

2. **Metaphor:** Wars and the battles they engender, in addition to being the central image to the poem, might also be a metaphor. How could this battle be said to be a metaphor, and what other metaphors does the poem contain?

   An essay on this topic would argue that the battle is a metaphor for any contest in life. Supporting evidence would be the broad statement of the poem's first two lines and the metaphor of the nectar.

3. **Diction:** Are there any unusual word choices in the poem that, upon inspection, prove the value of the poet's choosing?

   The word *nectar* is cited above as a word that bears further consideration. An essay discussing this word choice would likely touch on issues of alliteration and meaning. Other words from "Success is counted sweetest" that could bear further analysis are *purple* and *Host.*

4. **Use of senses:** How does Dickinson successfully engage the senses in this poem?

An essay on this topic might choose any one word, such as *purple,* and discuss how it has numerous sensory connotations. There is purple prose and purple music, the idea of the overwrought and excessive. There is also the idea of richness. Purple is thick like velvet or blood. You might also choose to catalog the way the senses are used here to give perspective to the plight of the dying soldier.

Compare and Contrast Essays

"Success is counted sweetest" is a poem whose message is repeated throughout Dickinson's work, so it is not difficult to find any number of poems to compare with it. As mentioned above, #135—"Water is taught by thirst" contains a similar message, though it does not concentrate on the battle. Instead, this poem shows how things are often defined by their lack.

"The Missing All—prevented Me" and "Your Riches—taught me—Poverty" are both suggestive of autobiography. The former depicts a speaker so taken over by "Missing All" that she cannot be distracted by the Sun being put out or the world dislodging from its axis, occurrences she refers to as "minor Things" (2). What the "All" is that she misses is unidentified. She cannot lift her head from her "work," which somehow is connected to the missing of all. In "Your Riches—taught me—Poverty," it is clearly a beloved who is missed. It is only the speaker who appreciates the true value of the missing beloved and who feels impoverished in his or her absence.

To compare or contrast another poem of battle, you might turn to #639—"My Portion is Defeat—today." You will find in it a number of similarities to "Success is counted sweetest." Both poems take the point of view of the defeated, and both emphasize the music of the victors as it is heard by the vanquished. But #639 has a graphic depiction of the battlefield and its corpses, and the conclusion is not as positive as in "Success is counted sweetest."

"My Portion is Defeat—today" might move you to consider Dickinson's attitude toward death and other losses as essentially positive. If so,

#816—"A Death blow is a Life blow to Some" might be another poem worthy of discussion. This poem, like "Success is counted sweetest," begins with a seeming contradiction. How can a death blow be a life blow? In this poem, Dickinson suggests that for some, living is death. For those people, it is death that allows them to finally live.

Sample Topics:

1. **Definitions:** How do Dickinson's poems suggest that only those who lack or lose what they desire know its true worth?

   "Water is taught by thirst" is very similar to "Success is counted sweetest" in defining an object by its absence. If you were to contrast these two poems, it would illustrate Dickinson's concern with this theme while also deepening your understanding of both. "Water is taught by thirst," you might say, explicitly shows what the poet values.

2. **Love poems:** How could you argue that "Success is counted sweetest" is a love poem?

   By looking at other poems that discuss the loss of love in similar terms as the loss that the vanquished soldier is experiencing in "Success is counted sweetest," you could write an essay that argues that love is the central loss that concerns Dickinson. Poems such as #985—"The Missing All prevented Me" or #299—"Your riches taught me poverty" suggest this idea. You might wish to concentrate on the sensual imagery of lines three and four from "Success is counted sweetest": "To comprehend a nectar / Requires sorest need."

3. **The battlefield:** How does Dickinson depict the battlefield in her other poems?

   Dickinson's #639—"My Portion is Defeat—today" could almost seem an extended version of "Success is counted sweetest." These two poems share a scene and have a similar message. However, their perspective is different. In #639 it is the speaker who is defeated. Comparing the two poems might lead you to argue that this change in perspective changes the message of #639 entirely.

4. **Paradox:** How does Dickinson reconcile the seemingly contradictory ideas that often begin her poems and are resolved by the poems' conclusions?

Her poem #816—"A Death blow is a Life blow to Some" begins in such a contradiction. Like "Success is counted sweetest," it elevates what is normally considered an unenviable fate, dying or losing. A comparison of these two poems could lead to a thesis such as Dickinson's poems force us to reconsider what it means to win or lose, live or die.

Bibliography and Online Resources

Baring-Gould, Sabiner, and Arthur S. Sullivan. "Onward, Christian Soldiers." HymnSite.com. 12 Aug. 2006 <http://www.hymnsite.com/lyrics/umh575.sht>.

Johnson, Thomas H., ed. *The Poems of Emily Dickinson.* 3 vols. Cambridge, MA: Harvard UP, 1979.

Johnson, Thomas H., and Theodora Ward, eds. *The Letters of Emily Dickinson.* 3 vols. Cambridge, MA: Harvard UP, 1986.

Pollak, Vivian R. "American Women Poets Reading Dickinson: The Example of Helen Hunt Jackson." *The Emily Dickinson Handbook.* Ed. Gudrun Grabher, Roland Hagenbuchle, and Cristanne Miller. Amherst: U of Massachusetts, P, 1998.

Sewall, Richard B. *The Life of Emily Dickinson.* Cambridge, MA: Harvard UP, 1974.

Whicher, George. *This Was a Poet: A Critical Biography of Emily Dickinson.* New York: Scribner's, 1939.

Wolosky, Shira. *Emily Dickinson: A Voice of War.* New Haven, CT: Yale UP, 1984.

#214—
"I TASTE A LIQUOR NEVER BREWED"

READING TO WRITE

I TASTE A liquor never brewed" was published on May 4, 1861, in Samuel Bowles's *Springfield Republican.* The poem was unsigned and bore the title "The May Wine." It is something of a rarity in poetry; it is a happy poem. Some would argue that it is a comic poem. Before you begin to write about it, you will first want to answer for yourself who the speaker is. Although it is easy to see the speaker as a representative of the poet, it has sometimes also been proposed that the speaker is a bird. If you believe that it is a person, you will also want to decide what sort of drunkenness this is.

Stanza two makes clear that the poem is not about any common liquor. Instead, the speaker is an "Inebriate of Air" and a "Debauchee of Dew," in the common parlance, "high on life." She is inebriated by the joy of living or the joy of nature. This bears no comparison to even the finest liquors, like those evoked in stanza one. What is more, she will continue to "drink" until the end of time.

Much of the imagery of the poem is from the natural world. The "drunken Bee" and the "Butterflies" of stanza three may drink from nature as she does, but she will drink longer than they. Dickinson writes of "Reeling—thro endless summer days," and readers of Dickinson's poems will recognize her affinity for the summer.

The poem concludes with the speaker "Leaning against the—Sun" (16). This ascent seems to have taken the speaker into heaven, where the "saints" and "seraphs" come to stare at her drunken state. At this point, you might ask yourself what sort of heaven is this. Is the little drinker a part of it? Or does her love for nature set her apart?

Although the imagery might be a little outrageous, the poem is essentially light. There is really no suggestion of darkness in it and no hint of unhappiness.

TOPICS AND STRATEGIES

This section of the chapter will seek to provide you with various approaches you might take in writing a paper about this poem. These ideas are by no means exhaustive and should be looked at as a starting point for your own investigation.

Themes

One theme evident in this poem is the effect nature has on the speaker. Nature is the source of her inebriation. Drunkenness is the extended metaphor that describes her state. Nature also comes to her service. Not only is it a source of sustenance, but her relationship is so close that she is "Leaning against the—Sun." There is perhaps some suggestion that she is closer to nature than she is to God. The speaker seems more at one with the natural world than the seraphs and saints in the poem.

The poem also has a theme of excess in that here excess is depicted as a positive, whereas it is generally thought of in negative terms. Drinking to excess is often used to comic effect by writers, but here it is less comic than virtuous. She drinks from something more valuable than "pearl." Pearl has connotations of virtue and rarity. Although the word *debauchee* usually signals someone corrupted, here the corruption takes place in "inns of Molten Blue" (8), the clear summer sky. Dickinson's poems often prize sensory experience, and here the experience is one of excess.

The treatment of the inebriate is kind. She is a "little Tippler" (15), and her exploits seem to be viewed affectionately by the poet. It is possible to see signs of transcendental thought in the poem, as the speaker perhaps reaches heaven with only her love of nature to take her there. She has no other intermediary. Here inebriation is depicted as an ecstatic state. It takes her beyond herself and provides a spiritual experience.

You can also see in this poem a theme Dickinson regularly returns to—the pleasures of her own home. In stanza one, the poet writes of liquors that can be found upon the Rhine, but they are no match for the air she is breathing. Through the transports of nature, the speaker is able to travel, even so far as the Sun. This poem is an example of Dickinson's preference for simple pleasures, and the ability she had to see in the most simple of experiences something unique and transcendent.

Sample Topics:

1. **Nature:** How does the speaker of "I taste a liquor never brewed" interact with nature?

   One thesis for an essay of this type would be that the poem depicts a speaker sustained by nature (the air she breathes is also the drink she takes). Other theses would be that she is un-self-conscious in her praise of nature or that her hunger for it is greater than that of the butterflies or bees.

2. **Excess:** How does "I taste a liquor never brewed" celebrate excess?

   An essay on this topic might talk about the imagery of the poem, which tends toward exaggeration. The metaphor of drunkenness is treated positively. The speaker ascends to the heavens eventually. Is she envied or condemned by those who come to see her?

3. **Inebriation:** What does it mean to be inebriated?

   The question might strike you as humorous, but consider how often this metaphor is used in daily conversation or how often people reach for other metaphors to describe this state. In "I taste a liquor never brewed," Dickinson attempts to depict a state of ecstasy. If you were to write on this, you might argue

that inebriation is too comic an idea to successfully convey a love of nature.

4. **Home:** How does Dickinson tend to enlarge our view of home?

"I taste a liquor never brewed" is about breathing, that most common activity, and being transported beyond. What happens in the poem could happen anywhere, although it might require a sensibility many of us do not have. If you were to write on this topic, you might have a thesis that says that in this poem Dickinson is able to show the magical in the commonplace.

Compare and Contrast Essays

The similarities between Ralph Waldo Emerson's "Bacchus" and Dickinson's "I taste a liquor never brewed" have been remarked upon by numerous critics. Emerson's poem begins with the following lines:

> Bring me wine, but wine which never grew
> In the belly of the grape,
> Or grew on vine whose tap-roots, reaching through
> Under the Andes to the Cape,
> Suffer no savor of the earth to scape (1–5).

As in Dickinson's poem, the extended metaphor is about drinking, perhaps to the point of excess. Unlike Dickinson's poem, the drunkenness is meant to result in poetry. Emerson's poem is a prayer for poetic inspiration.

Dickinson's early poem #128—"Bring me the sunset in a cup" asks to know "How many cups the Bee partakes, / The Debauchee of Dews!" (10–11). She uses the exact same phrase as in "I taste a liquor never brewed," but in #128, it applies directly to the bee. The first line, "Bring me the sunset in a cup," is another take on the metaphor of drinking in nature. She returned to this idea later in poem #1628—"A Drunkard cannot meet a Cork." In this poem, the speaker meets a fly in January, and this causes her to think about warmer weather. Dickinson writes, "The moderate drinker of Delight / Does not deserve the spring" (7–8).

Dickinson's #252—"I can wade Grief" is a moving poem that begins with a curious boast: "I can wade Grief— / Whole Pools of it— / I'm used to that" (1–3). As the poem continues, the speaker says it is joy that she cannot understand: "But the least push of Joy / Breaks up my feet— / And I tip—drunken— / Let no Pebble—smile— / 'Twas the New Liquor— / That was all!" (4–9). Although this poem is about grief and joy, the metaphor is a similar one. Joy, like nature in "I taste a liquor never brewed," has the power to intoxicate.

Dickinson's poem #1101 begins, "Between the form of Life and Life / The difference is as big / As Liquor at the Lip between / And Liquor in the Jug" (1–4). The metaphor of drinking is applied to life in this poem. The speaker says that "the form of Life" is inferior to life. The poem seems to urge the reader to partake of life as one might wine. The poem ends with a testimonial from a speaker who has known both life and the form of it: "The corkless is superior— / I know for I have tried" (7–8).

Sample Topics:

1. **Emerson's "Bacchus":** How does Emerson's poem contrast with "I taste a liquor never brewed"?

   If you wished to contrast these two poems, you might begin with a short discussion of how the imagery compares. Certainly, there are enough similarities to make you wonder whether Dickinson used Emerson's poem as her inspiration. However, the bulk of your essay would likely focus on how different the two poems are, perhaps discussing such things as their diction, imagery, and even their length. Another possible approach, and thesis, would be to argue that Dickinson asks less from nature than Emerson does from Bacchus.

2. **Drinking in nature:** How does Dickinson convey the idea of "drinking in" nature?

   You might compare or contrast "I taste a liquor never brewed" with any of the poems discussed above. In the case of "Bring me the sunset in a cup" it could be interesting to see the poet working earlier with ideas she returns to throughout her life, as well as trying out phrases she liked enough to use again. One possible thesis for a paper about those two poems would be that the earlier is a more explicit depiction of a love for nature. If you were to write about "A Drunkard cannot meet a Cork," you might focus on the idea of intoxication or remembrance.

3. **What we are awash in:** How does Dickinson use liquid as a metaphor for intense emotional states?

An essay on this subject might compare "I taste a liquor never brewed" with "I can wade Grief." One possible thesis is that these poems attempt to depict strong emotional states. Their way to depict grief and joy is to show the body coming into contact with liquids and either wading, drowning, or becoming drunk.

4. **Life:** When the speaker of "I taste a liquor never brewed" is intoxicated with nature, is that not also an intoxication with life?

If you wished to compare "I taste a liquor never brewed" with "Between the form of Life and Life," one possible thesis would be that "I taste a liquor never brewed" is really about being intoxicated with living. Evidence might come in the poem's focus on the breath.

Bibliography and Online Resources

Anderson, Charles R. *Emily Dickinson's Poetry: Stairway of Surprise.* New York: Holt, Rinehart & Winston, 1960.

Eby, Cecil D. "'I Taste a Liquor Never Brewed': A Variant Reading." *American Literature* 36.4 (Jan. 1965): 516–518.

Emerson, Ralph Waldo. "Bacchus." *EServer, Iowa State University.* 20 Oct. 2006 <http://poetry.eserver.org/Emerson(Bacchus).html>.

Fast, Robin Riley, and Christine Mack Gordon, eds. *Approaches to Teaching Dickinson's Poetry.* New York: MLA, 1989.

Garrow, A. Scott. "A Note on Manzanilla." *American Literature* 35.3. (Nov. 1963): 366.

Johnson, Thomas H., ed. *The Poems of Emily Dickinson.* 3 vols. Cambridge, MA: Harvard UP, 1979.

Johnson, Thomas, H., and Theodora Ward, eds. *The Letters of Emily Dickinson.* 3 vols. Cambridge, MA: Harvard UP, 1986.

Sewall, Richard B. *The Life of Emily Dickinson.* Cambridge, MA: Harvard UP, 1974.

#258—
"THERE'S A CERTAIN SLANT OF LIGHT"

READING TO WRITE

DICKINSON'S "THERE'S a certain Slant of light" looks at the external world in terms of the internal. As you read, you will very likely notice that the tone of the poem is oppressive or even depressing. The "heft" (3), or weight, of the poem is unrelenting. Words such as *oppresses, hurt, despair,* and *affliction* pile upon one another, and the final word of the poem is *Death*. Even "Air" has the ability to hurt. An essay could be written on the imagery of this poem and how it makes the reader feel. A reader would not necessarily have to understand the poem completely in order to understand the feeling it attempts to convey.

A writer might also wish to notice how time behaves in "There's a certain Slant of light." As Dickinson's poem progresses, how does time progress? What effect does time have on the poem's speaker? You will want to consider the connotations of the seasons and the times of day. Winter is often associated with death, despair, illness, and endings, as is the evening and the close of day. The future is night and darkness.

And yet, the despair of the poem is not without its merits. Notice that this hurt, for all it pains the speaker, is also "Heavenly" (5). She feels it inside, "Where the Meanings, are" (8). It is also "imperial" (11), and this word is suggestive of its worth.

TOPICS AND STRATEGIES

This section of the chapter will seek to provide you with various approaches you might take in writing a paper about this poem. These ideas are by no means exhaustive and should be looked at as a starting point for your own investigation.

Themes

One important theme in Dickinson's poems, illustrated in "There's a certain Slant of light," is the difference between the interior and the exterior world. She is concerned oftentimes with the boundary between the interior and the exterior. What is shown is often contrasted with what is felt. And it is the interior—"Where the Meanings, are"—that she values.

Sometimes, as in "There's a certain Slant of light," the interior landscape is suggested by the exterior. Outside it is "Winter" (2). The light is oppressive and indirect. Being indirect is often seen as positive in Dickinson. Her poem "Tell the truth—but tell it Slant" uses the same word to describe how best to approach a truth too great to approach headlong. Here, in #258, the "Slant of light" seems to penetrate into places the speaker would rather keep hidden, a pain too great to meet straight on. The "Landscape listens" (13) rather than sees, while the "Shadows—hold their breath" (14).

Line 10 speaks of "the Seal Despair," and despair seems to be the emotion that most governs the poem. One possible theme is that despair must be mastered as best it can. The speaker, though imprinted with it, shows "no scar" (6). The pain she suffers is extreme, "like the Distance / On the look of Death" (15–16), but she does not die. Moreover, the only outward expression of that suffering is the poem, and the poem is a controlled and measured response to it.

Many readers believe that "There's a certain Slant of light" is a poem of mourning. If so, then its theme might be that the death of one we love marks us with permanent sorrow. There is plenty of evidence in the poem to believe that it is about death. The "Cathedral Tunes" (4) are suggestive of funeral hymns or church services. "Heavenly Hurt" (5) suggests that this hurt comes from above or perhaps will be healed in heaven. The idea of its being sent from "Air" (12) and being "imperial" (11) supports this reading, as does the "look of Death" (16) and the "Distance" (15) it holds.

Sample Topics:

1. **Interior v. exterior:** How does "There's a certain Slant of light" seek to depict an interior and an exterior world?

In each stanza of this poem, an external and concrete image, such as the "scar" of line 6, results in "internal difference" (7). Outwardly, there is no change to show the despair. To an observer less afflicted, this would be just another winter sunset. One possible thesis on this topic would be that Dickinson's poem seeks to establish a boundary between what is internal and what is external in every image or stanza.

2. **Symbolic landscapes:** How does the landscape reflect the internal state of the poem's speaker?

An essay on this topic would likely discuss the connotations of winter. It might even attempt to conjecture what the landscape looks like, although the poem contains few hints. Does that suggest that the landscape is empty? Or do the shadows contain secrets?

3. **The mastery of despair:** How could "There's a certain Slant of light" be said to be about the mastery of despair?

As you read "There's a certain Slant of light," look for evidence of strength or even hope in the speaker. There are few tears in Dickinson's poems. Instead, there seems to be a premium placed on stoicism. It is almost a virtue to bear one's own cross and to bear it with grace and dignity. In #561—"I measure every Grief I meet," the speaker attempts to measure every grief she sees in others to see how it compares to her own. There may even be a certain pride in believing that one bears a greater grief than others.

4. **The pain of mourning:** What does this poem have to say about the pain that follows the death of one we love?

One possible thesis for a paper on this topic would be that Dickinson attempts, in "There's a certain Slant of light," to teach us how to mourn. To support such a thesis, you would want to present evidence about this death and perhaps the pain of letting the loved one go, as a season moves into another or as day moves into night. Although winter and night both come, one does not forget the summer or the light. Death marks the person left to mourn internally and forever.

Philosophy and Ideas

Dickinson writes, "I would not paint—a picture" (1) in poem #505. But "There's a certain Slant of light" is a particularly visual poem and has been compared to a visual performance. Yet there are very few visual cues in the poem. Still, readers feel they can "see" the scene presented. That sense seems to be conveyed by way of the other senses. The light, for instance, is given weight and sound.

Dickinson often uses religious imagery to convey a secular meaning. In "There's a certain Slant of light," the pain that is the subject of the poem is described as "Heavenly Hurt" (5). How can "hurt" be "heavenly"? Does the hurt originate in heaven, or does "heavenly" describe the pleasure of the pain?

It does seem that there is a certain pleasure in this suffering. It is without context, so the reader is left to wonder why the speaker feels so. Any physical distress is internalized. But even if "Cathedral Tunes" (4) are oppressive, they are also, usually, beautiful and uplifting.

Particularly in stanza three, the speaker expresses how exclusive her suffering is. When she says that "None may teach it—Any" (9), she is signaling that exclusivity. The line might be read to say that "none may teach this hurt anything" or "none may teach it, not anyone." With either reading, there is a sense of privilege attached to it. The hurt she has been given in line five is divine.

Sample Topics:

1. **Visual arts:** How does "There's a certain Slant of light" use painterly elements to convey its meaning?

An interesting essay could be written discussing why this poem "feels" visually apt. You might spend some time describing the scene as you imagine it. Then you would want to consider how you arrived at these impressions. This would involve consideration of the poem's imagery.

2. **Religious imagery:** How does the religious imagery of this poem take on secular meaning?

One possible thesis would be that the religious imagery of "There's a certain Slant of light" elevates the emotion she is describing.

3. **Suffering as bliss:** How can suffering be pleasurable?

An essay on this topic might argue that in "There's a certain Slant of light," Dickinson is showing the pleasure that can come with suffering. Although she feels despair, it is also "heavenly" and "imperial." Those cathedral tunes have their beauty, as does the winter landscape.

4. **The exaltation of the sufferer:** Is there not the sense that the suffering person is special because of his or her suffering?

A paper on this topic might concentrate on certain images or the choice of words such as *heavenly* or *imperial.* You might notice a claim for the speaker's heightened awareness. She is, for instance, in tune with what the light and the landscape are saying. The tone of this poem could be discussed. The speaker is not conversational; she is overheard, and she is magisterial.

Language, Symbols, and Imagery

Poets are meant to present their readers with images that are original but that are also recognized as true. There should be some sense of the accuracy of what is said. Dickinson often creates images by suggesting synesthesia, a confusion of the senses. But this confusion allows the reader to understand with some accuracy what is meant in a way that a more forthright description would not. In "There's a certain Slant of light," synesthesia is present in the image of the light

"That oppresses, like the Heft / Of Cathedral Tunes" (3–4). The light is given weight and by extension sound, as the "Cathedral Tunes" are said to have "Heft."

"There's a certain Slant of light," like many of Dickinson's poems, has oddities of syntax that require the reader to slow down to consider what is meant. At times, it seems hard to know, but usually, careful consideration will be rewarded, and you will find a startling insight or a number of valid and interesting meanings. There are a number of lines in this poem that might require that extra work. Line nine, "None may teach it—Any," is discussed above in the section on "Philosophy and Ideas." But why would she write, "Where the Meanings, are," with the comma added before the word *are?* What is the pronoun referring to in line 13: "When it comes, the Landscape listens"? Is "it" the "Slant of light" or the "imperial affliction"?

Dickinson's diction, or word choice, can always bear greater consideration. In this poem, there is one word, *heft,* that appears three times in Dickinson's work, and another, *light,* that appears 82 times. Poem #632—"The Brain—is wider than the Sky" is another poem where Dickinson talks of "heft." In #632's final stanza, she uses it as another word for "weigh" (or "to lift, lift up, or lift with the purpose of weighing," *Oxford English Dictionary*):

> The Brain is just the weight of God—
> For—Heft them—Pound for Pound—
> And they will differ—if they do—
> As Syllable from Sound—(9–12).

Since *heft* is used so seldom in Dickinson's poems, each instance could possibly help to clarify the connotations she attached to the word. (A concordance, such as S. P. Rosenbaum's *A Concordance to the Poems of Emily Dickinson,* will list each usage of a word throughout the poems.) In the poem above, *heft* seems to carry connotations of weight, the importance of the "Brain" and "God," and also the difficulty of measuring or lifting either of these. "Light" is an important motif in Dickinson's work because it returns to a central idea of hers: the importance of seeing as a metaphor for understanding.

Sample Topics:

1. **Synesthesia:** How does Dickinson's use of imagery that suggests synesthesia contribute to the overall effect of "There's a certain Slant of light"?

A paper on this topic would discuss how Dickinson's unusual imagery, combining sensory details in unexpected ways, deepens the symbolic weight of those images. How can "Cathedral Tunes" have weight? Or a "Slant of light" sound? How can a "Landscape" listen? How does the "look of Death" have "Distance"?

2. **Questions of syntax:** "There's a certain Slant of light" has various syntactical oddities. Dickinson's early editors thought this meant that she badly needed an editor, but this has come to be seen as one of the prized characteristics of her work. What do you think?

You might argue that Dickinson's syntax allows the reader to choose among meanings. For instance, the line, "None may teach it—Any," allows at least the two variant readings discussed in the section above on "Philosophy and Ideas." A paper on this topic would provide variant readings of some of the lines of "There's a certain Slant of light," showing the validity of each reading and arguing that these variants contribute to the richness of the poem.

3. **Weight:** How is weight conveyed in "There's a certain Slant of light"?

"Heft," in "The Brain—is wider than the Sky," takes on connotations of weight, importance, unwieldiness, and more. In "There's a certain Slant of light," oppressiveness prevails. An essay on the topic of weight in this poem might look at a concordance to find other instances when Dickinson used such words as *heft* or *weight* or *oppress*. A possible thesis would be that Dickinson uses *heft* and other synonyms for weight to convey an overall sense of oppressiveness in "There's a certain Slant of light."

4. **Light:** What does light come to mean in "There's a certain Slant of light"?

This poem begins with an image of light. Light, as an idea, is important in Dickinson's poetry. An essay on this topic might have a thesis that states, "Emily Dickinson often uses light as a synonym for understanding, but the understanding that comes in 'There's a certain Slant of light' is not uplifting. The 'light' brings confirmation of the speaker's despair."

Compare and Contrast Essays

Dickinson is known for employing religious or sacred imagery in unusual ways, as she does in "There's a certain Slant of light," where "Cathedral Tunes," "Heavenly Hurt," and "Seal Despair" all come to mean something more than they might in a religious context. Poem #528—"Mine—by the Right of the White Election!" is a curious poem that has been assigned meanings both religious and secular. Is it a poem about the exaltation of religion, or poetry, or love? Does the religious imagery somehow serve to sanctify the emotion?

What is impossible to miss in "There's a certain Slant of light," as in many other Dickinson poems, is that it expresses acute suffering. If you were to compare or contrast this poem with poems such as #341—"After great pain a formal feeling comes" or #1540—"As Imperceptibly as Grief," you would perhaps have more to say on how Dickinson so successfully depicts pain. In "As Imperceptibly as Grief," the pain is linked to the movement of the seasons, something all readers can identify with. She uses the concrete—"Cathedral Tunes"—to show the abstract—"Heavenly Hurt."

The pain in "There's a certain Slant of Light" is internal; outwardly, it is not given expression. In Dickinson's poems, the interior world is the most important, for it is "Where the Meanings, are" (8). "There's a certain Slant of Light" could be discussed alongside some of Dickinson's other notable poems of interior hurt. "I felt a funeral in my brain" and "I felt a cleaving in my mind" depict the sort of internal hurt that scars the person it befalls in such a way that she will never recover. The hurt is a sort of death to the one who experiences it. Poem #510—"It was not death, for I stood up" makes this clear. In that poem, you will also find the word *despair* to describe the emotion, as in "There's a certain Slant of light."

One obvious way Dickinson tries to reveal an inner state is by depicting an exterior that mirrors it. "There's a certain Slant of light" is set in winter, a season Dickinson herself dreaded, as any who has experienced the long New England winter might. An essay could be written contrasting this winter poem with one of another season. "There came a Day at Summer's full" is a poem of unrelenting joy. "I dreaded that first robin so" discusses a dread of spring felt by someone in such despair that she would have the winter continue indefinitely. Still, she cannot help but be "lifted" by the changes spring has brought.

You might notice that some of the poems mentioned in one category also could be discussed in another. For instance, #130—"These are the days when Birds come back," could be discussed in terms of religious imagery or images of the seasons. A poem such as "As Imperceptibly as Grief" could be discussed in terms of the seasons as well as pain.

Sample Topics:

1. **Religious imagery:** How does Dickinson subvert religious imagery in her poems?

   You might choose to compare "There's a certain Slant of light" with one of Dickinson's other poems that uses religious imagery in an orthodox way. Two possible poems to consider would be #130—"These are the days when Birds come back" and #528—"Mine—by the Right of the White Election!" A possible thesis would be that the use of sacred images is an attempt by Dickinson to render the secular sacred.

2. **Poems of pain:** How do Dickinson's poems so convincingly express pain?

   You might compare "There's a certain Slant of light" with another of Dickinson's famous poems of pain, such as #341—"After great pain a formal feeling comes" or #1540—"As Imperceptibly as Grief." You might want to focus on the qualities she gives to pain, such as weight, shadow, or a coldness that can freeze.

3. **The interior:** Dickinson is so skilled at depicting interior fracture that many critics have surmised she herself underwent some psychological crisis that was akin to mental illness. What do her poems of interior fracture suggest to you?

One possible thesis here is that poems such as #280—"I felt a funeral in my brain," #510—"It was not death, for I stood up," or #937—"I felt a cleaving in my mind" convincingly portray an internal crisis, but the speaker always remains in control so that there is no external evidence of the pain she is in.

4. **Seasons:** How does Dickinson use the weather, the landscape, or the changing seasons to depict psychological, interior states?

There are a number of poems you could turn to for an essay on this topic. You could even rephrase the question above into a statement and simply show Dickinson doing just this in a number of ways. In #322—"There came a Day at Summer's full," Dickinson writes of a day in summer that is of unbounded joy. The poem contrasts interestingly with "There's a certain Slant of light." You might want to focus on images of the sacred or of time if you were to contrast these two poems. As Dickinson often sets poems of happiness in the summer, #348—"I dreaded that first robin so" compares interestingly to "There's a certain Slant of light" for the speaker's dread of summer and the alleviation of her pain that she knows will come with it.

Bibliography and Online Resources

Anderson, Charles. *Emily Dickinson's Poetry: Stairway of Surprise.* New York: Holt, Rinehart, & Winston, 1960.

"Emily Dickinson (1830–86)." *American Literature on the Web.* 28 Aug. 2000. 3 Aug. 2006 <http://www.nagasaki-gaigo.ac.jp/ishikawa/amlit/d/dickinson19re.htm>.

Johnson, Thomas H., ed. *The Poems of Emily Dickinson*. 3 vols. Cambridge, MA: Harvard UP, 1979.

Johnson, Thomas, H., and Theodora Ward, eds. *The Letters of Emily Dickinson*. 3 vols. Cambridge, MA: Harvard UP, 1986.

Perrine, Laurence. "Dickinson's 'There's a Certain Slant of Light.'" *The Explicator* 11 (May 1953), Item 50.

Rosenbaum, S. P. *A Concordance to the Poems of Emily Dickinson*. Ithaca, N.Y.: Cornell UP, 1964.

Sewall, Richard B. *The Life of Emily Dickinson*. Cambridge, MA: Harvard UP, 1974.

Simpson, J. A., and Edmund S. Weiner, eds. "Heft." *The Oxford English Dictionary*. Oxford: Oxford UP, 1989.

Winters, Yvor. "Emily Dickinson and the Limits of Judgment." *In Defense of Reason*. 3rd ed. Denver: Swallow Press, 1987. 283–299.

#280 —
"I FELT A FUNERAL, IN MY BRAIN"

READING TO WRITE

A S YOU read "I felt a Funeral, in my Brain" with an intent to write about it, a central question you will want to answer for yourself is, What is the subject? Paula Bennett, in *Emily Dickinson: Woman Poet*, writes, "On the surface, this poem is about death or, possibly, madness. But, finally, effectively, if it is 'about' anything, it is about dread. . . . She tells what it *feels like* to realize that nothing can be known at all" (68). Many readers have believed that the poem is about the speaker's descent into madness and that the funeral (and the eventual burial) is a metaphor for that descent. The loss of reason, then, would be a death of sorts to the individual. One aspect of the poem's power derives from the way the speaker is both participant and observer in the funeral. From the beginning of the poem, it is as if she is two people, both relatively emotionless. By the end of the poem, those people have experienced a permanent break.

Of course, there are other interpretations available, and one way to approach writing about this poem is to offer and then defend one of your own. It could be argued that "I felt a Funeral, in my Brain" is simply about death. It could be argued that in the poem, death is a metaphor for a psychological crisis (something less than madness, though tragic enough to the one who experiences it). Support for this argument might come from the tone of the poem. Perhaps the speaker is too rational for true madness. It has been suggested more than once that the poem is about fainting. Dickinson's final illness, many years after this poem, involved a sudden collapse, such as may be suggested here. If it is a deathbed poem, where the speaker is moving into death, perhaps the final lines suggest, as many believe the ending of "I felt a fly buzz—when I Died" does, a disappointment at not finding God at the end. The speaker, instead, finds nothingness: "And then a Plank in Reason, broke, / And I dropped down, and down— / And hit a World, at every plunge, / And Finished knowing—then—" (17–20).

A Freudian reading might argue that "I felt a Funeral, in my Brain" is about repression, a calculated burial of something in the mind that the speaker wishes to keep hidden, even from herself. But contradicting this idea is the tone of the poem, which seems to want to relate, as matter-of-factly as possible, exactly what occurred inside the speaker's brain. It is equally possible to see the speaker as a madman much like one out of Edgar Allan Poe's work. Like the narrator of Poe's "The Tell-Tale Heart," the speaker here attempts to be calm and straightforward, but the poem's repetitions undermine the attempt. When, in line seven, the speaker of #280 refers to the incessant drum that "kept beating—beating," or in the opening stanza, where the "Mourners" (2) are "treading—treading" (3), there is the sense that the speaker is obsessively bothered by what she senses. You would notice, too, the many lines that begin with "And," lending a speed and urgency to the poem.

TOPICS AND STRATEGIES

This section of the chapter will seek to provide you with various approaches you might take in writing a paper about this poem. These ideas are by no means exhaustive and should be looked at as a starting point for your own investigation.

Themes

The theme of isolation is present in "I felt a Funeral, in my Brain." The isolation is both physical and psychological. In stanza four, the speaker describes herself as "wrecked" (16) and "solitary" (16). She feels she is, like "Silence" (15), a member of "some strange Race" (15). As the poem concludes and the speaker describes a fall through space and a movement through other worlds, the isolation seems to grow until she is in a world that only she knows and can inhabit. The speaker also seems isolated from herself as she watches the funeral taking place in her brain.

This division of self may allude to madness as another possible theme in "I felt a Funeral, in my Brain." The funeral can be seen as a metaphor for the end of the speaker's rationality. The speaker's alienation is symptomatic of her loss. In the final stanza, Dickinson writes of dropping from "a Plank in Reason" (17). That the loss of one plank was enough to precipitate the plummeting leads the reader to believe that her hold on reason was not strong. In the poem's final line (20), the speaker has "Finished knowing." However, the poem does not conclude with these words. They are followed by a dash, the word *then,* and yet another dash. Has the speaker "finished knowing," or is there something to know beyond what the poem tells us? As so often in Dickinson, the words are open to some interpretation. The word *then* could lead us to consider what might happen to the speaker after all that is described ends. Or the line could be read in the sense of "Then I finished knowing." Dickinson's final dash seems to leave the reader in a netherworld—a place that the reader cannot imagine fully. Is it a void? Has the speaker reached its bottom, or is there the possibility of falling further still?

Perhaps this is less madness than the repression, or burial, of an unpleasant memory or aspect of the speaker's character. Sharon Cameron, in *Lyric Time: Dickinson and the Limits of Genre,* believes this to be the case. The funeral and subsequent burial, then, would depict the act of repressing. Line four, where the speaker says, "That Sense was breaking through," and the poem's end, where she has "Finished knowing," would show, first, the threat that awareness poses to her and then the relief of no longer knowing what she found so troubling.

On the other hand, the speaker may be confronting an aspect of herself that she finds difficult to face. The difficulty may prove so great that the poem's end represents a psychotic break. Less than the full madness discussed above, this would be a momentary break with reason, perhaps one where the final outcome is a loss of consciousness. Stanza four would depict the pain of being fully aware of the "funeral" she is feeling inside. Stanza five would show that this awareness is psychologically unbearable.

Sample Topics:

1. **Isolation:** How would you characterize the speaker's isolation in "I felt a Funeral, in my Brain"?

   Often in Dickinson's poetry, isolation is a desirable state. It connotes privacy and freedom or a certain status of the individual that makes him or her special and set apart from others. The isolation of the speaker in this poem seems different, though, almost like a metaphorical death sentence has been imposed.

2. **Madness:** Does the poem's audience, along with the speaker, observe her descent into madness?

   One possible thesis is that this poem attempts to depict the onset of madness in the speaker. A paper on this topic might chart that descent, relying on evidence from the poem.

3. **Repression:** Does "I felt a Funeral, in my Brain" seem to depict the process of repression?

   An essay on this topic might argue that "I felt a Funeral, in my Brain" shows a speaker repressing, or burying, an aspect of herself that she cannot face. Evidence could come from the poem in a discussion of tone, imagery, and language.

4. **The pain of awareness:** Does "I felt a Funeral, in my Brain" depict the crisis that comes with full experience or awareness of a painful event?

   Perhaps "I felt a Funeral, in my Brain" shows the effect of not repressing what pains an individual. It could be argued that the mind of the speaker confronts the pain she is feeling and therefore experiences a psychological break or loss of consciousness at the poem's conclusion. Evidence in the poem that supports this reading might include the sensory details, particularly those related to hearing. The speaker seems to be in a heightened state of awareness.

History and Context

One curious fact about the history of this poem is that when it was first published, the editors chose to remove the final stanza. How does it change your reading of the poem to omit that final stanza? While we can only guess why the editors made this decision, the guessing could lead us to draw some conclusions. Perhaps the final stanza points too much to the idea that Dickinson had at some point lost her senses. Perhaps the omission of the final stanza makes the poem seem more conventionally about a funeral.

In Dickinson's time, the funeral served as a narrative, both in the actions taken and the recalling of the events of the life. The descent of the body into the grave was not to be considered terrible, because the true self, the soul, had already ascended into heaven. One troubling aspect of Dickinson's poem is that there is no ascent. The poem concludes with a fall that does not end. In the tradition of the funeral narrative, this would be akin to damnation. "I felt a Funeral, in my Brain" encourages the reader to examine the conventions of the funeral. The reader knows how the funeral is supposed to go and what each step of the ritual is meant to represent. Here, the steps are taken, but they fail to have the desired outcome or meaning. Expectations are further undermined by the poem being spoken by the deceased.

The poem touches upon the fantasy of seeing one's own funeral. In its most idealized version, the deceased would hear kind words spoken about her, see the grief that overtakes all who know her, and be made certain of the value of her life. There is perhaps also an element of vindication, where all concerned would be made sorry not to have valued her more or sorry for the wrongs done her in life. This funeral, however, offers none of these consolations. Instead, there is only further separation from humankind.

Elizabeth Phillips links "I felt a Funeral, in my Brain" explicitly to the Civil War and the death of Emily Dickinson's close friend Frazer Stearns. John Cody believes this poem to be an expression of intense emotional pain, such as one might feel if grieving for a close friend. These readings do not see the funeral as something that is happening to the speaker, but rather something that the speaker observes. It could be the funeral of Stearns or that of any number of young men killed in the war.

Sample Topics:

1. **Editing:** How is "I felt a Funeral, in my Brain" changed by the presence of the final stanza?

   It is always strange to think that an editor would change the work of a poet such as Dickinson. It can be similarly fruitful to look at differing versions of a poem that the poet herself created. If you were to write an essay on this topic, you might form a thesis that argued that the final stanza is necessary to the poem. The final stanza brings the reader back to the image first presented in the opening stanza that "Sense was breaking through."

2. **Funerals:** How does Dickinson use the image of the funeral as a metaphor?

   A paper on this subject might begin by discussing the events of the funeral as depicted in Dickinson's poem and then discuss how these events conventionally happen versus how they happen here. Does Dickinson cause you to reexamine your beliefs about the funeral ceremony? What does it mean to have a narrator who is the dead person for whom this ceremony is performed?

3. **Seeing your own funeral:** How does this poem upend the fantasy of seeing one's own funeral?

   That "I felt a Funeral, in my Brain" offers none of the consolations typically seen in this fantasy is one possible thesis. Evidence you might use may include such things as the absence of dialogue. No one speaks of the deceased. She cannot hear, if they do, because language has been replaced by ominous sound and she is "Wrecked, solitary, here" (16).

4. **The Civil War and the death of Frazer Stearns:** Is this a Civil War poem?

A paper that wished to address this issue would perhaps want to look at Dickinson's letters and the Sewall biography to see the effect Frazer Stearns's death had on her. A possible thesis could be that "I felt a Funeral, in my Brain" was likely composed during the Civil War and was perhaps Dickinson's reaction to the funerals of the many war dead.

Philosophy and Ideas

"I felt a Funeral, in my Brain" looks at ideas of the interior and exterior, as well as the boundaries that may or may not exist between them. The poem seems to begin inside the brain of the speaker. By the end, the speaker appears to be falling through endless space. Although the space holds worlds, its vastness makes it seem frighteningly empty. The physical world that would usually form a support has been lost. All the normal frames of reference, such as the identity of the self or others, are also lost.

Dickinson's poems often concern her desire to understand her experiences. Perhaps most readers of literature approach poems in a similar way, hoping to make sense of their own experience. Here, the poem begins with a situation that is puzzling, but the ending of the poem does not help us to understand. As in many Dickinson poems, "I felt a Funeral, in my Brain" seems to posit death as the ultimate knowledge. It does this, again, by using a speaker who may, depending on your interpretation of the poem, be speaking from the grave. Even if the situation presented here is allowing us to follow a speaker into the grave, we are no less puzzled. The deceased does not know any more about death than the living do.

Time as we understand it is disarranged in "I felt a Funeral, in my Brain." The funeral seems to precede the true death. The time that is portrayed, like the duration of the funeral, moves rapidly toward the conclusion. Other markers of perception are similarly deranged. The funeral is "felt." The service is "like a Drum" (16) that is beating in the speaker's mind. She hears a box lift and "creak across" (10) her soul. These are only a few instances.

Sample Topics:

1. **Interiors and exteriors:** Where does the poem take place?

An essay on this topic would try to describe the setting of this poem. Is it inside the speaker's head? Do you feel a sense of claustrophobia at the beginning of the poem give way to a wish for some enclosure by the end? A close look at the diction used in the poem might help: words such as *breaking through, broke,* and *dropped.* You would also want to discuss line 12, where "Space—began to toll."

2. **Understanding:** Can this poem be said to be about a failure to understand?

"I felt a Funeral, in my Brain" begins with an image the speaker seems to be trying to understand, the "funeral" that is "felt." At the conclusion of the first stanza, she says that "it seemed / That Sense was breaking through." Using that image in concert with the final stanza might allow you to argue that the poem concerns a failed attempt at understanding or knowing.

3. **Death as the ultimate knowledge:** How does "I felt a Funeral, in my Brain" challenge the idea that death is the ultimate knowledge?

An essay on this topic might argue that this poem, like other Dickinson poems, does not portray death as the ultimate knowledge. If the speaker is dead, as many readers believe, the result is not a greater understanding, only a greater separation from the living.

4. **Derangment of the senses:** Is death a loss of the senses?

A thesis for an essay on this topic might say that in "I felt a Funeral, in my Brain," the only sense the speaker has left is hearing, which is lost by the poem's conclusion. You could also choose to write about how time is not arranged as we usually know it or simply explore some of Dickinson's odd imagery. For instance, how does one "feel" a "funeral"?

Language, Symbols, and Imagery

The entire poem could be considered a metaphor. You could argue that it is an extended metaphor for death, psychological crisis, or mourning. Isolated images could also be considered. For instance, the mourners may be a metaphor to express the speaker's pain. You might argue that "Space" (12) is a metaphor for purgatory or psychological isolation.

The repetitions in "I felt a Funeral, in my Brain" set an ominous tone. In the first stanza, the mourners are "treading—treading" (3). In the second, the service is "beating—beating" (17). In the concluding stanza, the speaker describes herself dropping "down, and down" (18). All of these words indicate a downward pressure, as if some force is pushing the speaker down. You will notice the many lines that begin with "And," making the words seem hurried. You may imagine a speaker who has to talk hurriedly in order to say all she can before she meets her end or perhaps a speaker who is frenetic in the way of a character out of Edgar Allan Poe's writing.

One notable aspect of this poem is that it is in the past tense. We know, therefore, that the conclusion of the poem is not the conclusion of the ordeal. After the speaker finishes "knowing," she is still able to relate what has happened to her. Is this another of Dickinson's speakers who is already deceased? Even though the poem is clearly in the past tense from the first line, the poem has a strange urgency, as if it is all happening now.

A valid way to approach any work of literature is to consider one image and its connotations. One of the more curious images in this poem is the "Plank in Reason" of line 17. What could Dickinson possibly wish for a reader to take from this image? Perhaps it brings to your mind the image of the planks holding the coffin aboveground before it is lowered. If so, that would explain the fall that happens when the plank breaks. But since the speaker falls and hits "worlds," it might also suggest that the movement into the grave is also a movement into hell. Or it may be just a movement into darkness and isolation, again, an image of the grave. But since this is a "Plank in Reason," it must have other possibilities as well. If someone's hold on reason is not firm, if he or she lacks a foundation, the person might be imagined to be balancing on a plank. His or her position would be precarious.

Sample Topics:

1. **Metaphor:** Is there an extended metaphor at work in the poem?

If you wished to argue that "I felt a Funeral, in my Brain" is about the process of grieving, you might try to explain the metaphors you find in each image. For instance, you might argue that a funeral can indeed be "felt" as well as attended and that to truly "feel" a funeral is to grieve. In truth, attendance does not matter much at all, for you might be able to feel funerals that you do not attend. You could attempt to "read" the metaphors no matter what your interpretation of the poem might be.

2. **Repetition:** How does Dickinson use repetition in "I felt a Funeral, in my Brain"?

To argue this topic, you might say the repetitions in the poem are what lead readers to believe the speaker is mad. You could also discuss how the use of the word *and* speeds up the reading and makes the poem seem hurried and rushed. Does this lead you to trust or distrust the speaker?

3. **Tense:** Why is the poem in the past tense?

An essay on this topic might argue that setting the poem in the past tense tells the reader more about how the poem concludes. For instance, you might argue that whatever tragedy befell the speaker, she has survived it. We know because she is able to communicate something of it to us now.

4. **The plank:** What does the image of the "Plank in Reason" suggest to you?

You might wish to say that the plank is an image of the speaker's precarious hold on reality. You could also argue that the plank is a fitting description of the support a corpse would feel before being lowered into the ground. Whatever interpretation you give to the plank would have to be supported by the other imagery of the poem and would influence your interpretation of the whole.

Compare and Contrast Essays

One Dickinson poem "I felt a Funeral, in my Brain" very much resembles is #465—"I heard a fly buzz—when I Died." In both poems, there is, possibly, a speaker who has already died. Both are entirely in the past tense while leaving the present unaccounted for. At the conclusion of each poem is what appears to be a fall into unconsciousness or certainly darkness. You might also wish to compare how both poems feature distorted sensory perception. "I felt a Funeral, in my Brain" concerns itself mostly with the sense of hearing. "I heard a fly buzz—when I Died" shares that interest, as the first line will tell you, but seems to focus most on seeing.

You could argue that "I felt a Funeral, in my Brain" is about spiritual paralysis, and go on to compare or contrast it with any number of the many poems Dickinson wrote on this subject. If the speaker is experiencing some sort of paralysis, that would explain her inability to act or to communicate. In #341—"After great pain, a formal feeling comes," the physical body is also compared to a funeral. In that poem, the paralysis is compared to freezing to death. Dickinson's #512—"The Soul has Bandaged moments," is a bit more straightforward and could easily be contrasted with "I felt a Funeral, in my Brain." In "The Soul has Bandaged moments," the soul is actually shown dancing and swinging in stanza three, when it breaks from its captivity. But the beginning and end of the poem are a vision of gothic horror, with the soul kept enchained by a demon, unable to speak.

Three poems that could be used in a compare and contrast essay about pain in Dickinson are #305—"The difference between Despair," #396—"There is a Languor of the Life," and #875—"I stepped from Plank to Plank." There is no shortage of Dickinson poems on the subject of pain. "I stepped from Plank to Plank" could be interesting in comparison to "I felt a Funeral, in my Brain" because it revisits this image of the plank. In "There is a Langour of the Life," Dickinson writes of a pain so great that death is the only release. "The difference between Despair" shows a paralysis like those discussed above and also a loss of the ability to see.

Karen Ford in *Gender and the Poetics of Excess: Moments of Brocade* says that poem #937—"I felt a Cleaving in my Mind" is the companion

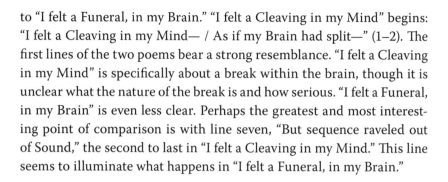
to "I felt a Funeral, in my Brain." "I felt a Cleaving in my Mind" begins: "I felt a Cleaving in my Mind— / As if my Brain had split—" (1–2). The first lines of the two poems bear a strong resemblance. "I felt a Cleaving in my Mind" is specifically about a break within the brain, though it is unclear what the nature of the break is and how serious. "I felt a Funeral, in my Brain" is even less clear. Perhaps the greatest and most interesting point of comparison is with line seven, "But sequence raveled out of Sound," the second to last in "I felt a Cleaving in my Mind." This line seems to illuminate what happens in "I felt a Funeral, in my Brain."

Sample Topics:

1. **The fall into unconsciousness:** Can a comparison of this poem with Dickinson's "I heard a fly buzz—when I Died" show that both poems are about a fall into unconsciousness?

   An essay on this topic might argue that both poems show that Dickinson feared death was a losing of conscious perception. Comparing the endings of "I felt a Funeral, in my Brain" and "I heard a fly buzz—when I Died" presents a striking similarity in their concern with not knowing.

2. **Spiritual paralysis:** How can "I felt a Funeral, in my Brain," like other Dickinson poems, be said to be about spiritual paralysis?

   "The Soul has Bandaged moments" would be an interesting poem to contrast or compare with "I felt a Funeral, in my Brain." "After great pain, a formal feeling comes" could be discussed in a comparative essay, too. One possible thesis is that these poems (whichever you choose) show that Dickinson portrayed intense suffering as paralyzing.

3. **Representations of pain:** How does "I felt a Funeral, in my Brain" compare to other Dickinson poems in its representation of pain?

   You could choose to compare "I felt a Funeral, in my Brain" to one of the three poems mentioned above, #305—"The difference between Despair," #396—"There is a Languor of the Life," or #875—"I stepped from Plank to Plank," or you could choose another you have read. The poem you choose will dictate the direction of your essay.

4. **Loss of reason:** Is "I felt a Funeral, in my Brain," like "I felt a Cleaving in my Mind," about a loss of reason?

If you were to pursue this topic, you would want to read Karen Ford's discussion of these two poems. You might decide to either agree or disagree with her argument. There is evidence to support both readings.

Bibliography and Online Resources

Bennett, Paula. *Emily Dickinson: Woman Poet.* Iowa City: Iowa UP, 1991.

Budick, E. Miller. *Emily Dickinson and the Life of Language.* Baton Rouge: Louisiana State UP, 1985.

Cameron, Sharon. *Lyric Time: Dickinson and the Limits of Genre.* Baltimore: Johns Hopkins UP, 1979.

Cody, John. *After Great Pain: The Inner Life of Emily Dickinson.* Cambridge, MA: Harvard UP, 1971.

Ford, Karen. *Gender and the Poetics of Excess: Moments of Brocade.* Oxford: UP of Mississippi, 1997.

Johnson, Thomas H., ed. *The Poems of Emily Dickinson.* 3 vols. Cambridge, MA: Harvard UP, 1979.

Johnson, Thomas H., and Theodora Ward, eds. *The Letters of Emily Dickinson.* 3 vols. Cambridge, MA: Harvard UP, 1986.

Phillips, Elizabeth. *Emily Dickinson: Personae and Performance.* University Park: Pennsylvania State Press, 1988.

Sewall, Richard B. *The Life of Emily Dickinson.* Cambridge, MA: Harvard UP, 1974.

Wolff, Cynthia Griffin. *Emily Dickinson.* New York: Knopf, 1986.

#288—
"I'M NOBODY!
WHO ARE YOU?"

READING TO WRITE

"I'M NOBODY! Who are you?" is one of Dickinson's most popular poems. It is a poem often taught in high school classrooms and remembered even when the reader no longer recalls the name of the poet. "I'm Nobody! Who are you?" seems to speak to a universal feeling of being on the outside. It appears to validate that experience. The "nobodies" of the poem revel in their status.

In addition, the speaker of the poem is defiant in the face of the powers that be. As stanza two says of those others, "How dreary—to be—Somebody! / How public—like a Frog!" (5–6). As Dickinson wrote elsewhere, "My barefoot rank is better" (*Letters* 408). And there is a bit of satire in poem #288. It may be directed toward authority figures. It may be directed at those who value public status. It could be directed toward those who would publish their poems.

As you read the poem and consider how to write about it, a central question you might ask is why this poem has proved so popular. One possible answer is in the conspiratorial tone. How do you picture the sound of the speaker's voice? It seems it is a whisper directed at one special other. That special other, gifted with an understanding of the speaker's innermost self, is the reader. You might compare it to another well-known American poem, Walt Whitman's "Song of Myself." In that poem, Whitman introduces himself as "Walt Whitman, an American, one of the roughs, a kosmos" (449). How different he is from Dickinson! Whereas a reader might read the first line of Whitman and admire Whitman, the first line of "I'm Nobody! Who are you?" might lead the reader to think Dickinson is saying, I am just like you. In some respects, this poem seduces the reader into complicity with its writer.

TOPICS AND STRATEGIES

This section of the chapter will seek to provide you with various approaches you might take in writing a paper about this poem. These ideas are by no means exhaustive and should be looked at as a starting point for your own investigation.

Themes

"I'm Nobody! Who are you?" is a poem, in part, about anonymity. Most of us would not, on first glance, want to consider ourselves "nobody." This poem praises the state. Those who are "somebody," on the other hand, are portrayed as pompous and egotistical. They are also rendered comical, because the "Bog" does not care what their names are.

As discussed above, the poem mounts a bit of a conspiracy with the two "nobodies" in league against those who would be "somebody." "I'm Nobody! Who are you?" becomes a poem of us against them. Looking just at the structure of the poem, you will see that the two stanzas evenly divide. The first stanza is dedicated to the "nobodies." The second stanza is about being "somebody." The two nobodies of the first stanza remain quiet, while the frog of the second stanza speaks incessantly.

Gudrun Grabher in *The Emily Dickinson Handbook* states that this poem exemplifies "the voice made audible and the person invisible" (231). The voice is another theme of "I'm Nobody! Who are you?" The division between the two groups, those who are nobody and those who are somebody, is a division in the manner of speaking. The speech of the first stanza is private and intimate. The speech of the second stanza is public and self-promoting.

Along the same lines is another theme: recognition. The speaker recognizes another who is also a "nobody." Readers recognize themselves in the poem. Who recognizes the frog? He tells his name, but only "to an admiring Bog." The poem does not identify him with any particulars. The bog, even though described as "admiring," likely does not care. What does it matter if you are admired by a bog? But to be recognized by another who truly understands you is a gift.

Sample Topics:

1. **Anonymity:** How does this poem raise anonymity to a virtue?

One thesis on this topic would be that "I'm Nobody! Who are you?" reverses the usual signs of status so that to be nobody is a more valued state than being somebody. If you were to pursue this argument, you might discuss the image of the frog. You might also discuss Dickinson's own preference for a reclusive existence.

2. **Us v. them:** How is "I'm Nobody! Who are you?" another of Dickinson's poems about exclusion?

If you were to pursue this argument, you might argue that Dickinson sets up a hierarchy wherein to be "nobody" is far more valued than to be "somebody." To begin, you might discuss the structure of the poem. How do the two groups stand in contrast to each other?

3. **The voice:** What is the importance of the voice in this poem?

If you agree with what was stated by Grabher above, you might argue that this poem is about claiming the voice while disavowing the body. In the second stanza, the only sound the frog can make is self-referential. He speaks only his name. If you have come into contact with a bog, you know that the croaking drowns out the individual frog, leaving only the sound of an unidentifiable mass. You might also want to talk about what the voice of the frog is like. This is not Dickinson's beloved Bobolink or any other songbird.

4. **Recognition:** How is "I'm Nobody! Who are you?" about the importance of recognition?

Again, this poem subverts expectations. In general, it is considered positive to be recognized. In this poem, it is just the opposite. One possible thesis on this topic is that "I'm Nobody! Who are you?" shows that true recognition from another is better than being superficially known by many.

Language, Symbols, and Imagery

In a poem of only eight short lines, the imagery does a great deal of the work. The basic images here are the frog, the bog, the name, and nobody. Any of these could make an interesting discussion for the purposes of an essay. To begin, you would consider the positive and negative connotations of each. What are the connotations of the frog? Although frogs sometimes are transformed into princes, frogs are largely viewed in a negative light. They are slimy and bloated, and the noise that they make—the croak—is not pretty or especially expressive.

The word *bog* also has negative connotations. We speak of being "bogged down," stuck in the mire or otherwise held back. Bogs are muddy and wet. It seems unlikely that anything positive could come from one.

No one is "named" in this poem, while the frog repeats his. The two "nobodies" are identified only by that term. But, in a sense, they have the same name. Or, keeping their names to themselves is what distinguishes them from others. As the poem says in line four, "Don't tell! they'd advertise—you know!" Privacy was highly valued by Dickinson. She considered keeping one's self private a sign of self-respect.

The usual connotations of "nobody" are all negative. To say someone is nobody is considered insulting. Think about the connotations of *nobody* within this poem. The word comes to mean something quite different. You might also break the word down into the way it would be heard: no body. Would it ever be desirable to have no body? Would such a creature be only spirit, or, in the case of a poet, would she perhaps be only a voice?

Sample Topics:

1. **Frog:** How does the image of the frog contribute to Dickinson's poem?

An essay on this topic might argue that this essentially comic image explains why Dickinson's poem is so memorable. Who can forget this great, pompous, overblown frog repeating his name over and over?

2. **Bog:** What does the image of the bog tell you about the frog's admirers?

This is such a negative image. In a bog, everyone melds together, becoming prisoners of the slime and muck they live in. The frogs (or people) of the bog stand in stark contrast to the two nobodies of stanza one.

3. **Name:** Why would it be considered a positive to keep your name a secret?

This has to do with identities and perhaps knowing oneself. One possible thesis on this topic would be that the name is the most valued aspect of the person. It is who one is. "To tell one's name," then, would be to give one's self away. In this sense, this poem shares a great deal with Dickinson's #709—"Publication is the auction."

4. **Nobody:** What is the image of nobody in "I'm Nobody! Who are you?"

How does this poem upend expectations about what it means to be nobody? You might approach an essay on this topic with a discussion of being nobody in terms of being without a physical body. Another means of approach would be to simply discuss the connotations of nobody and how the poem shows its virtues. In this poem, to be somebody is laughable.

Compare and Contrast Essays

Other Dickinson poems that share the theme of us versus them are #435—"Much Madness is divinest Sense" and "The Soul selects her own Society." "Much Madness is divinest Sense" makes clear that the majority rules when it comes to making distinctions between madness and sense. She writes that all you need do is "Demur—you're straightway

dangerous— / And handled with a Chain" (7–8). "The Soul selects her
own Society" is similar to "I'm Nobody! Who are you?" in its recognition
of one likeminded soul who is taken in. Together, these two form their
own "majority."

Sometimes it can be fun to trace an image through an author's work.
This can show you how an author thought about this particular idea
and perhaps allow you to find more meaning in any one instance of
its use. Dickinson frequently revisits images, ideas, and motifs. The
image of the frog is an interesting one to consider. You will find frogs
in poems #1359—"The long sigh of the Frog" and #1379—"His Mansion
in the Pool." "The long sigh of the Frog" provides another view of the
frog's croaking, which is more in line with Dickinson's exaltation of the
natural world. "His Mansion in the Pool" shows what could be a more
sharply drawn portrait of the same frog met in "I'm Nobody! Who are
you?"

In Dickinson's #1465—"Before you thought of Spring," a bird heralds
the change in season with "shouts of joy to Nobody / But his seraphic
self" (15–16). As in "I'm Nobody! Who are you?" the bird is admired for
his independence. He does not care about his listener on the ground,
although for a moment she flatters herself that he does.

"I died for Beauty," Dickinson's poem #449, is an interesting one to
pair with "I'm Nobody! Who are you?" The speaker has died and next to
her is lain one who has "died for Truth" (3). Automatically, these would
seem to have more status than the nobodies of the latter poem. Like the
two nobodies, they recognize their kinship. Dickinson writes: "And so, as
Kinsmen, met at Night— / We talked between the Rooms— / Until the
Moss had reached our lips— / And covered up—our names" (9–12). The
covering up of the names is the end of the poem. What does that mean to
the two who died for truth and for beauty? Does their anonymity obliter-
ate them, or does it free them?

Sample Topics:

1. **Majority vs. minority:** How does Dickinson portray the majority versus the minority?

Many Dickinson poems reveal a love for the underdog. If you
were to compare "Much Madness is divinest Sense" to "I'm

Nobody! Who are you?" you might discuss how both poems emphasize the need to keep quiet. There is a threatening aspect to what will happen if the majority finds out about them. If you were to compare "The soul selects her own Society" to "I'm Nobody! Who are you?" you might choose to discuss the importance of belonging and recognition, or how a minority can take on the strength of a majority.

2. **Other frogs:** How can looking at other examples of frogs in Dickinson's poems shed light on the frog from "I'm Nobody! Who are you?"

A comparison of #1359—"The long sigh of the Frog" with "I'm Nobody! Who are you?" could be useful, particularly if you wished to discuss voice in both those poems. It would be very interesting to write an essay comparing #1379—"His Mansion in the Pool" to "I'm Nobody! Who are you?" In the former poem, Dickinson depicts a frog as "Orator of April" (7). Unlike the frog of "I'm Nobody! Who are you?" this one disappears when applauded.

3. **The pleasures of nobody:** How does Dickinson make her admiration for "nobody" clear?

In #1465—"Before you thought of Spring," Dickinson introduces another "nobody." If you were to write an essay comparing this poem to "I'm Nobody! Who are you?" you might argue that Dickinson's admiration for the natural world stems in part from its indifference to its human inhabitants. This is seen, also, in "His Mansion in the Pool." The animals have an anonymity that the poet considers enviable.

4. **Names:** What does it mean to lose your name?

Poem #449—"I died for Beauty" ends with the loss of names. "I'm Nobody! Who are you?" features a frog who trumpets his name all day long. What is the significance of the name in these two poems? One possible thesis is that Dickinson portrays anonymity as necessary for getting to the essence of an individual.

Bibliography and Online Resources

Grabher, Gudrun, Roland Hagenbuchle, and Cristanne Miller, eds. *The Emily Dickinson Handbook.* Amherst: U of Massachusetts P, 1998.

Johnson, Thomas H., ed. *The Poems of Emily Dickinson.* 3 vols. Cambridge, MA: Harvard UP, 1979.

Johnson, Thomas H., and Theodora Ward, eds. *The Letters of Emily Dickinson.* 3 vols. Cambridge, MA: Harvard UP, 1986.

Sewall, Richard B. *The Life of Emily Dickinson.* Cambridge, MA: Harvard UP, 1974.

#303—
"THE SOUL SELECTS
HER OWN SOCIETY"

READING TO WRITE

MUCH LIKE "I'm Nobody! Who are you?" "The Soul selects her own Society" is a poem about two who are uniquely set apart; however, "I'm Nobody! Who are you?" is often read as comic in its intent, and its tone is markedly lighter than in Dickinson's poem #303. "The Soul selects her own Society" describes the way the soul chooses "One" (10) as her own. The nature of that one is something you will want to reflect upon. The process the soul goes through in the choosing resembles a wedding ceremony wherein all others are forsaken. There is a solemnity and beauty to the idea that the soul will "close the Valves of her attention" (11) and then admit in no one, not even an "Emperor" (7).

The soul is personified as female in line one, but it might be equally as valid to see her as a fortress or a woman enclosed in such a structure, for this soul has a door, a gate, a mat, and those "Valves of . . . attention." The tone and diction of the poem lead the reader to picture someone stately and regal; if an emperor does not move her, it is possible that she is an empress. She does have a "divine Majority" that she shuts out.

In the second stanza, the reader sees how uncompromising she is. No entreaty will cause her to open her door another time. The repetition of the word *unmoved* at the beginning of lines five and seven underscores this.

In the third stanza, Dickinson makes clear how exclusive the soul is. From an "ample nation" (9) the soul chooses only one. All others are excluded not only from her soul but from her own attention. The overwhelming sense is that the soul is abrupt but sure. There is something impressive about the certainty of its choosing and the valves that close "like stone" (12), as the final line says. In Western culture, "The Soul selects her own Society" might be read as representing an ideal of romantic love. In a Christian culture, the poem could be read as an ideal of Christian commitment.

TOPICS AND STRATEGIES

This section of the chapter will seek to provide you with various approaches you might take in writing a paper about this poem. These ideas are by no means exhaustive and should be looked at as a starting point for your own investigation.

Themes

When people use the word *society*, they generally mean a large group, people like themselves, or an elite group. Dickinson's poem introduces the idea of a society of a few or only two, depending on your interpretation of the poem. The idea that this is an elite group is still there, however. Whoever is admitted to the soul's society must first have moved the soul to open itself, and one can imagine how difficult this might be.

This poem is often considered a love poem. Generally, when we think of allowing someone into our soul (or heart), we think of one beloved person and then no other. As in Dickinson's poem, the choice admits no argument. And, as in her poem, the position of the other is of no matter. That is, not even an emperor could usurp the beloved's position. "The Soul selects her own Society" has often been considered an autobiographical poem, answering the question of why Dickinson never married. In that reading, Dickinson chose one, and though that one could not marry her (was perhaps already married) or did not choose her in return, for Dickinson, all choosing ended.

But the emphasis in the poem seems less on the choosing than on the act of excluding all others. This is a rather common Dickinson trait. You might ask yourself why exclusion would be important to the poet. Does it somehow make her special, too, like the beloved one? Is it a testimony to her wisdom in choosing? Is it a testament to her loyalty? You might consider the diction in the poem as you think about these questions. In the second line, she writes, the soul "shuts the Door." Shutting a door may be an innocuous act, but more often it is a rejection. In stanza two, she twice opens a line with "Unmoved" (5, 7). There is some suggestion that the people outside who would have her attention are intruding upon her.

This is another poem that shows Dickinson's self-reliant attitude. The right of the soul to make her choice is unassailable. The soul's wisdom is taken for granted. This might be seen as an assertion of self. The soul knows better than the "divine Majority" (3).

Sample Topics:

1. **Society:** What sort of society is intended in "The Soul selects her own Society"?

   A paper on this topic might argue that Dickinson uses the conventional definition of society in this poem but changes it to suit her message. This society remains elite and select. It is so select that it may be a society of one.

2. **Love:** How can this be said to be a love poem?

   Certainly, "The Soul selects her own Society" adheres to the conventions of romantic love. In this reading, the poem is about finding what we now call the "soul mate."

3. **Exclusion:** Why is the act of excluding emphasized in "The Soul selects her own Society"?

   An essay on this topic might argue that the poem's audience is not the beloved, but all of those people who would ask for the speaker's attention. Evidence might come in the form of an analysis of Dickinson's diction in the poem. You might also note that the one chosen is not described, as if who has been chosen is unimportant.

4. **Self-reliance:** How does this poem display the self-reliance of its speaker?

One possible thesis is that "The Soul selects her own Society" displays a particularly American faith in the individual. Does the "divine Majority" include God? Can no one, not even a deity, open the doors to the soul again? The answer seems to be no.

Philosophy and Ideas

Discussions of the soul are often religious in context. Do you think that is what is meant here? Could the "soul" of this poem also be a synonym for what we routinely call the "heart"? Generally, the soul is considered the essence of the person and the part that continues after the mortal body dies. This lends value to the idea of being chosen by the soul. The implication is that this choice will continue beyond death.

The phrase *divine Majority* is a curious one. It is tempting to think that the majority are those excluded. However, the use of the adjective *divine* leads to other readings. It seems that now that the soul has selected, those two have formed a majority. Or, at least to the speaker this is what they represent. The word *divine* elevates the "society."

E. Miller Budick makes an interesting observation in *Emily Dickinson and the Life of Language*. She writes: "Phrases like 'The Soul selects', 'her divine Majority', 'an ample nation', and 'Choose One' are intended to call to mind several of the platform doctrines of Puritan faith—the Calvinist principle of divine, inscrutable selectivity, for example, the covenant of grace, and the analogy between the individual saint and the chosen nation, Israel" (139). The poem on a first reading announces its religious language; further research would help you to decide about its Puritan influences or ideas.

Overwhelmingly, "The Soul selects her own Society" is about the virtue of fidelity. Whether it is a love poem, a religious poem, a poem of friendship, or any of the other possible readings, it is a poem that praises the idea of loyalty. Evidence in the poem to support this reading can be found in each stanza. In the first, words such as *society* and *divine* let the reader know how the one the soul has selected is valued. The stanza concludes with the demand: "Present no more" (4). The soul no longer wishes to have anyone presented to her. As the second stanza continues, it is made clear that no person, no matter how exalted, will be admitted. The soul is "unmoved." The word *unmoved,* repeated as it is, gives the sense of the stony silence the soul now maintains. The doors are shut and the valves closed, even the "Valves of her attention."

Sample Topics:

1. **The soul:** What do you think Dickinson means when she refers to the "soul" in this poem?

   An essay on this topic might argue that Dickinson means the seat of romantic love. It might also argue that she is referring to the innermost self. Some evidence supporting the idea that she is referring to the heart are the references to "valves" and to "stone." The heart has valves and is sometimes described as being hardened like stone.

2. **Divinity:** How can the "society" of the soul be like divinity?

   If you take "The Soul selects her own Society" to be a love poem, this is another instance in which Dickinson gives to love the importance of religion. Of course, this would mean that the one housed in her soul is of a rank greater than an emperor and certainly greater than all those nameless personages whose chariots pause at her gate.

3. **Puritanism:** Is "The Soul selects her own Society" a poem born out of Puritanism?

   An essay on this topic would likely start by looking at Budick's text. Other than the images she has identified as Puritan in origin, what other images are perhaps also Puritan? While the possibility that the poem is particularly American was raised above, it also has echoes of the royalist about it, as well as the fairy tale.

4. **Fidelity:** How can "The Soul selects her own Society" be said to be a poem of fidelity?

Fidelity is usually considered a virtue. Here, fidelity is raised to the level of religion. The evidence to make this argument is ample in the poem. You might discuss the tone, the imagery, and the diction.

Language, Symbols, and Imagery

Dickinson writes compact and concise lyrics. It might be useful to puzzle about how she packs such a great deal of meaning into what is usually between eight and 12 lines. In "The Soul selects her own Society," the 12 lines are organized in units of two. That is, every two lines of the poem is an independent phrase or thought unit. All expected rhymes are present, though they are not exact rhymes in most cases. Dickinson relies heavily on alliteration. In lines one and two, the alliteration seems to emphasize the important words: *Soul, selects, Society,* and *shuts.* The rhyme scheme of ABAB reinforces the unity of the phrases and the stanzas.

Of the many ways the soul has been characterized, this is the only instance the author of this book knows of when it has been depicted as a house. In "The Soul selects her own Society," the soul controls a space that resembles a humble house. It has a door, a gate, and a mat. Outside is the great world of people and emperors. The house, however, is inviolable. She is in strict control of who enters. If you have read even a little of Dickinson, you are aware how important the idea of home was to her.

The choice of the word *stone* to conclude the poem is meant to show how fixed the soul is once it has made its decision. Even as Dickinson repeats the word *unmoved* in lines five and seven, there is the suggestion of something stony, maybe statuelike. Has the soul become hardened? Souls, though they are thought to endure, seem ethereal.

You may notice that in the last stanza, the second and fourth lines are shorter than in the preceding stanzas. In the first two stanzas, the second and fourth lines are four syllables in length; in the final stanza, they are each two syllables. Dickinson may have chosen to do this in order to emphasize these two lines. In other chapters, it has been noted that the dash that often ends her poems gives the work a sense of openendedness. It does not seem to have the same effect here.

Sample Topics:

1. **Compression:** Why does Dickinson's typically compressed form work so well in this poem?

One possible thesis for an essay on this topic would be that Dickinson's "The Soul selects her own Society" is a perfect example of the marriage of form and subject. The poem mirrors the locked box of the soul. Analysis of the formal elements of the poem would assist you in making this argument.

2. **Soul as house:** What are the connotations of home?

If you feel comfortable in doing so, it might be interesting to approach this topic by discussing what the connotations of home were to Dickinson specifically. However, this is not required. Building upon the most general knowledge, you could write a paper that discusses the image of the soul as a house. Why would the soul be homelike? What makes this image so unusual? What makes it apt?

3. **Stone:** Is *stone* an apt word in this poem?

A bit like the image of the soul as a house, the idea of a soul closed as stone may strike you as odd. What are the connotations of this word? When you think of valves, are they ever like stone? Does the image strike you as overly cold and unyielding?

4. **Conclusion:** Does "The Soul selects her own Society" close satisfactorily?

This may take you back to some of the previous discussions in this chapter. This poem, unlike many other Dickinson poems, seems to close "like stone." An essay on this topic would argue that this is the only way to end a poem on this subject. The conclusion admits no argument.

Compare and Contrast Essays

Dickinson's #683—"The Soul unto itself" discusses the soul's ability to take care of itself. In it, the soul becomes a sort of kingdom unto itself. The soul is "friend" (2), "enemy" (4), and "Sovereign" (7). As in "The Soul selects her own Society," this soul is also a stronghold. Dickinson suggests that because the soul needs no one else, it "should stand in Awe" (8) of itself.

Most discussions of the soul center on religion, and many of Dickinson's poems discuss the soul's relationship to God. As you may imagine, however, her approach to this is unconventional. In #357—"God is a distant—stately Lover," the portrayal of God as lover startles in the opening line. As the poem continues, the triangle of God, Jesus, and the soul is compared to the triangle of Miles Standish, Priscilla Mullins, and John Alden. The story of the Pilgrim love triangle is taken from Henry Wadsworth Longfellow's *The Courtship of Miles Standish* (1858). While the idea of God as lover does not begin with Dickinson, it retains some power to shock, particularly when aligned with a popular romance.

"He fumbles at your Soul" shares the mingling of the religious and the romantic. How you interpret the poem hinges upon who you decide the "He" is. "He" may be God; "He" may be a lover. His power is absolute.

You might choose to see in "The Soul selects her own Society" a statement of Dickinson's own power. As the soul in that poem knows and makes its choice, so does Dickinson. This sets her apart from what is generally accepted as society. In #508—"I'm ceded—I've stopped being Theirs," you'll see a similar statement of power. In the first stanza, the speaker puts away her name, her childhood, and her occupations. In the second, she is baptized anew, this time by her own choice. She takes a new name and existence. The identity she has outgrown is replaced. She writes that she is now "Crowned—Crowing—on my Father's breast— / A half unconscious Queen" (15–16).

It is a very different speaker in #1055—"The Soul should always stand ajar." It is a bit difficult to imagine that this and "The Soul selects her own Society" come from the same poet. "The Soul should always stand ajar" appears to be a more conventionally religious poem. Its message is related by its first line: The soul should remain with its door always open so that, if God calls, He can easily enter.

Sample Topics:

1. **The soul alone:** How is "The Soul unto itself" like "The Soul selects her own Society"?

   In both poems, the soul is personified. In both, they exhibit tremendous self-reliance. A thesis comparing these two poems might say that the soul in "The Soul unto itself" is very like the soul in "The Soul selects her own Society," except that in the former poem the soul is its own society. It needs no other.

2. **God and the soul:** How does Dickinson approach the subject of God and the soul?

If you were to write an essay comparing "God is a distant— stately Lover" to "The Soul selects her own Society," you might begin by saying that the former poem is evidence that the society admitted in the latter poem is God. If you were to contrast #315—"He fumbles at your Soul" with "The Soul selects her own Society," one place to begin would be with a discussion of the power of the soul in both poems. You will notice that in the latter, the soul maintains absolute control. In "He fumbles at your Soul," it is a powerful "He," perhaps God, but certainly someone godlike, who overpowers the soul.

3. **Set apart:** How does #508—"I'm ceded—I've stopped being Theirs," like "The Soul selects her own Society," show a speaker set apart from her peers?

A paper that compared these two poems might focus on the idea of choice. How are both speakers exalted? What part does royalty play in both poems? What part does religion play? Would you say that these poems are primarily religious or romantic in focus? How would you characterize the speakers of these poems?

4. **Two souls:** How different is the message of #1055—"The Soul should always stand ajar" from that of "The Soul selects her own Society"?

You might argue that the difference between these two poems is the difference between the secular and the religious. Of course, there are similarities in the characterization of the soul as a house with a door and those who would be housed in the soul as callers. It is also interesting that Dickinson personifies the soul, each time, as "she."

Bibliography and Online Resources

Budick, E. Miller. *Emily Dickinson and the Life of Language*. Baton Rouge: Louisiana UP, 1985.

Cameron, Sharon. *Choosing Not Choosing: Dickinson's Fascicles*. Chicago: U of Chicago P, 1992.

Hecht, Anthony. "The Riddles of Emily Dickinson." *Obbligati: Essays on Criticism*. New York: Atheneum, 1986. 85–117.

Johnson, Thomas H., ed. *The Poems of Emily Dickinson*. 3 vols. Cambridge, MA: Harvard UP, 1979.

Johnson, Thomas H., and Theodora Ward, eds. *The Letters of Emily Dickinson*. 3 vols. Cambridge, MA: Harvard UP, 1986.

Juhasz, Suzanne. *The Undiscovered Continent: Emily Dickinson and the Space of the Mind*. Bloomington: Indiana UP, 1983.

Longfellow, Henry Wadsworth. *"The Courtship of Miles Standish."* Worldwide School. 8 Oct. 2006 <http://www.worldwideschool.org/library/books/lit/poetry/TheCompletePoeticalWorksofHenryWadsworthLongfellow/chap10.html>.

Lutscher, Robert M. "An Emersonian Context of Dickinson's 'The Soul selects her own Society.'" *ESQ: A Journal of the American Renaissance* 30 (1984): 111–116.

Monteiro, George. "Dickinson's Select Society." *Dickinson Studies* 39.1 (1981): 41–43.

Sewall, Richard B. *The Life of Emily Dickinson*. Cambridge, MA: Harvard UP, 1974.

#324—"SOME KEEP THE SABBATH GOING TO CHURCH"

READING TO WRITE

"**S**OME KEEP the Sabbath going to Church" was one of those handful of poems published during Dickinson's lifetime. The poem appeared in a publication called the *Round Table* on March 12, 1864. It was printed with the title "My Sabbath," and it is possible that Dickinson herself gave it this title.

As you read this poem and consider how to write about it, you will find fewer problems of interpretation than you are likely to encounter in other Dickinson poems. "Some keep the Sabbath going to Church" announces its subject in the first line. The idea behind the poem, though it may have been shocking to some readers in 1864, will not trouble many now. The poem's speaker suggests that while some go to church to practice their religion and to be close to God, it is possible to be close to Him (perhaps closer than one can be in the church) in nature. The speaker says of the Sabbath: "I keep it, staying at Home" (2). In that line is one theme of this poem and of many of Dickinson's other works, the superiority of home to anywhere else.

As the poem continues, an elaborate metaphor of home as church is developed. Every element you might expect to find in a conventional church service is here replaced by a natural occurrence. Dickinson moves the reader to consider whether the service humankind has created could ever rival God's own creation. Although the answer may seem blasphemous, it is rather obvious that it could not.

If you read biographical material about Dickinson, you will learn that she did not attend church services after she began to seclude herself. You will also learn that home was to her a sacred place and perhaps that she lavished much care upon the gardens of her home. In such lines as "God preaches, a noted Clergyman— / And the sermon is never long" (9–10), you may recognize Dickinson's satiric tone. The poem concludes with the following statement: "So instead of getting to Heaven, at last— / "I'm going, all along" (11–12). In those lines you might hear Dickinson's self-confidence, as well as her belief that she was able to approach God without a mediator.

TOPICS AND STRATEGIES

This section of the chapter will seek to provide you with various approaches you might take in writing a paper about this poem. These ideas are by no means exhaustive and should be looked at as a starting point for your own investigation.

Themes

Although this poem sings the virtues of "staying at Home," its real setting is a garden. The garden is a common setting for a religious experience. The Garden of Gethsemane, for instance, and Jesus' time there, is a well known biblical story. The garden is also a setting of beauty and abundance, and so may be considered symbolic of God's wonders and gifts. The poem follows the biblical injunction to remember the Sabbath and keep it holy (Exodus 20:8–11). The Bible does not say that this should be done in a church.

For Dickinson, there was no one place as important to her as the house that is now called the Dickinson Homestead. Reading through her poems or letters, the idea of home occurs often. She seemed to have conceived of her home as its own universe. And so it is not surprising that her home should have also had a church. For some people, church is an idea that is carried along inside. Worship, of course, needs no specific place.

Another theme present in Dickinson's poem is the idea that paradise may be present in this world. Certainly, the scene described by the poem is idyllic. The final two lines are: "So instead of getting to Heaven, at last— / I'm going, all along" (11–12). There is something quite moving about those lines. Not only do they show Dickinson's self-assurance—she does not seem to doubt that heaven is her clear destination—but they also show disbelief that any idea of renunciation or unhappiness on Earth will guarantee a later reward. All rewards are already present.

Inherent in the poem is the idea of a personal religion. To those who were seated at a Sunday service while Dickinson was in her garden, this idea would likely seem blasphemous. However, in Dickinson's work, personal conversations with God are the norm. He does not necessarily answer, but Dickinson is not shy about speaking to him and believes he hears.

Sample Topics:

1. **The garden:** How does "Some keep the Sabbath going to Church" make the argument that a garden is an apt place for worship?

   To make the above argument, Dickinson draws parallels between her garden and the church. One way to write this paper would be to discuss each of those parallels and how accurate they seem to be. For instance, when she talks of wearing her "wings" (6), Dickinson refers to a 19th-century fashion in the drape of her sleeve. But, for many readers, "wings" will evoke a picture of the angelic.

2. **Church vs. home:** How is the value of a place determined?

   One possible thesis on this topic is that Dickinson's "Some keep the Sabbath going to Church" argues that home is superior to a church for religious experience. Some evidence in support of this would be that "God preaches" (9) the speaker's service. Is God both in her garden and at the church? Or is he just in her garden?

3. **Paradise vs. this world:** How does one obtain paradise while yet in this world?

   "Some keep the Sabbath going to Church" portrays paradise as easily reachable. Dickinson often expressed disbelief that paradise could be superior to the world we know. One thesis that you might pursue on this topic is that Dickinson portrays the world as if it were paradise. Therefore, trying to "reach" paradise becomes unnecessary.

4. **Personal religion:** How does "Some keep the Sabbath going to Church" seem to form the tenets of a personal religion?

Dickinson's poem replaces the usual characters and events of a Sunday service with the creatures and occurrences in her garden. When line two of the poem opens, "I keep it," the reader is alerted to the fact that while "some" may keep the Sabbath one way, this is the way "I" keep it. The speaker lets us know this is a solitary activity. You might approach an essay on this topic by discussing other instances of "I" in the poem. What does the speaker do? How does her religion differ from most? How close is she to God and to heaven?

Compare and Contrast Essays

Poem #1591—"The Bobolink is gone" is one of many Dickinson poems, including "Some kept the Sabbath going to Church," that features the bobolink, a songbird. In the latter poem, the bobolink is Dickinson's "Chorister" (3). In "The Bobolink is gone," he plays a similar role. When he departs, "The Presbyterian Birds / Can now resume the Meeting" (4–5). Unlike those birds, he has no sense of decorum. For the bobolink, religion is passionate and personal. It knows no rules.

In #18—"The Gentian weaves her fringes," Dickinson makes the connection she sees between religion and nature even more explicit than she does in "Some keep the Sabbath going to Church." Again, the bobolink appears. Here, he and Dickinson meet, along with an "aged Bee" (11), to mark the passing of summer. The conclusion of the poem is a prayer, but one uniquely addressed to the natural world: "In the name of the Bee— / And of the Butterfly— / And of the Breeze—Amen!" (17–19).

Poem #1545—"The Bible is an antique Volume" draws parallels between the biblical stories and romantic tales. Even more than "Some keep the Sabbath going to Church," this poem might be judged as blasphemous. The first three lines are as follows: "The Bible is an antique

Volume— / Written by faded Men / At the suggestion of Holy Spectres."
Line five identifies "Eden—the ancient Homestead," and we again meet
the idea of paradise as a homelike place. She puts the words *believe* and
lost in quotation marks, throwing their common usage in Christian
teaching into question. The poem's final lines suggest that poetry would
be a welcome replacement for Christianity. Dickinson writes, "Had but
the Tale a warbling Teller— / All the Boys would come— / Orpheus' Sermon captivated— / It did not condemn" (13–16).

The first line of Dickinson's #79—"Going to Heaven!" seems to echo
the final line of "Some keep the Sabbath going to Church." "Going to
Heaven!" reflects on the idea that the poem's speaker will eventually
reside there. The first stanza lets her surety of this be known. She writes
that "it will be done / As sure as flocks go home at night / Unto the Shep-
herd's arm!" (8–10). In the second stanza, the poet refers to heaven as
"home" (19). The third stanza makes clear her love for the world she cur-
rently dwells in. If you were to contrast this poem with "Some keep the
Sabbath going to Church," you might remark on the similarities these
two poems share while pointing out that "Going to Heaven!" displays a
very conventional religious belief.

Sample Topics:

1. **The bobolink:** How does Dickinson portray this bird as the
   speaker's kin?

A possible thesis on this topic would be that in #1591—"The
Bobolink is gone" and in "Some keep the Sabbath going to
Church," the bird is a stand-in for the poet. The idea of the poet
as bird is a common one. They both create song. In these two
poems, the bird worships alongside her. Like the speaker, he is
disruptive. He does not belong in a more conventional service.

2. **Prayer:** How do nature and religion coexist in these two
   poems?

In "The Gentian weaves her fringes," another church service
occurs in nature. This time, it is a funeral service. If you were to
compare this poem to "Some keep the Sabbath going to Church,"

you might argue that Dickinson finds in nature all the elements required for religious practice.

3. **Poetry:** Does Dickinson suggest that the Bible is just another set of stories, better told by a poet?

"The Bible is an antique Volume" contrasts nicely with "Some keep the Sabbath going to Church." In both poems, you will see some mention of home. Perhaps in the adjective *warbling,* you will be reminded of the bobolink. Both poems share a distrust or disdain for conventional religious thought and practice. However, one poem sees in nature an alternative for religion, while the other sees poetry as its proper replacement.

4. **Heaven:** How does Dickinson's view of heaven change, while her belief in heaven as her final destination does not waver?

"Going to Heaven!" displays, like "Some keep the Sabbath going to Church," a surety about heaven and the speaker's place there. If you were to write an essay contrasting these two poems, you might focus on the more conventional message of "Going to Heaven!" You might also argue that there are signs of doubt about religion in both or that her love of the things of this world shows in both poems.

Bibliography and Online Resources

Donoghue, Denis. "Emily Dickinson." *Six American Poets from Emily Dickinson to the Present.* Ed. Allen Tate. Minneapolis: U of Minnesota P, 1965. 9–44.

Eyler, Audrey S. "An Explication of Poem #354: 'Some Keep the Sabbath going to Church.'" *Dickinson Studies* 29 (1976): 40–43.

Johnson, Thomas H., ed. *The Poems of Emily Dickinson.* 3 vols. Cambridge, MA: Harvard UP, 1979.

Johnson, Thomas H., and Theodora Ward, eds. *The Letters of Emily Dickinson.* 3 vols. Cambridge, MA: Harvard UP, 1986.

Sewall, Richard B. *The Life of Emily Dickinson.* Cambridge, MA: Harvard UP, 1974.

#341—"AFTER GREAT PAIN, A FORMAL FEELING COMES"

READING TO WRITE

DICKINSON'S POEM "After great pain, a formal feeling comes," like all good poems and especially Dickinson's, can only be written about after it has been closely read. Its imagery, themes, and ideas are all ripe for discussion in an essay.

The first line of the poem establishes its subject. What follows is a description of what occurs after a person has suffered "great pain." The nature of this pain is nonspecific, but its effects are not. An essay might be written about the effects of great pain and how Dickinson uses imagery to help the reader understand those effects. Such an essay would analyze the images of the poem. Although the poem is only 13 lines long, it is packed with unusual and telling images.

Already, in this first line, the reader meets a word that might strike him or her as odd or particularly weighty. Why is the feeling that comes "formal," and what does this word suggest? It seems to set the tone of the poem. What will come after the pain will be something "formal": perhaps ceremonial, circumscribed, stiff, or uncomfortable. Such word choice, or diction, could be analyzed in an essay.

Already, it is evident that this poem is somewhat unusual and provides, perhaps, a new way of seeing or thinking about the reaction to pain. What follows only becomes odder still, for in the second line the reader is introduced to Dickinson's unorthodox use of capitalization. "Nerves" here is capitalized either because it is being personified or because it is an important word, as Dickinson will often capitalize any word she seems to assign importance to in the poem (often, but not always, the nouns). The poem will travel from these nerves to other places in the body where the pain is felt or reacted to: the "Heart" (3) and the "Feet" (5). The nerves "sit" (2), and the image conjured is, while highly imaginative, not that difficult to summon. They are like people sitting calmly, like one would at a ceremony, but the nerves are also like tombs, and this enlarges the image to people sitting calmly in rows like those in a cemetery. The people, the nerves, and the tombs are conflated together. The cemetery and the ceremony might also come together in the reader's mind as a funeral, where people sit ceremoniously and are but one step removed from the tomb. The funeral is, as well, an event that follows after great pain, the pain at the death of a loved one. You might be able to compose an essay that conjectures what kind of pain Dickinson is referencing in this poem.

Line three of the poem opens itself up to at least two interpretations due to Dickinson's capitalization of the pronoun "He" and the unusual syntax. "The stiff Heart questions was it He, that bore, / And Yesterday, or Centuries before?" (3–4), asks the speaker. The reader understands that the heart is here personified. Since there is no "I" in this poem, the one who has suffered the great pain is unidentifiable. But not only is the sufferer, and the speaker, nameless and faceless, but the sufferer might also be said not to be whole. Instead, the sufferer is reduced to body parts, and these body parts are reduced to only their ability to feel and react to the blow they have received. So the heart here "bore" the great pain, or at least in its suffering questions whether it was truly he or another. The heart asks was it "He," and this capitalization of the masculine pronoun leaves open at least two possible readings. Generally, we know that a masculine pronoun when capitalized refers to the deity or to Christ. The reader must therefore wonder if the poet means to compare the suffering of this heart to Christ's suffering on the cross, or does the poet simply want us to read the "He" as referring back to the heart? Or does the poet wish for us to consider both? You could write an essay that attempts to answer that question.

In this first stanza, Dickinson has given us much to think about. A powerful essay can be written on the experience of pain in this poem and how Dickinson's imagery contributes to our understanding of it: how it reduces an individual to sensations, or only to isolated parts of the body; how it takes away individuality; or how suffering is suffering, whether it is experienced by a lover, a mourner, or Christ. Continuing through the poem are images in each line that can sharpen the reader's perception of pain, and a strong essay can be built out of a discussion of these images.

TOPICS AND STRATEGIES

This section of the chapter will seek to provide you with various approaches you might take in writing a paper about this poem. These ideas are by no means exhaustive and should be looked at as a starting point for your own investigation.

Themes:

The poem takes on various themes, although some less directly than others. Some of those that might be considered are survival, hurt, numbness, and death. Its central theme might be to look at how an individual reacts to any "great pain," lending a universal quality to the poem. A writer might want to look at one concept, such as "freezing" (12), and find other poems by Dickinson to better elucidate what she seems to be saying about this. It might also help to attempt to summarize the poem. For instance, the overarching theme of the poem might be stated thusly: "After a great pain has been inflicted, it is still to be endured."

Sample Topics:

1. **Survival:** What does the poem seem to be saying about survival? How might a person be changed by the experience of pain if it is, as the poet says, "outlived" (11)?

A paper that approaches the poem this way would consider the fate of the "person" or persons in the poem. First, you must notice that the poem begins only after the initial pain has been experienced, so initial hurt has been survived, at least for the moment. Do you think it is ultimately survived? And, if so, how has the one who has felt great pain been changed, if at all? To arrive at an answer, you should look closely at each metaphor Dickinson offers for describing the aftermath of pain.

2. **Hurt:** In poem #241, Dickinson wrote, "I like a look of Agony, / Because I know it's true" (1–2). What do you make of Dickinson's interest in pain? How would you characterize her interest as depicted in "After great pain, a formal feeling comes"?

An essay could be written arguing either that the poem is overwhelmed by the pain that is its subject or that the close examination of pain is a way to conquer it. A paper on this topic might look to other poems of Dickinson's that deal with pain or hurt, such as #241. It might also compare poems on this subject by some of Dickinson's contemporaries to see if her attitude toward suffering is markedly different from others'. Another approach would be to consider this an "opinion" paper, looking at your own reactions to "After great pain, a formal feeling comes."

3. **Numbness:** The poem offers several metaphors for numbness. Does numbness alter through the poem? Can there be said to be stages of numbness?

To begin an essay such as this, you would list all of those metaphors and prepare yourself to explain them. Such a paper would involve a discussion of the metaphors, the numbing effects that are represented by them, and how Dickinson moves through the poem and the various characterizations of numbness to arrive at the conclusion.

4. **Death:** This poem could easily be read as the reaction of the speaker to the death of a loved one, and often is. What does this poem have to say about death or mourning?

The occasion for this poem is unstated, so the reader has no way to truly determine if a death is involved; however, there is evidence to support this reading. A strong paper would make the case that the poem is about death by carefully discussing this evidence. Interpreting that same evidence would provide the answer to what the poem might be trying to say about death or bereavement.

History and Context

To some extent, the power of Dickinson as a poet rests on her work being almost outside time. The bulk of her poems were published beginning in 1890, and it was not until 1945 that Dickinson's complete works were published. Somehow Dickinson has a way of always sounding current. "After great pain, a formal feeling comes" is particularly devoid of any historical context. It might be argued that some of its power comes from this absence of historical context. But you should certainly be aware that in 1862, a prolific year for Dickinson the poet, the Civil War was at its height. You might want to know that Austin Dickinson, Emily Dickinson's beloved older brother, was able to pay another to fight in his place, thus avoiding conscription. The war resulted in the deaths of many of Dickinson's young friends and acquaintances. It was impossible not to be touched by what was happening in the country. Dickinson's home on Main Street in Amherst afforded easy viewing of funeral processions making their way to the town cemetery. The high mortality rate of the 19th century, even without the war, occasioned much of Dickinson's verse and certainly contributed to the sense held by some that Dickinson was overly interested in death as a subject. There was, in short, a great deal of suffering that could not fail to move the most casual observer, and it was keenly felt by Dickinson.

"After great pain, a formal feeling comes" can be viewed in other contexts as well. Dickinson wrote in her letters that she thought "New Englandy." She hailed from one of the more prominent New England families, and she was wholly involved in the life and activities of Amherst when she was young. Therefore, it might be fruitful to look at this poem as a particularly "New Englandy" exercise. Then, in Dickinson's own history and context, 1862 was an important year: She wrote 366 poems in 1862. By 1862, she had also written her letters, three of which survive, to an unidentified person she addressed only as "Master." These "Master Letters," as they came to be called, offer perhaps some clue to Dickinson's growing isolation from others. The letters show the writer in tremendous emotional pain and hint at a catastrophic disappointment in love. An essay might reasonably look at poem #341 in light of the history and context of Dickinson's own life.

Sample Topics:
1. **The Civil War:** The poem makes no explicit reference to the Civil War, so how could it be said to be a "Civil War poem"?

   A paper on this subject might look at a history of the year 1862. You may wish to look at Mathew Brady's Civil War photographs, particularly those of soldiers in snow. You might look to Dickinson's letters for discussion of how her family and friends were affected by the war efforts. The thesis of the paper could seek to prove that this poem is a "war poem."

2. **"New Englandy":** Rather stereotypically, the people of New England have been characterized as stoic, reserved, sometimes cold. Some of this comes from the combined strains of Puritanism, Protestantism, and the sheer tenacity it took to eke out an existence in such an unforgiving terrain. How could this poem be said to be the product of a New England sensibility?

   Do a bit of research on the characteristics of New England people and how Dickinson conformed or rebelled against them. Do you see evidence in her work of a New England reserve? You might consider how pain is sometimes represented and reacted to. How does this poem subvert our expectations of how an individual might react to pain?

3. **The absence of context and time:** "After great pain, a formal feeling comes" is approximately 150 years old. How can it be said to be a modern poem?

   An essay on this topic would likely dwell on the universality of the poem. You might want to look at how pain is considered today or how this poem would be applicable to pain in many instances, many times. Modern poetry is somewhat defined by the confessional movement, where writers write directly of their own and most personal experiences. You might be able to think of examples of poems written for specific occasions or about specific people. You might consider why Dickinson did not write more specifically of the year 1862 or designate a clear speaker or event in the poem.

4. **Biographical reading:** Dickinson wrote the bulk of her poems in 1862. It has been theorized that she underwent some personal crisis in that year, likely having to do with disappointment in love. How could "After great pain, a formal feeling comes" be read in light of Dickinson's biography? This was also the year that marked her growing seclusion.

An essay such as this could be approached in a number of ways. You could look at Dickinson's Master Letters to see other descriptions and images Dickinson provides to describe a great pain that has afflicted her, or you could read her letters or other poems from 1862 in an attempt to draw a conclusion about Dickinson's own experience of "great pain."

Philosophy and Ideas

What does the poem "After great pain, a formal feeling comes" have to say about philosophy and ideas? Consider the idea of pain and what profound pain may do to an individual. Dickinson's poem seems to suggest that pain is dehumanizing, and this is perhaps part of the reason the speaker is unidentified, as is the nature of the pain. The poem may have something to say about the universality of pain. Perhaps, the agent and cause of the pain does not matter because all pain is relative to the one who experiences it, and all pain is painful. The poem can cause us to think about life and death. If you believe the speaker to be reacting to the death of a loved one, the result is that the speaker is alive and yet numb to life. What the poem depicts, then, is a living death. The poem considers the nature of time, for time seems to have a distinct effect on pain, or else pain has a distinct effect on time. You might consider paralysis, both emotional and physical. How can pain be said to somehow "paralyze" the person experiencing it? Finally, the poem suggests a line between the exterior and the interior of the sufferer. The damage, as it were, is internal. Perhaps we can never know another's pain.

Sample Topics:

1. **Interiority:** What does the poem seem to be saying about the inner life? Is it more or less real than what is external to the individual and observed in the external world?

   It has already been established that the speaker of "After great pain, a formal feeling comes" is nameless and faceless. Perhaps this is even more suggestive than previously considered. Is Dickinson trying to say something about our inner lives? Look at the imagery of the poem, particularly the "quartz content-ment" (9). Think about the process of freezing, how cold moves slowly through the body. Think about, as well, the particulars that are personified: nerves, heart, and feet. You could then write an essay that argues that pain is experienced on the inside more than it is expressed outwardly.

2. **Time:** In the poem, time is referred to specifically as "Yester-day" (4), "Centuries" (4), and the "Hour" (10). How does time function in the poem?

   Clearly the poem is concerned with time. What does Dickinson seem to be saying about time and its effect on pain? Does the pain grow less over time? Does pain even know time? Look at the imagery related to time, specifically "the Hour of Lead" (10). Does such an hour ever advance? You might write an essay that looks at time in the poem and whether pain can be outlived, or is it always a part of an individual, once experienced.

3. **Death:** The person who has experienced the pain is not dead, at least not yet. But what she is experiencing is so like death that you might wonder if death would be preferable. What does the poem tell us about death?

   This could be approached in one of two ways. A writer could consider this a poem of bereavement. In that case, you would talk about the ways we react to death. Does Dickinson offer us a guide to accepting our losses? Another would be to construct a paper around the idea that death deals a blow of equal power to those who remain alive.

4. **Paralysis:** What does the poem have to say about paralysis, either emotional or physical? How can a person be paralyzed in both ways? Is paralysis a fitting reaction to extreme pain?

Think about the images of paralysis in the poem. Nerves, which you might consider somewhat active, "sit ceremonious" (2). The feet, though they move, move in a "mechanical" (5) and a "wooden" (7) way. They also move on "ought" (6), a word you would want to seek out in a dictionary for a full rendering of all its possible meanings. *Ought* could be read as meaning "nothing," like zero, saying that the feet move on the ground, the air, and the nothing or nothingness, as if it is all of no matter. It could also be read that the feet move as they ought to, doing what they must. As you read on, there is the stone, the lead, and the freezing persons, all of which might lead you to write an essay on the subject of paralysis in this poem.

Form and Genre

Dickinson is noted for her form: the ballad stanza, the oddities of punctuation, the curious syntax. It is usually not hard to tell a Dickinson poem at a glance. "After great pain, a formal feeling comes" is not an exception, though it has some deviations. The poem's first stanza is written in iambic pentameter (10 syllables falling in iambs, so that the first syllable of every two syllable foot is unstressed while the second is stressed), but the meter is not consistent. Her rhyming is fairly consistent, though Dickinson uses slant rhymes, sometimes also called "off" or "half" rhymes (rhymes that rely on similar consonant or vowel sounds to create the effect of rhyme) in many places throughout this poem. (The first example in this poem is in lines one and two: "comes" and "Tombs.")

"After great pain, a formal feeling comes" is also an example of how Dickinson used the dash as her chief mark of punctuation. Students will wish to consider the dash and what it may suggest and what it might "do" in this particular poem. Although Dickinson might be characterized as a "formal" poet (she tends to adhere to standard metrical forms), "After great pain, a formal feeling comes" shows that she would deviate from form where it served her purposes. To look at the places a poem deviates from its form is always useful when writing and thinking about poetry.

Finally, this poem is also a lyric and exhibits the compression of that genre. The internal elements of the poem are in service to the form of the whole.

Sample Topics:

1. **The dash:** Dickinson employs punctuation that English teachers everywhere would fault their students for. Her use of the dash is an example of "poetic license," the ability of the poet to deviate successfully from the rules of prose. It is allowed only when the poet can justify such deviation within the work. How could you argue that Dickinson's dash is the most effective punctuation for this poem?

A paper such as this would look carefully at the punctuation of the poem. You might be interested to know that there are scholars who have measured Dickinson's dashes to find out if their length (in her handwritten manuscripts) was significant and that her first editors thought it necessary to "clean up" her punctuation and sometimes her rhymes as well. However, Dickinson's use of the dash here, particularly the final one, appears to have much method in it. You will want to ask yourself how the poem might be changed if that final mark of punctuation were a period. Would this be an improvement, or would it somehow lessen the effect of the whole?

2. **Meter:** Dickinson was very proficient in the use of meter. This poem begins in strict iambic pentameter; however, the meter is broken in the second stanza. What effect does this have on your reading?

Although Dickinson's line break at five is not the expected one, reading the poem aloud—as you should always do—will prove that lines five and six together read as a line of iambic tetrameter (eight syllables of iambs, alternating between unstressed and stressed syllables), so the break is a decision on the poet's part. How does this change stanza two? How does it change the poem as a whole? Scanning the poem (counting the syllables and trying to determine where the stresses fall) would be helpful here.

3. **Use of rhyme:** The poem is rhymed—basically, *AABB*. The first two lines of stanzas one and three have a slant rhyme; the last two lines of every stanza have an exact rhyme. Those exact rhymes have the effect of "closing" up every stanza like a box. How does rhyme work to create meaning in "After great pain, a formal feeling comes"?

Try to map out the rhyme scheme of the poem. Consider the rhymes and the diction of those end words. Pay particular attention to the final two lines of each stanza and the final word of the poem. Why might these be particularly significant? Try to reach a conclusion about the rhymes and their effect on the reader.

Bibliography and Online Resources

Chase, Richard. *Emily Dickinson.* New York: Dell, 1965.

Cody, John. *After Great Pain: The Inner Life of Emily Dickinson.* Cambridge, MA: Harvard UP, 1971.

Crumbley, Paul. "Emily Dickinson's Life." *Modern American Poetry.* 1995. 27 Apr. 2006 <http://www.english.uiuc.edu/maps/poets/a_f/dickinson/bio.htm>.

Farr, Judith. *The Passion of Emily Dickinson.* Cambridge, MA: Harvard UP, 1992.

Farr, Judith. ed. *Emily Dickinson: A Collection of Critical Essays.* New York: Prentice Hall, 1996.

Franklin, R. W., ed. *The Manuscript Books of Emily Dickinson.* 2 vols. Cambridge, MA: Harvard UP, 1981.

———. *The Master Letters of Emily Dickinson.* Amherst, MA: Amherst College Press, 1986.

———. *The Poems of Emily Dickinson: Reading Edition.* Cambridge, MA: Harvard UP, 1999.

———. *The Poems of Emily Dickinson: Variorum Edition.* 3 vols. Cambridge, MA: Harvard UP, 1998.

Johnson, Thomas H., ed. *The Poems of Emily Dickinson, including Variant Readings Critically Compared with All Known Manuscripts.* 3 vols. Cambridge, MA: Harvard UP, 1955.

——. *Complete Poems.* Boston: Little, Brown, 1960.

——. *Selected Letters.* Cambridge, MA: Harvard UP, 1971.

Johnson, Thomas H., and Theodora Ward, eds. *Emily Dickinson: An Interpretive Biography.* Cambridge, MA: Harvard UP, 1955.

——. *The Letters of Emily Dickinson.* 3 vols. Cambridge, MA: Harvard UP, 1979.

"On 341 ('After great pain, a formal feeling comes')." *Modern American Poetry.* 26 Apr. 2006 <http://www.english.uiuc.edu/maps/poets/a_f/dickinson/341. htm>.

Poet's Corner: "Emily Dickinson." *Thomson Gale. Authors and Artists for Young Adults,* Vols. 7–26. Gale, 1992–99. 28 Apr. 2006 <http://www.gale. com/free_resources/poets/bio/dickinson_e.htm>.

Reuben, Paul P. "Chapter 4: Nineteenth Century to 1865: Emily Dickinson." *PAL: Perspectives in American Literature—A Research and Reference Guide.* 27 Apr. 2006 <http://www.csustan.edu/english/reuben/pal/chap4/dickinson. html>.

Sewall, Richard B., ed. *Emily Dickinson: A Collection of Critical Essays.* Englewood Cliffs, NJ: Prentice-Hall, 1963.

——. *The Life of Emily Dickinson.* New York: Farrar, Straus & Giroux, 1974.

Whicher, George F. *This Was a Poet: A Critical Biography of Emily Dickinson.* Ann Arbor: U of Michigan P, 1957.

#435—
"MUCH MADNESS
IS DIVINEST SENSE"

READING TO WRITE

"**M**UCH MADNESS is divinest Sense" is one of Dickinson's most commonly taught poems. The poem begins as a definition, but it is a definition built upon a paradox. The two states of madness and sense, she implies, are generally mislabeled. It takes a "discerning Eye" (2) to recognize the difference. Presumably, the poem's speaker is in possession of the necessary discernment. The first three lines say that madness and sense are often confused. The dense repetitions of consonants in the poem's opening require the reader to read slowly and to take in the message. Lines four and five let us know who it is that makes the determination between them. The majority rules, but perhaps the majority itself is mad. The last three lines of the poem address the reader as "you." Dickinson writes: "Assent—and you are sane— / Demur—you're straightway dangerous— / And handled with a Chain" (6–8). The implication is that it should be important to everyone to question the majority, for there is no predicting when the majority will decide that you are "dangerous." The more direct implication is that the majority decides what "sense" is and what matters. If you question the majority's definition, you are deemed mad. Diction choices such as *assent* and *demur* make the poem's ending all the more threatening. If all it takes is mild demurral to earn one a "Chain," then it is very easy indeed to be deemed one of the mad. The lyric is firmly on the side of the individual and not the majority.

TOPICS AND STRATEGIES

This section of the chapter will seek to provide you with various approaches you might take in writing a paper about this poem. These ideas are by no means exhaustive and should be looked at as a starting point for your own investigation.

Themes

One theme or series of themes evident in the poem relates to madness. These include the definition of madness, who decides, and what is done to those who are mad. In a poem as short as this one, you will want to pay close attention to every diction choice. Dickinson writes that "Much Madness is divinest Sense." How can madness be divine, or, as the word seems to imply, the most divine? The use of this word brings to mind the "madness" of saints, or even the persecution of Christ. You may also be reminded of the idea of the holy fool. He who is considered mad in this world might be truly divine, while the one considered wise might be deemed foolish in the next.

"Much Madness is divinest Sense" can be read as a critique against conformity. It is hard not to read the words *assent* and *demur* as being tinged with sarcasm. Certainly one message of the poem is that if you "assent" to the crowd you will be judged sane. This, of course, makes any individualism impossible. And anyone who behaves differently from the majority will be accused of demurral.

Returning to the idea of divinity, consider what it is to be divine. This was an adjective Dickinson employed more than once. By definition, to be divine is to emanate from God or to be of him. A lesser meaning would be simply to be lovely or ideal. Line five suggests that the majority always has its way, but the majority may be in darkness when it comes to the divine. Presumably, perseverance in a state that is "divine" would be rewarded in heaven, and the most "discerning Eye" must certainly be God's.

Perception is another theme of this poem. Madness is a state perceived, as is sanity. These labels are determined by what the majority perceives to be real and true. In another time or another place, all could be perceived differently. Perception returns to another common theme in Dickinson: seeing.

Sample Topics:

1. **Madness:** How does "Much Madness is divinest Sense" make a case for the divinity of madness?

   There are at least three ways of talking about madness in this poem. One is that madness here may be wisdom. Another is that since the majority decides, the majority could be wrong. Still another is that the poem makes a case for the gentle treatment of those termed *mad* by the majority.

2. **Conformity:** How does the poem reveal Dickinson's attitude toward conformity?

   It is curious that a poet deemed "eccentric" and "cracked" wrote a poem such as this one. It could almost be seen as speaking directly to her critics. One possible thesis, if you wished to talk about conformity in "Much Madness is divinest Sense," is that this poem is firmly on the side of the nonconformist.

3. **Divinity:** How can madness and divinity coexist?

   The poem suggests that these two go hand in hand. One possible thesis on this subject would be that Dickinson implies in "Much Madness is divinest Sense" that the behaviors that are deemed odd by the vast majority of people may very well be divine in origin.

4. **Perception:** How much is determined by who is doing the seeing?

   An essay on this subject would likely focus on the "discerning Eye" of line two. The "discerning Eye" can see the truth. (Is the

"Eye" a pun on *I,* and another nod toward the virtues of individuality?) The majority are without such perception.

Compare and Contrast Essays

"Much Madness is divinest Sense" echoes Ralph Waldo Emerson's essay "Self-Reliance." In it, Emerson writes that there

> are the voices which we hear in solitude, but they grow faint and inaudible as we enter into the world. Society everywhere is in conspiracy against the manhood of every one of its members. Society is a joint-stock company, in which the members agree, for the better securing of his bread to each shareholder, to surrender the liberty and culture of the eater. The virtue in most request is conformity.

Emerson's essay also includes these lines: "Pythagoras was misunderstood, and Socrates, and Jesus, and Luther, and Copernicus, and Galileo, and Newton, and every pure and wise spirit that ever took flesh. To be great is to be misunderstood." You might wish to read Emerson's essay in order to argue that Dickinson's poem is Emersonian.

The threat of "Much Madness is divinest Sense" is the poem's final word, the "Chain," which may represent imprisonment. In poem #613—"They shut me up in Prose," Dickinson puts imprisonment in terms of prose. Freedom is represented by poetry. One possible way to interpret "Much Madness is divinest Sense" is that the life of the poet, which may be divinely led and inspired, might be seen by the vast majority as madness. The poet often has the reputation of being slightly debauched and disrespectable. Poetry is also often seen as the province of the unstable and the odd.

The idea of the individual versus the masses, or the majority against the minority, is a theme of "Much Madness is divinest Sense." There are a number of Dickinson poems with this theme. Two well-known ones are "I'm Nobody! Who are you?" and "The Soul selects her own Society." If you were to compare "I'm Nobody! Who are you?" to "Much Madness is divinest Sense," an obvious place to begin might be the croaking frog. Although the majority admires the frog's repetition of his name, the two nobodies know better. "The Soul selects her own Society" speaks of a "divine majority," but the sense seems to be that this majority is divine because it consists of only two.

An interesting subject for investigation could be how Dickinson uses the word *divine* in her poetry. In #593—"I think I was enchanted," the speaker describes the situation of being overwhelmed, while reading, by the power of the words. One of the phrases she uses to describe her feeling is "a Divine Insanity" (25). Probably the most famous of Dickinson's uses of this adjective is #1072—"Title divine—is mine!" This poem is difficult to decipher, but the suggestion is that she has, by divine decree or blessing, been made wife, although her status is not known by any but herself and her "husband."

Sample Topics:

1. **"Self-reliance":** How does "Much Madness is divinest Sense" compare to Emerson's essay "Self-Reliance"?

   An essay on this topic might argue that Dickinson's focus is on madness. Another possible argument is that while Emerson's essay is an exhortation to defy the majority, Dickinson never goes that far.

2. **Imprisonment:** How can imprisonment reflect the plight of the poet?

   You might wish to enlarge this topic to talk about any sensitive person who is unlike the majority of people. However, if you wished to compare #613—"They shut me up in Prose" with "Much Madness is divinest Sense," you might focus on the way the poet might be judged, like a loud little girl, a threat to the peace of the majority. You might also look at #454—"It was given to me by the gods," which seems to be a poem about the poetic gift and how it distances one from the rest of the world.

3. **Majority and minority:** How does Dickinson characterize the majority and the minority in her poetry?

   You might arrive at a different answer to this question depending on which poem you choose to compare with "Much Madness is divinest Sense." An appropriate thesis for comparing either "The Soul selects her own Society" or "I'm Nobody! Who are you?" with that poem would be that Dickinson proves herself to be on the side of the minority.

4. **The divine:** What does Dickinson mean when she writes of the divine?

If you wished to write on this topic, you might use a concordance to find other instances of Dickinson's use of this word. If you wished to compare "Title divine—is mine!" to "Much Madness is divinest Sense," you might focus on the idea that the true self has to be kept hidden from the majority of people. An essay that compared "Much Madness is divinest Sense" to "I think I was enchanted" might argue that *divine* is a word Dickinson often uses to describe poetic inspiration.

Bibliography and Online Resources

Emerson, Ralph Waldo. "Self-Reliance (1841)." *infoUSA*. 23 Oct. 2006 <http://usinfo.state.gov/usa/infousa/facts/democrac/14.htm>.

Johnson, Thomas H., ed. *The Poems of Emily Dickinson*. 3 vols. Cambridge, MA: Harvard UP, 1979.

Johnson, Thomas H., and Theodora Ward, eds. *The Letters of Emily Dickinson*. 3 vols. Cambridge, MA: Harvard UP, 1986.

Sewall, Richard B. *The Life of Emily Dickinson*. Cambridge, MA: Harvard UP, 1974.

#441—
"THIS IS MY LETTER TO THE WORLD"

READING TO WRITE

"THIS IS my letter to the World" is a poem that seems quintessential Dickinson. The first two lines, "This is my letter to the World / That never wrote to Me," seem to underscore the perception of Dickinson as a reclusive poet, unable to confront the world directly but attempting to do so in her work. Since most readers know that the majority of Dickinson's poems were not discovered until after her death, the idea that the poems are her "letter" gains some poignancy. This poem, then, is often taken to be a direct statement of her intent.

As you read, you will want to consider the meaning of the word *this*. When Dickinson uses the pronoun to open her poem, she causes us to ask if it is the poem itself that is her letter. One question you might ask yourself is if there are any other possible candidates for her "letter to the World." You will want to look carefully at Dickinson's word choice. For instance, what does she mean when she states "the world?" Is the "world" a future audience, as it is often taken to be, or are there other possibilities here, too? Her letter is, she says in line three, "The simple News that Nature told." And yet the poem contains no description or discussion of nature.

In the second stanza, nature seems to be the antecedent for the pronoun "her" (5). The poet appears to plead with her future "countrymen" (7) to judge her with the same kindness and consideration they would afford to nature. Although there is evidence here to believe that this poem is characteristic of a shy and self-effacing poet only able to face the public after her death and only after making a plea for understanding, you would also want to note the assurance of Dickinson's belief in a future audience who will read her poem.

TOPICS AND STRATEGIES

This section of the chapter will seek to provide you with various approaches you might take in writing a paper about this poem. These ideas are by no means exhaustive and should be looked at as a starting point for your own investigation.

Themes

Among the themes present in "This is my letter to the World" is the love of nature. One interpretation of the poem is that the "News that Nature told" is the only news of any import. This news is described as "simple" (3), although it is told "With tender Majesty" (4). That people, even far into the future, should regard nature with love is taken for granted.

A theme that is perhaps less obvious is the independence of the spirit of the poet and the poem. Although the poet has not been addressed by the "World," she is still sending her letter. Its reception concerns her, but not so much that she will not send it. There seems to be some assurance that the world will not be indifferent to the letter, and her appeal for the tenderness of her readers seems almost to ask that their regard for her work be elevated to their level of regard for nature.

The idea that the word might allow the poet some level of immortality is also here. In "This is my letter to the World" Dickinson writes, "Her Message is committed / To Hands I cannot see" (5–6). Although the pronoun "Her" here refers to nature, the message is also Dickinson's. The poem, or letter, is being sent to the future. Dickinson seems certain that the future will read it. She is a bit less certain of how it will be regarded. But whatever feeling her readers have for the poem she believes will be transferred to her. As she asks in the final line, "Judge tenderly—of Me" (8).

Although an argument can certainly be made for the boldness of "This is my letter to the World," another reader might see humility in the poem. The tone could be described as quiet and respectful. Dickinson asks where another poet might demand. The voice is unfailingly polite. The nature that she seeks to align herself with is not violent or volatile; it is the nature that is tender and simple.

Sample Topics:

1. **Love of nature:** How does "This is my letter to the World" reveal a love of nature?

Joy in the natural world is an important motif in Dickinson's poetry. "This is my letter to the World" is a poem that expresses the poet's pleasure in nature. An essay that discussed this might begin with a statement such as, "Emily Dickinson believed that no one could be indifferent to nature. In this poem, she attempts to align her poems with the natural world."

2. **Independence:** What does it take to send a letter to someone who has not first written to you?

Dickinson's characteristic independence is evident in this poem. An essay might focus on the idea of sending a letter to an unknown recipient. It could also focus on the idea of presuming to speak for nature.

3. **Words as immortality:** How does this poem speak to the belief in the immortality of the poet?

An essay on this topic might argue that "This is my letter to the World" exhibits a remarkable level of forethought regarding a future audience. The poem has the quality of speaking directly to the reader. It asks the reader to consider the feelings of the writer. One point of discussion could be the manner of direct address, the idea that the reader is reading a "letter" rather than a poem.

4. **Humility:** Is the poet as tender and simple as nature?

This is a relatively short poem of eight lines. It is direct. An argument could be made that it reinforces the idea of Dickinson's humility. Knowing that this poem was found after her death, along with the vast majority of her work, seems to offer evidence that she felt uncertain about the reception her work would receive.

History and Context

One way to view this poem is in the context of Dickinson's letters. *The Letters of Emily Dickinson* is a three-volume set, and the set represents only a fraction of the letters written by Dickinson. The prose in the letters is very similar to the voice of the poems, so reading the letters is a literary experience—that is to say, Dickinson's letters are unlike anyone else's. It is very obvious that the letter was a form of great importance to her. Although Dickinson retired into relative seclusion in the latter half of her life, her extensive correspondence ensured that she was not isolated.

There is a traditional idea that poets possess a certain amount of prescience. If you ascribe to this idea, "This is my letter to the World" would be reflective of Dickinson's abilities. Dickinson's work has grown steadily in its popularity since its first publication. Her current reputation is that she is the preeminent American woman poet.

What has often been termed the *Dickinson myth* is that Dickinson was a certain type of eccentric whose habits resemble what would now be diagnosed as agoraphobia. It is true that she rarely left her home; she dressed only in white; she saw and spoke to only a select few. It is possible to read "This is my letter to the World" in terms of these behaviors. The statement that the world "never wrote" to her suggests a withdrawal from the world. The idea that the poem is a message to that world suggests an inability to communicate with the world directly.

"This is my letter to the World" has an interesting publication history. It was chosen as the frontispiece to the *Poems of Emily Dickinson* compiled by Mabel Loomis Todd and T. W. Higginson. It is interesting to consider why, of all of Dickinson's work, this poem would be chosen as representative. Would our conception of Dickinson be changed if this poem were less popular?

Sample Topics:

1. **Importance of letters:** Is it possible to view "This is my letter to the World" as another example of Dickinson's correspondence?

If you wished to pursue this as a paper topic, you might want to turn to Richard Sewall's biography, where, in the glossary, you will find a reference to letters and the importance of letter writing. You would also want to look at *The Letters of Emily Dickinson,* edited by Thomas H. Johnson and Theodora Ward. You would not need to read far to gain an understanding of the part letters played in her life. Dickinson's poem #636—"The Way I read a Letter's—this" might also be of interest to you.

2. **Popularity:** How has Dickinson's "letter to the World" been received?

If you were to consult a publication such as Jeanetta Boswell's bibliography of secondary sources for Dickinson, you would see how reviews and commentary on her and her work have grown over the years, as well as how reservations about her work have largely disappeared. Given the evidence of her stature, you might be able to argue that Dickinson's poem "This is my letter to the World" was not only received by the world but also judged "tenderly."

3. **Myth:** How does "This is my letter to the World" support the Dickinson myth?

An argument could be made that this poem is a reflection of the behavior that moved Samuel Bowles to call Dickinson "the Queen recluse" (Sewall 99). A line-by-line explication would offer evidence for this reading. Dickinson's biography would offer further evidence.

4. **Publication:** What is the significance of this poem in the history of the publication of Dickinson's work?

Dickinson's poems took a circuitous route to publication. A paper that wished to examine this poem in light of that might argue that "This is my letter to the World" is an apt introduction to Dickinson's work. Such an essay would argue that Todd and

Higginson chose the appropriate poem to introduce Dickinson to the world.

Language, Symbols, and Imagery

"This is my letter to the World" is built upon contradictions. As in many Dickinson poems, the first two lines provide a sort of twist, where the statement made in the first is either contradicted or qualified by the second line. She writes, "This is my letter to the World / That never wrote to Me." The next couplet speaks of a "simple" message delivered with "tender Majesty," another seeming incongruity. In the second stanza, "Her Message is committed / To Hands I cannot see," and the image of those hands is evoked, even if the hands cannot be seen by the eyes.

A teacher once said to the author of this book: As you read a poem, you should picture the expression on the poet's face as she or he composed it. What do you imagine was the expression on Dickinson's face when she wrote "This is my letter to the World"? The answer to that question would perhaps help you decide the tone of the poem. Although there are some wrong answers, there are several that could be said to be right and that could be defended. The success of this poem comes, in part, from the relative lightness of tone.

Dickinson had a fondness for repetition. In this poem, you might wish to consider the repeated sounds. In the first stanza, for instance, the repetition of the "t" sound transitions the reader from line to line. In the second stanza, look at the repetitions of *h, s,* and *m*. You might also look at the internal rhymes. The final line of the poem, "Judge tenderly— of Me," rhymes the words *tenderly* and *me*. And there are other sound repetitions to follow, such as the final stanza's repeated "e" sound in *see, sweet,* and *me*.

To trace just one of the images in a poem can be a useful way to approach the work and lead to an essay topic. In this poem, you might want to consider the image of hands. In poetry, a synecdoche is the use of a part of a thing to represent the whole. A common synecdoche is to use the term *wheels* when you refer to a car. Here, "Hands" can stand for the people who will read Dickinson's poem, but you should try to think what further ideas are evoked by the image of hands. We commonly refer to hands when we mean "help," as when people ask to be given a hand. Sometimes hand is used to refer to a lover or a parent or other caretaker. From there, we get such sayings as a "raised with a firm hand" or "don't bite the hand that feeds you." What does Dickinson mean when she writes, "Her Message is committed / To Hands I cannot see"?

Sample Topics:

1. **Contradictions:** How do the contradictions and reversals of ideas work in "This is my letter to the World"?

   An argument on this topic might have a thesis such as, "The contradictions in this poem instill a sense of surprise in the reader." Or you could argue that the poem is perfectly balanced, with every idea given its opposite.

2. **Tone:** What is the tone of this poem? How does it help you to understand "This is my letter to the World"?

   Although important ideas are addressed in this poem—life, death, nature, literary fame, personal reputation, and more—they are not approached with reverence. There are clues in the rhythm of the poem and also in such word choices as *sweet* to describe future readers. An essay on this topic might talk about the conscious decision a poet makes about tone, how the tone works to get the message across to readers, or how the tone, here, surprises.

3. **Repetition:** How does Dickinson use repetition to build "This is my letter to the World"?

   An essay on this topic might argue that given Dickinson's penchant for compression, repetition is necessary in her work. The repeated sounds, rhymes, and words lend coherence and unity to this short, eight-line poem. Like a couplet, they serve to tighten the composition.

4. **Hands:** How does the image of hands contribute to the power of "This is my letter to the World"?

N

After you consider the many possibilities of this image, you might arrive at any number of possible theses. Here is but one: "The image of 'Hands' in "This is my letter to the World" evokes the physical presence of future readers. Since Emily Dickinson is putting the poem in our 'hands,' she is showing she trusts us to take good care of it. This sets up a relationship between the reader and the poem that inclines us toward liking it."

Compare and Contrast Essays

An essay that compared or contrasted "This is my letter to the World" to other poems by Dickinson might focus on themes she often revisited. One of these is the idea of being entrusted with a message. In poem #827—"The Only News I know," for instance, she writes: "The Only News I know / Is Bulletins all Day / from Immortality" (1–3). It is a poem that seems to exhibit Dickinson's awareness of her power as a poet. When compared with "This is my letter to the World," the latter poem may strike you as more self-assured, as if she recognized, over time, her abilities. It might, on the other hand, lead you to think that "This is my letter to the World" is not really such a humble performance.

Another important theme in Dickinson's work is the importance of secrets: secret identities and secrets kept. Her #288—"I'm Nobody! Who are You?" touches on this theme. The speaker has a secret, the secret of her status. She shares it with only one special other. The secret knowledge of the two "nobodies" makes them an elite group. Referring again to a special knowledge of immortality, Dickinson writes in #1748—"The reticent volcano keeps": "The only secret people keep / Is Immortality" (11–12). The comparison between the poet and the volcano was made famously in #1705—"Volcanoes be in Sicily," the last line of which is "Vesuvius at Home" (8).

Another fruitful line of inquiry might be to compare or contrast Dickinson's poem with poems by other writers who seemed to attempt to speak directly to an audience of readers who would only come to know them after the poets themselves had died. One example of this might be seen in John Keats's "This Living Hand," quoted here in its entirety:

This living hand, now warm and capable
Of earnest grasping, would, if it were cold

And in the icy silence of the tomb,
So haunt thy days and chill thy dreaming nights
That thou wouldst wish thine own heart dry of blood
So in my veins red life might stream again,
And thou be conscience-calmed—see here it is—
I hold it towards you.

Another example can be seen in Walt Whitman's *Song of Myself,* particularly section 52 and the conclusion, where he writes:

If you want me again look for me under your boot-soles.

You will hardly know who I am or what I mean,
But I shall be good health to you nevertheless,
And filter and fibre your blood.

Failing to fetch me at first keep encouraged,
Missing me one place search another,
I stop somewhere waiting for you.

It is interesting to note their similarities and differences to "This is my letter to the World." A good essay could be made by examining either poem.

Sample Topics:

1. **Messages:** A number of Dickinson's poems evince the idea that the poet has been entrusted with a message. Does comparing or contrasting one of these poems with "This is my letter to the World" allow you a fuller understanding of that poem?

   The very idea that the poet has been entrusted with a message, whether it is from nature, immortality, or God, betrays a certain confidence. "The Only News I know" suggests that she is in direct communication with a mysterious world beyond the visible. Such a statement could serve as a thesis for an essay on Dickinson's "messages."

2. **Secrets:** What does it mean to keep a secret, particularly if that secret is God's or nature's or immortality's?

You might use a concordance to find other Dickinson poems about secrets or news. "This is my letter to the World" seems to position Dickinson as the bearer of news entrusted to her by nature. In "I'm Nobody! Who are You?" the speaker keeps the secret of her identity, entrusting it only to one special other who is like herself. In the volcano poems, the speaker has special knowledge that others do not have, and so the speaker is elevated and isolated by what she knows. One possible thesis on this topic is that the use of secrets in Dickinson's work tells us something about Dickinson herself. Another might be that Dickinson's poems convey that to have a secret separates you from others. It is a unique privilege.

3. **Keats's "This Living Hand":** How does "This is my letter to the World" compare to Keats's "This Living Hand" as a message from beyond the grave?

One interesting way to approach this poem in concert with Dickinson's would be to contrast the way both poets use the image of hands. Keats's hand is a chilling image because it seems to reach from the grave out to the reader. Dickinson, alternatively, trusts her poem to the reader's living hands. In both poems, the image of hands creates a peculiar intimacy between the poet and the reader.

4. **Whitman's** *Song of Myself:* How does Whitman's interaction with his future readers differ from Dickinson's?

Whitman's poem sets up an intimacy between himself and his readers, whereas Dickinson puts the poem between to act as intermediary. This says a lot about these two great American poets, sometimes called the patriarch and matriarch of American poetry. Whitman seems to say that he will physically be in the world, even after his death. You might look at Sewall's biography or her letters to find Dickinson's reply to T. W. Higginson's question about whether she had read Whitman. Dickinson wrote that she had not but had heard he was "scandalous."

Bibliography and Online Resources

Boswell, Jeanetta. *Emily Dickinson: A Bibliography of Secondary Sources, with Selective Annotations, 1890 through 1897.* Jefferson, NC: McFarland & Co., 1989.

Doriani, Beth Maclay. *Emily Dickinson: Daughter of Prophecy.* Amherst: U of Massachusetts P, 1996.

Farr, Judith. *The Passion of Emily Dickinson.* Cambridge, MA: Harvard UP, 1992.

Gelpi, Albert J. *Emily Dickinson: The Mind of the Poet.* Cambridge, MA: Harvard UP, 1966.

Higginson, T. W., and Mabel Loomis Todd, eds. *Poems by Emily Dickinson.* Boston: Roberts Brothers, 1890.

Johnson, Thomas H., ed. *The Poems of Emily Dickinson.* 3 vols. Cambridge, MA: Harvard UP, 1979.

Johnson, Thomas H., and Theodora Ward, eds. *The Letters of Emily Dickinson.* 3 vols. Cambridge, MA: Harvard UP, 1986.

Keats, John. "This Living Hand." *Academy of American Poets.* 7 Aug. 2006 <http://www.poets.org/viewmedia.php/prmMID/15800>.

Paglia, Camille. *Sexual Personae: Art and Decadence from Nefertiti to Emily Dickinson.* New York: Vintage, 1991.

Rich, Adrienne. "Vesuvius at Home: The Power of Emily Dickinson." *On Lies, Secrets, and Silence: Selected Prose 1966–1978.* New York: Norton, 1979. 157–183.

Sewall, Richard B. *The Life of Emily Dickinson.* Cambridge, MA: Harvard UP, 1974.

Whitman, Walt. "Whitman's 'Song of Myself.'" *Modern American Poetry.* 7 Aug. 2006 <http://www.english.uiuc.edu/maps/poets/s_z/whitman/song.htm>.

#448—
"THIS WAS A POET—
IT IS THAT"

READING TO WRITE

IN ORDER to write about Dickinson's "This was a Poet—It is That" you will need to untangle the language of her poem. In the first line, she uses two pronouns without clear antecedents. When she writes, "This was a Poet," what does the *this* refer to? *This* could refer to someone either male or female. It is possible that *this* refers to one of Dickinson's flowers. It could possibly be a poem. In the final stanzas, however, the poet is clearly "He."

And what does the phrase "It is That" mean? It might be of help to paraphrase what Dickinson seems to be saying. In the first stanza, it seems that she wishes to say that the poet is the one who can, by compression of thought, show the rest of us the wonder of what passes unnoticed before us. This poem is a paean to the power of the poet.

Stanza two refers to the idea that the poet shows us what we know so that we wonder why we have never thought of it in quite that way before. It is as if the poet can put into words what would otherwise pass without comment. In the second half of the poem, Dickinson introduces a metaphor that you might find puzzling. Basically, she says that next to the poet, we are poor. She includes herself among the impoverished. However, the beauty of that poverty is that we are justified in robbing the poet. And the poet is so rich, what we take from him will in no way harm him. He is his own fortune, and the fortune goes beyond time.

TOPICS AND STRATEGIES

This section of the chapter will seek to provide you with various approaches you might take in writing a paper about this poem. These ideas are by no means exhaustive and should be looked at as a starting point for your own investigation.

Themes

Dickinson's poem introduces a definition of what it is to be a poet. Although some of the definition will hinge upon your interpretation of the poem's first word, much of it is clear. The poet, she writes, "distills" (2). The poet is the "discloser" (9). And the poet is rich. What this seems to add up to is a definition by value; the poet's value rests upon his or her ability to do what the rest of us cannot.

The verb *distill* suggests that something vaporous (in terms of meaning, perhaps something that is in the air but hard to apprehend) is changed into small drops of liquid (something we are able to touch and see). It also hints at the idea of compression, which you might recognize as an essential element in Dickinson's verse. One way to understand the poet, Dickinson suggests, is to know that the poet can apprehend the significance of life and compress it into a small verse that is packed with meaning.

This meaning is essential to the poet's audience, which should be everyone. The poet shows us what we need to know but are unable to see clearly. He turns "sense" into "Attar so immense" (4); he reduces sense into the essential. In the second stanza, Dickinson writes of "the familiar species / That perished by the Door" (5–6). This image will perhaps cause you to think of plants that might have been distilled into attar (an essential oil) but, instead, were allowed to die. The image could also be a metaphor for words. These words, which might have amounted to something precious, were treated as everyday things and allowed to die. No one recognized their value.

Likewise, the poet is rich because he sees the value in all. This ability makes him rich. It is also inseparable from who he is. In stanzas three and four, Dickinson explains how our transactions with the poet work. Her analogy has a bit of the Robin Hood about it. In stanza three, she writes: "The Poet—it is He— / Entitles Us—by Contrast— / To ceaseless Poverty" (10–12). Basically, next to the poet, any of us is poor. The poet, on the other hand, is so rich that "robbing" could not harm him.

Sample Topics:
  1. **The value of the poet:** What is the value of the poet?

> If you were to write an essay arguing that Dickinson's "This was a Poet—It is That" is a poem whose theme is the value of the poet, you might begin by examining the poem's verbs. What does it mean to "distill" or "disclose"? Why is it important that someone be able to do this?

  2. **Compression:** How does "This was a Poet—It is That" argue for compression in poetic thought?

> An essay on this subject might focus on the process of distillation. How are essential oils made? How does value arise from the process? How can something common be lent value by a process of compression? One possible thesis is that Dickinson uses her knowledge of botany to create an arresting metaphor for poetry.

  3. **Essence:** What does it mean to be essential?

> *Essential* has the connotation of vital. That is, what is essential is also necessary for life to continue. An essay that wished to explore the idea of essence in this poem might argue that Dickinson sets forth in "This was a Poet—It is That" her belief that poetry is essential to life.

  4. **Riches:** When we read a poem, are we "robbing" the poet?

> Dickinson presents a curious image at the end of "This was a Poet—It is That." She says that we are justified in robbing the poet because the poet is so rich he will not miss what is taken. He is his own fortune, always renewable and "exterior—to Time" (16). If you were to write on this topic, there are many possible approaches available to you. One possible thesis is that this poem shows Dickinson's belief in the poet's unique "ownership" of his or her poems, an idea that obviously had resilience for her in light of her reticence about publishing.

Compare and Contrast Essays

Another way to approach the idea of essence in this poem is to consider the idea of what the poet creates, or what is left when the poet is no more. There are at least two Dickinson poems where she approaches this idea in a similar way to "This was a Poet—It is That." In #675—"Essential Oils—are wrung," Dickinson returns to the exact image of the former poem, the attar that comes from pressing flowers. "Essential Oils—are wrung" is a more explicit development of that one idea. The poem shows the rose as the flower that is being pressed, and if you were to compare this poem to "This was a Poet—It is That," you would likely want to consider and discuss the connotations of the rose. This poem also resonates because of what we know of Dickinson's life. Like the fascicles and poems found in Dickinson's drawer after her death, the poems referred to in this poem make the poet immortal. Poem #883—"The Poets light but Lamps" continues the discussion of immortality, but the imagery is different. Here, Dickinson writes that poets light lamps of enduring, "vital" (4) flame. Their light continues after the poets themselves "go out" (2).

If you see the "familiar species" (5) by the door of lines five and six as the common words we use without recognizing their import, you might choose to compare or contrast "This was a Poet—It is That" with other Dickinson poems that emphasize the importance of words. Some poems you might want to look at in this case include #1126—"Shall I take thee, the Poet said," #1651—"A Word made Flesh is seldom," and #1261—"A Word dropped careless on a Page." "Shall I take thee, the Poet said" describes the importance of the word to the poetic process. Here, finding the right word is a mystical process. It is a similar situation in "A Word made Flesh is seldom," where the imagery is essentially biblical. The addition to this poem is the idea that people are only allowed to understand or partake up to their capacity. In "A Word dropped careless on a Page," Dickinson cautions against using words too lightly. Again, she seems to assign a mystical component to words. And here, a process takes place like the earlier distillation of attar, only the result is "Malaria" (8).

If you wanted to talk about the importance of the poet in Dickinson's poetry, you might turn to a poem such as #569—"I reckon—when I count at all." In that work, Dickinson writes that the poet is "all." She places the poet above heaven and nature. Perhaps you see something similar in "This was a Poet—It is That."

It has been proposed that "This was a Poet—It is That" is a reaction to Ralph Waldo Emerson's essay "The Poet." The imagery is similar. It might be interesting to contrast Dickinson's handling of the topic. If the two agree that the poet is the "discloser," where do they disagree?

Sample Topics:

1. **What is left:** How does Dickinson return, in various poems, to the idea of immortality?

   You might choose to compare "Essential Oils—are wrung" or "The Poets light but Lamps" to "This was a Poet—It is That." All three poems return to the image of what the poet leaves behind, or what is left after the poet's death. You could focus on the image of distillation. Another possible way to approach these poems is to focus on the idea of vitality and words that signal vitality, such as *life, essence, vital, light,* and *summer.*

2. **The importance of the word:** How do Dickinson's poems show a belief in the power of words?

   Comparing Dickinson's "This was a Poet—It is That" with any number of her poems, but particularly "Shall I take thee, the Poet said," "A Word made Flesh is seldom," or "A Word dropped careless on a Page," might lead you to argue that Dickinson believed words had mystical properties. You might also isolate imagery from any two of the poems to create your own argument.

3. **Poets and poetry:** Where do poets and poetry rank in Dickinson's hierarchy?

   If you were to compare #569—"I reckon—when I count at all" with "This was a Poet—It is That," you might write an essay with a thesis stating that Dickinson places poets above all. But you might also find yourself inclined to argue that Dickinson still places the poet in service of something higher, either God or a mystical process.

4. **Emerson's "The Poet"**: How is Dickinson's poet different from Emerson's?

Contrasting Dickinson's poem with Emerson's essay may lead you to argue that Dickinson essentially agrees with Emerson's thesis. However, you might decide that Emerson had a less religious and less democratic view of the role of the poet.

Bibliography and Online Resources

Emerson, Ralph Waldo. "The Poet." *RWE.org.* 14 Sep. 2006 <http://www.rwe.org/works/Essays–2nd_Series_1_Poet.htm>.

Johnson, Thomas H., ed. *The Poems of Emily Dickinson.* 3 vols. Cambridge, MA: Harvard UP, 1979.

Johnson, Thomas H., and Theodora Ward, eds. *The Letters of Emily Dickinson.* 3 vols. Cambridge, MA: Harvard UP, 1986.

Sewall, Richard B. *The Life of Emily Dickinson.* Cambridge, MA: Harvard UP, 1974.

#465—"I HEARD A FLY BUZZ—WHEN I DIED"

READING TO WRITE

Dickinson's "I heard a Fly buzz—when I died" is primarily a poem about death, but also about memory, religion, the senses, and many other ideas and experiences. The ideas and associations in this poem make it ripe for consideration. As a result, many critics have written about it, and it is not a hard poem to locate secondary source material about.

From the first line, the reader is made aware of two unusual conditions: The speaker of the poem has died, and the moment of dying coincided with the speaker's perception of the sound of the fly's buzzing. The presence of the fly and the speaker's heightened awareness and fixation on it both seem less than fitting the dignity of the deathbed scene. The fly's buzzing stands out in sharp relief to the silence maintained by those surrounding the dying person. In order to write about this poem, you would want to arrive at an understanding of the fly for yourself. What does the fly mean? Why is it here? Why would Dickinson choose to place a fly in this most solemn of scenes?

Any writer would also likely want to ask how this poem differs from other poems about dying and how it goes against most readers' expectations for a scene such as this. One noted difference in Dickinson's poem from other poems of death is the tone: It is basically devoid of sentiment. The speaker, while relating the circumstances of her dying, is to some extent a detached observer. The choice of the word *onset* in line seven also complicates. Although one can experience the onset of an illness, and *onset* does signify a beginning, in Dickinson's poem the word seems to carry its more negative connotation, as if it is an onslaught that is anticipated, or the beginning of a battle.

Writing about "I heard a Fly buzz—when I died" requires some attention to the way the senses are used in the poem. Much of the poem is devoted to sensory description, what the speaker perceives. The second stanza describes what the dying person "sees" in the room. In line five, the speaker says: "The Eyes around—had wrung them dry." The people who have gathered to witness the death are reduced to "Eyes" in this line and then "Breaths" in the next. These are perhaps the two characteristics the speaker equates with the living. These eyes have apparently already done their crying; they know that the death is imminent. They have steeled themselves to this.

Their "Breaths were gathering firm / For that last Onset—when the King / Be witnessed—in the Room" (6–8). They are waiting, breath held in, for the speaker's last breaths and for the moment when the divine will make its entrance. That the divine presence is characterized as a "King" lets the reader know that the expectation is for something magisterial, an authority beyond any they have ever encountered, far beyond their limited human knowledge. This is a sort of threshold moment, and the tension in the poem, now at its halfway mark, is running high. A writer will want to consider how the poem concludes—whether that king comes and in what form, and how the dying speaker moves toward and into death.

TOPICS AND STRATEGIES

This section of the chapter will seek to provide you with various approaches you might take in writing a paper about this poem. These ideas are by no means exhaustive and should be looked at as a starting point for your own investigation.

Themes

One theme present in "I heard a Fly buzz—when I died" addresses the boundary between life and death. How great is that boundary? Can we "see" or experience it, either by watching or by crossing it ourselves? As the first stanza shows, "The Stillness in the Room / Was like the Stillness in the Air— / Between the Heaves of Storm" (2–4). The room is still (the repetition of the word *stillness* in lines two and three serves to emphasize this fact), but for the fly; that stillness is pregnant with anticipation. Like the proverbial calm before the storm, the witnesses are quietly anticipating something tremendous: the passing of the loved one into eternity. Dickinson curiously places this stillness "between the Heaves of Storm," so there is the suggestion that as life is difficult or trying, like a storm, so might life after death be a similar sort of storm, with its own attendant difficulties. This runs contrary to the common idea of death as a peaceful place, a rest and reward.

Another question the poem moves its readers to ask is, What does Dickinson seem to suggest happens to the soul after death? Although Dickinson knew much of the Bible by heart and was an essentially spiritual person, she was not religious in the outward and conventional sense. Dickinson was the only member of her immediate family not to undergo the public conversion to Protestantism. Her refusal to do so at Mount Holyoke Female Seminary, where such a public proclamation of faith was expected, was also cause for personal difficulty. Her inability to conform in matters of faith set her apart from her contemporaries and from her family.

Dickinson's poem explores in depth the metaphoric implications of "seeing." It asks what it means to see, and that word can be understood in many ways—as understanding, perceiving, witnessing, knowing, and so on. Other senses are also elevated, such as hearing and the act of breathing. The people who are present at the deathbed are described only by those sensory acts: watching and breathing. Another theme introduced in part by this emphasis on the senses is the nature of the dying person. Is a person essentially an animal or a spiritual being? How does the act of dying serve to show us the essential self?

Sample Topics:

1. **The boundary between life and death:** What does "I heard a Fly buzz—when I Died" suggest about the boundary between life and death?

How great does this boundary seem to be? Can anyone observe another's crossing of it? How much does the dying speaker understand about her own crossing over? What composes the boundary? How much do we rely on our senses to show us we are alive? These are only a few questions you might want to consider as you write an essay that tries to explain how this poem illustrates the boundary between life and death.

2. **Life after death:** What do you think this poem is trying to say about life after death?

The poem features a speaker who has already died, so there is some sort of existence for that speaker beyond her earthly one. What kind of existence do you think it is? How does it differ from life? How does it differ from conventional religious representations of life after death?

3. **The metaphor of seeing:** Consider the poet's use of metaphor. How might death be like the closing of the windows or the closing of the eyes? How might death be like blindness?

A paper on this topic would look at the poem's many references to seeing, eyes, light, windows, and other forms of sensory perception. What does it mean to "see" in the poem? Also consider words such as *witnessed* (line eight) and *vision*, which does not appear in the poem but is suggested. A paper like this need not "explain" what Dickinson means by seeing in this poem; it could be enough to explore how richly loaded this metaphor is.

4. **The nature of man:** How much is the dying person a part of the natural, physical world? How much is the dying person a part of the spiritual?

In Dickinson's poem readers have a chance to, in a sense, be present at a deathbed scene. The poem may lead you to consider what Dickinson is saying about the nature of our selves. Is the dying person largely animal or spiritual? You could write an essay that attempts to answer these questions for yourself and your audience.

History and Context

Thomas H. Johnson dates "I heard a Fly buzz—when I died" to the year 1862, coincident with the Civil War (*Poems* 224). Although Dickinson has been sometimes taken to task for not addressing the war explicitly in her poetry, it should also be noted that the Civil War years were Dickinson's most productive. It would not be unreasonable to expect a writer working during a national crisis such as a civil war to exhibit an interest in mortality.

Even without the war, mortality was high in the 19th century. Many of Dickinson's letters are letters of condolence. So, while her interest in death should not be seen as unusual, her treatment of death in "I heard a Fly buzz—when I died" is. It notably lacks the sentimentality or religiosity common to 19th-century depictions of the deathbed scene. This death, also, is without context. We do not know who the dying person is, how she is dying, or any other details that might lend specificity to the scene. Therefore, it could be the death of anyone at anytime.

As critic Sabine Sielke writes, Dickinson "kept a clear, often ironic distance from Victorian values, Calvinist traditions, and conventional thinking" (388), but she was not unschooled in any of these. One Calvinist tradition important to this poem is that of watching the death of someone for a sign of the hereafter. Congruent with this is the idea of the "good" death. It was thought that if a person died well—peacefully, composedly, in little pain—this person was likely a member of the elect and would enter the kingdom of God. What happened at the deathbed, then, became a window into the hereafter and the dying person's fate.

The reader waits to learn what will happen, and what does and does not happen says a great deal about what differentiates Dickinson from her peers. For, even at a remove of 150 years, we know how we expect this scene to be depicted. There is something essentially unsettling about the death that occurs in "I heard a Fly buzz—when I died," and it is conveyed even in that first line. Dickinson's fly is completely unexpected, and this death goes against our conventional views of how a person should die.

Sample Topics:

1. **The context of the Civil War:** Can this poem be read in terms of the war?

   This poem showcases an intimate view of death, one more intimate than contemporary readers will generally possess. Although the death here is considerably more peaceful than that of a soldier on the battlefield, the many deaths that occurred during the Civil War could have easily moved the poet to a consideration of the experience of dying. A paper could be written arguing that this rather unsentimental look at death was a result of the tremendous amount of dying that Dickinson witnessed during the war years.

2. **The context of 19th-century death:** How does Dickinson's poem illuminate dying in 19th-century America?

Dying was once a much more intimate affair, usually done at home, not in a hospital. The dying person was surrounded by friends and family. The corpse was prepared by the family and exhibited in the home. Putrefaction came quickly, and little could be done to hide the decay of the body. Dickinson's poem provides a window into the history of death, but it also moves us beyond these particulars. An essay could be written that discussed how "I heard a Fly buzz—when I died" makes us more aware of what it might have been like to die in 19th-century America.

3. **Calvinist beliefs:** How does this poem illuminate Calvinist beliefs and traditions?

You may wish to consult Richard B. Sewall's biography of Dickinson for discussion of beliefs and traditions as they were practiced by the Dickinson family and their neighbors. After some research, an essay could be written that explained how this poem is and is not reflective of the Calvinist belief system.

4. **Irreverence:** An essay could be written discussing the ways Dickinson's poem thwarts our expectations. How does this death differ from what we might expect death to be?

A paper such as this could contrast the attitudes of the witnesses with that of the dying person. It could also look at other representations of death or simply discuss conventional notions of what the deathbed is like. The very unusual nature of this poem is what makes it memorable, and a promising essay could be written discussing what is unusual about "I heard a Fly buzz—when I died."

Philosophy and Ideas

As death comes closer, the speaker makes further preparation for it: "I willed my Keepsakes—Signed away / What portion of me be / Assignable" (9–11). This last action, while not unusual, is also filled with significance. The willing away of the possessions is certainly meant, but as these "keepsakes" are also "portions" of the speaker's self, the reader is invited to consider that the speaker is somehow willing away the earthly self. What constitutes a life? What is left after the possessions are signed away? The reader is assured that not everything that belongs to the speaker is assignable. What the speaker is left with after earthly possessions are stripped away is the body and the soul, and can either of these be said to belong to him or her?

The poem also reveals Dickinson's interest in the consciousness, intellect, or understanding of an individual. To what extent is a person what he or she knows and perceives? Here is the moment where the poem turns, because at the moment of death, "There interposed a Fly" (12). She seems to wish for the reader to consider what happens to the mind after death, just as those gathered are interested in the soul.

As a scientific document, "I heard a Fly buzz—when I died" does attempt to answer the question of what happens, physically, at the moment of death. For Dickinson, one possible explanation, and perhaps a particularly frightening one for her as she was experiencing problems with her own vision at this time, is that death was a failure of the senses. There is a certain underlying terror in the failure of the eyes and the way the hearing seems to isolate the buzzing of the fly so that it, faint as we know it to be, is the last sound to remain. Of course, the fly's presence invites us to consider the fate of the body after death. The blowfly (often large and blue-green in color) can pick up the faintest odor of decay in the search for a corpse in which to lay its eggs. The fly is a certain, physical sign of the death of the body.

"I heard a Fly buzz—when I died" reveals to us a deathbed scene of the 19th century. The assembled company waits for a sign of the soul of the loved one's acceptance into a heavenly company. We must assume they are disappointed. Further, the poem suggests that the private relationship between an individual and God is superior to any public one. "I heard a Fly buzz—when I died" might also ask how great an ability does any individual have to know God. But, for many readers, "I heard a Fly buzz—when I died" is a poem of doubt.

Sample Topics:

1. **What makes a life?:** The poem seems to ask this question. When the speaker wills away what she can, what is left?

   An essay could be written that attempts to identify what the speaker possesses. Is she in possession of her body? Does she possess her soul? What does "I heard a Fly buzz—when I died" suggest is the "assignable" portion of an individual, in this case, the dying speaker? Here, the poet's diction seems particularly important. Why this choice of words?

2. **Perception:** What does awareness consist of in the poem? What does Dickinson seem to be saying about consciousness?

   One possible thesis is that "I heard a Fly buzz—when I died" is a poem about perception. It is also possible to imagine an argument that says that in this poem, death is the loss of perception. A paper such as this would focus on the many sensory details given.

3. **Decay:** Seek out a scientific discussion of what happens to the body at death. How does Dickinson's poem compare?

   A paper could be written arguing that "I heard a Fly buzz—when I died" is a straightforward examination of the death of the body. This would involve reading the fly more literally and less symbolically. Dickinson and her contemporaries were well aware of how a corpse progressed through the process of decay.

4. **Religion:** What does Dickinson seem to be suggesting about Christian beliefs concerning life after death?

Does the fly mock their belief by underscoring the physicality of death? Does the replacement of the "King" with a fly somehow suggest that there is no king and that the waiting for his appearance is an exercise in futility? Or does the fly suggest that God is in the smallest things, even the lowly fly? The last might come closest to being a tenet of Dickinson's own spiritual belief. After all, she is the poet who wrote, in poem #324, "Some keep the Sabbath going to Church— / I keep it, staying at Home" (1–2), which suggests that faith is a private matter.

Form and Genre

The poem consists of four quatrains. Typical of Dickinson's poems, these quatrains are ballad stanzas following hymn, or common, meter. Each stanza in this meter should rhyme at the second and fourth lines so that the rhyme scheme would be *ABAB* or, less often, *ABCB*. The meter is iambic, with four iambs in the first and third lines and three iambs in the second and fourth. It is the meter used for most Protestant hymns, such as "Amazing Grace." Dickinson and her contemporaries would have been familiar with the sound and rhythm of this meter from their church services and hymnals.

Also present are Dickinson's oddities of punctuation and capitalization, along with the disrupted syntax that opens up the poem's meanings to multiple interpretations. The only punctuation used throughout this poem is the dash, and it appears in places where the reader might expect a comma, semicolon, or period. The dash does seem to lend Dickinson's poems a sense of speed or urgency. The pauses that would normally occur with conventional punctuation seem hurried over. The lack of the final period seems to leave, particularly in this poem, a sense of something more to come. The significance of Dickinson's inconsistent capitalization is also uncertain, but, in general, the scattered words throughout the poem that she chooses to capitalize might be seen as particularly important to the poem's meaning. They tend to be words that are stressed by the meter as well, although not all stressed words are capitalized. (This is a characteristic of Dickinson's prose as well.) The rhymes are irregular for the ballad stanza until the last stanza of the poem. Until that point, each stanza has had a slant rhyme in lines two and four. The whole, or perfect, rhyme of "me" with "see" in the final stanza gives the poem a certain closure, even without a final period to mark its end.

Sample Topics:

1. **Hymn meter:** Is there any significance to the use of hymn meter in this poem?

   Dickinson often wrote in hymn meter, but the choice here could be significant. Using the tune to "Amazing Grace," try to hum "I heard a Fly buzz—when I died" and read the poem with attention to its music. Does this reveal anything further about the poem?

2. **Punctuation:** How does Dickinson's unique punctuation help you to understand this poem?

   You might wish to consider how Dickinson's punctuation helps the reader to understand "I heard a Fly buzz—when I died." An essay could be written discussing the effect her use of the dash has on your reading.

3. **Capitalization:** Can isolating the capital words of this poem give you a deeper understanding of it?

   An essay could be written that discusses the capitalized words in "I heard a Fly buzz—when I died." Read the poem out loud, giving those words extra emphasis. List the capitalized words on a separate sheet of paper. Can you find any particular logic behind the choices Dickinson made?

4. **Rhyme scheme:** Similar to the topic above, can you discover more about "I heard a Fly buzz—when I died" by isolating its rhymes?

   Paying careful attention to Dickinson's rhymes could help you create an essay that discusses their significance. You would want to look at rhymes that occur between stanzas, such as "was" in line 11 and "Buzz" in line 13. You would also want to look at internal rhymes and repetitions, such as "Stillness" in lines two and three.

Language, Symbols, and Imagery

Your reading of this poem hinges on your interpretation of the symbolic meaning of the fly. The fly disrupts the deathbed scene and upsets the speaker's expectations. The fly does not seem to be the expected king. It could be that the fly is a last worldly distraction. Perhaps, the fly has come to appropriate the body and is a sign or reminder of deathly decay. It may be that the fly's presence suggests that there is no king and that the only future for the dying is decomposition, not a life beyond the current one. The fly is the last presence of which the speaker is conscious: seeing and then lastly hearing it. The fly is heard even after the "Windows" (15) fail, when the speaker can no longer "see to see" (16).

Synesthesia is when one perceives one sort of sensory experience when, in fact, another sort of stimulus was received, such as when one can "hear" a certain color. Synesthesia can also be the describing of one sensory experience by using another. In this poem it occurs frequently, such as when the fly moves with a "Blue" (13) buzz. This produces a rare and unusual sort of imagery, an almost multilayered sensory experience.

"I heard a Fly buzz—when I died" is also a poem whose language, symbols, and imagery suggest much about religion. Any reader is likely to have his or her own interpretation of what the poem says in this respect. One possible way to approach an essay on this topic would be to consider this poem as another example of Dickinson's unique view of religious belief.

Sample Topics:

1. **The fly:** Why does she use a common insect? Why does the writer move from hearing the fly in the first stanza to seeing it in the third?

An essay could attempt to state what the "Fly" in this poem symbolizes. What language and imagery is used in reference to the fly? Is there more than one possible interpretation of the fly?

2. **The king:** Is the king death or Jesus? How is the buzzing fly related to the king?

An essay on this topic would attempt to explain the symbolism of the "King." Exploring the questions above would be one place to begin. You might also wish to think about the word *king* and all that it connotes. Why did Dickinson choose this particular word? Why does the juxtaposition of king and fly seem so unlikely?

3. **Synesthesia:** This poem is curious in its emphasis on sensory experience, particularly the overlapping or confusion of the senses. Do you think this confusion arises only because the speaker is coming closer to death? Do the sensory details help you to understand the experience of the speaker?

Pay attention to the poet's use of the senses. How many can you identify and how are they used? Some are fairly obvious, but look also for those less so, such as the insistence on breath, air, and the "Heaves of Storm." If synesthesia is a failure of the mind and body to work in congress with each other, how does this inform your reading of the poem?

4. **Religious imagery:** Various images and words in the poem—from the "Heaves of Storm," the "Onset," and the "King," to the use of "witnessed"—have religious connotations. Does the poem hold to their conventional meanings?

You might want to write an essay discussing the religious imagery of this poem. One possible thesis would be that although the poem has a great deal of religious imagery, the imagery is employed in unorthodox ways. Dickinson's poem #324—"Some keep the Sabbath going to Church" could be considered another poem useful for comparison to "I heard a Fly buzz—when I died" if you wanted to pursue the thesis that both poems showcase Dickinson's independent and idiosyncratic view of religion.

Compare and Contrast Essays

There are any number of ways to construct an essay that compares or contrasts Dickinson's "I heard a Fly buzz—when I died" with another work of literature, whether a poem by Dickinson herself or another work that you find relevant. "I heard a Fly buzz—when I died" depicts the process of death from the perspective of the one who has already completed it, as do some other important poems by Dickinson, notably, #712—"Because I could not stop for death" and #449—"I died for Beauty—but was scarce." These are some other obvious poems to look at for a possible essay that compares or contrasts Dickinson poems. The following have death as their subject: #216—"Safe in their Alabaster Chambers," #389—"There's been a Death, in the Opposite House," #856—"There is a finished feeling," #860—"Absence disembodies—so does Death," #922—"Those who have been in the Grave the longest," #943—"A Coffin—is a small Domain," and #949—"Under the Light, yet under."

The deathbed poem was tremendously popular in 19th-century America. A poet who produced them in bulk, Julia A. Moore, was satirized by Mark Twain in *Huckleberry Finn.* In that novel, the character Emmeline Grangerford writes the hysterically funny elegy for Stephen Dowling Bots. An interesting essay could be written looking at the work of Twain writing as Emmeline Grangerford ("Every time a man died, or a woman died, or a child died, she would be on hand with her 'tribute' before he was cold. . . . The neighbors said it was the doctor first, then Emmeline, and then the undertaker" [139]) or contrasting instances of other deathbed poems contemporary to Dickinson's. There are also at least two short stories that famously depict the deathbed scene: "The Death of Ivan Ilyich" by Leo Tolstoy and "The Jilting of Grannie Weatherall" by Katherine Anne Porter. You might find it interesting to look at either for another depiction of the act of dying.

Sample Topics:

1. **Other voices of the dead:** In at least two other poems, Dickinson has a speaker who is already dead. What effect does a deceased speaker have on the message delivered?

   Looking at either #712—"Because I could not stop for death" or #449—"I died for Beauty—but was scarce," compare or contrast the speaker of one of those poems to the speaker of "I heard a Fly buzz—when I died." Are their voices similar? Are their concerns the same? Do the poems exhibit any similar theme, such as death as the gradual loss of sensory feeling?

2. **Other views of death:** You might choose any number of Dickinson poems about death to compare or contrast with "I heard a Fly buzz—when I died." How does Dickinson represent death throughout her work? How is her view of death unique? What gives her the reputation in some circles as a morbid poet?

Dickinson has a reputation, which you might give more or less credence to, as a poet of death. You could choose a poem from the list above or another of your own choosing and profitably compare or contrast it with "I heard a Fly buzz—when I died."

3. **Contemporary views of death:** Death was a much greater preoccupation in 19th-century America than it is today, and poems, photographs, obituaries, and epitaphs all reflect this. If you look at a poem by one of Dickinson's contemporaries, such as Julia A. Moore, you will find a very different view than the one presented in "I heard a Fly buzz—when I died." How is Dickinson unlike her contemporaries?

You might write an essay contrasting Dickinson's deathbed scene in "I heard a Fly buzz—when I died" with other presentations of the same scene by other writers contemporary to her. It might also be fun to look at Twain's characterization of Emmeline Grangerford in *The Adventures of Huckleberry Finn* for one writer's view of deathbed poetry.

4. **Prose depictions of the deathbed:** Leo Tolstoy and Katherine Anne Porter are two writers who have depicted death through the eyes of the dying protagonist. Either of their stories might further illuminate your reading of "I heard a Fly buzz—when I died." How do different writers, here prose writers, depict the deathbed?

In Porter's "The Jilting of Granny Weatherall," the bridegroom (perhaps, like the fly, a stand-in for Christ) fails to appear. Tolstoy's Ivan Ilyich achieves grace at the very final moment. You might write an essay comparing or contrasting either of these figures with the speaker of Dickinson's poem.

Bibliography and Online Resources

Cameron, Sharon. "*Et in Arcadia Ego:* Representation, Death, and the Problem of Boundary in Emily Dickinson." *American Woman Poets: 1650–1950.* Ed. Harold Bloom. Philadelphia: Chelsea House Publishers, 2002. 45–86.

Johnson, Thomas H., ed. *The Poems of Emily Dickinson.* 3 vols. Cambridge, MA: Harvard UP, 1979.

Johnson, Thomas H., and Theodora Ward, eds. *The Letters of Emily Dickinson.* 3 vols. Cambridge, MA: Harvard UP, 1986.

"On 465 ('I Heard a Fly Buzz When I Died')." *Modern American Poetry.* <http://www.english.uiuc.edu/maps/poets/a_f/dickinson/465.htm.> 12 Jan. 2006.

Porter, Katherine Anne. "The Jilting of Granny Weatherall." *The Collected Stories of Katherine Anne Porter.* New York: Harvest Books, 1979. 80–89.

Ryan, Michael. "How to Use a Fly." *American Poetry Review* 33.2 (Mar.–Apr. 2004): 15–17.

Sewall, Richard B. *The Life of Emily Dickinson.* Cambridge, MA: Harvard UP, 1974.

Sielke, Sabine. "Emily Dickinson." *The Greenwood Encyclopedia of American Poets and Poetry.* Ed. Jeffery Gray. Vol. 2. Westport, CT: Greenwood Press, 2006. 387–392.

Tolstoy, Leo. "The Death of Ivan Ilyich." *The Classical Library.* 17 Jun. 2006 <http://www.classicallibrary.org/tolstoy/ivan/>.

Twain, Mark. *The Adventures of Huckleberry Finn.* New York: Penguin, 2002.

#569—"I RECKON—
WHEN I COUNT
AT ALL"

READING TO WRITE

IN A sense, this is one of Dickinson's "definition" poems. Here, she defines the poet by creating a hierarchy. She writes: "First—Poets— Then the Sun— / Then Summer—Then the Heaven of God" (2–3). With that, her list ends. You get a sense of what the poet values from what she has chosen to include. You also get a sense of the value she places on poets. She puts poets before nature and heaven. She concludes this part with "Poets—All" (8). She decides that poets encompass all of those things she has mentioned earlier.

A person of faith might take exception to Dickinson's list. To begin, she has placed poets above not only "the Heaven of God," but also the "Sun" and "Summer." If you consider God's creations to be analogous to God, this might seem blasphemous. In the second stanza, Dickinson goes further by dismissing the other components of her list and replacing all of it with poets alone. She says that "the Others look a needless Show" (7). As she goes on to explain why the Sun and summer can be discounted, she seems to refer not only to the poet's gift for creation but also to the poet's ability to create a world that will last. The Sun and summer of the poet have permanence.

As you consider how to write about this poem, you will want to come to some understanding of the difficult final stanza. The thought related in it begins in line 12, where Dickinson writes: "And if the Further

Heaven— / Be Beautiful as they prepare / For Those who worship Them" (12–14). The problem comes in interpreting the referent to the pronoun *they*. The "Further Heaven" may be taken to mean the heaven beyond this world or the heavens created by poets. For the referent to "they" in line 13, you most likely will look back to line eight, where she writes, "Poets—All." All pronouns from that point on seem to refer back to the poets, so Dickinson seems to be saying that if there is a heaven beyond the one that the poets create "For Those who worship Them," it is more than can be conceived in our imaginations.

What may be troubling here, and you would have to consider this as you write, is the idea she introduces of worshipping poets. If this is the correct interpretation, then the poem is making a religion of poetry. The poem's final lines imply a doubt that there could be a heaven better than that created by poets and, therefore, a doubt that there is a heaven outside of our known world.

TOPICS AND STRATEGIES

This section of the chapter will seek to provide you with various approaches you might take in writing a paper about this poem. These ideas are by no means exhaustive and should be looked at as a starting point for your own investigation.

Themes

That poetry deserves the same treatment as a religion is not an unusual assertion in Dickinson's poems. "I reckon—when I count at all" is perhaps the most extravagant in its claims for poetry and poets. The phrase "when I count at all" suggests that the preeminence of poetry is so well established for the speaker that it does not warrant consideration.

The poem has as its theme the question of faith, both religious and otherwise. While many people have faith in "the Heaven of God," this poem expresses some uncertainty. The question is not so much whether that heaven exists, but whether it could be superior to that created by the poets. To some extent, this puts the poet on an equal footing with God, as the creator of worlds.

It may strike some as odd that the sun and summer, Dickinson's favorite season, are also placed before heaven. Thematically, this could be described as reflective of a love of nature, perhaps at odds with Christian faith. It would also be in keeping with another theme in Dickinson's work: the primacy of what we can experience with our senses. The only failing in nature the poem points to is that it fades. The summer does not last, and sometimes the Sun is not visible.

Summer has a number of connotations. It is associated with heat, passion, leisure, youth, and the fullness of life. Another idea attached to summer is that it quickly fades. In "I reckon—when I count at all," the summer of the poets "lasts a Solid Year" (9). The summer of poets, then, is without end. To have a season that does not end might be perceived as more gratifying than "the Heaven of God" because that heaven still requires dying before one can be admitted. The summer of the poets might be seen as life without end, a different sort of immortality.

Sample Topics:

1. **Poetry:** What does "I reckon—when I count at all" say about poetry?

   This poem makes tall claims for poetry. If you were to write on this subject, you would want to discuss the hierarchy of her list: "Poets," "Sun," "Summer," and "the Heaven of God." You would also want to talk about the poem's ending and the final comparison between heaven and poetry.

2. **Faith:** What does this poem have to say about faith?

   The faith in "I reckon—when I count at all" is in poetry. If you choose to write on this topic, you might argue that Dickinson's placement of the poet above all shows a faith in poetry as strong as that which others reserve for religion.

3. **Nature:** How can the poet justify putting the Sun and summer before heaven?

   One possible thesis for an essay on this topic would be that the speaker of this poem values what can be experienced over that

that must be imagined. Perhaps this translates to an absence of faith. You could also call it a love of the things of this world.

4. **Summer:** Why is summer an important idea in this poem?

To write about summer in "I reckon—when I count at all" would be a less obvious choice, perhaps, than some of the others mentioned above. Sometimes choosing a less obvious topic can be rewarding, as you find more to say about it and are forced to think a bit harder about the poem than you might otherwise. One possible thesis might be the following: Summer is the central theme of Dickinson's poem because the poem's true subject is immortality.

Compare and Contrast Essays

Dickinson wrote a great number of poems about poets and poetry. You may want to consult a concordance to find other references to these subjects in her work. In poem #448—"This was a Poet—It is That," Dickinson praises the poet as the "Discloser" (9) of pictures and one whose wealth is himself. If you were to compare this poem with "I reckon—when I count at all," you might talk about the importance Dickinson assigns to the poet. For her, the poet is a subject of adoration, not unlike a god.

Dickinson's #1651—"A Word made Flesh is seldom" uses transubstantiation and the taking of Communion as a metaphor for the poetic act. This might again strike some as slightly blasphemous. If you were to compare this poem to "I reckon—when I count at all," you might see a similarity in the use of biblical metaphors. You might want to discuss how both poems relegate a power to the poet that is more usually reserved for God.

That could also lead you to another topic, which is the idea of being godlike. The fascination with being godlike is another commonly recurring idea in Dickinson's work. Poem #724—"It's easy to invent a Life" begins: "It's easy to invent a Life / God does it—every Day" (1–2). The poem's conclusion might remind you of "I reckon—when I count at all." Dickinson writes that God continues on, "inserting Here—a Sun— / There—leaving out a Man" (11–12). There is something cavalier in her portrayal of God, as if his choices were more random and less considered than a poet's. A more respectful poem is #945—"This is a Blossom of the Brain." This poem seems to trace poetic inspiration to God so that the nurturing of the poem is a religious act. If one allows the poetic thought to die, Dickinson writes, this is "The Funeral of God" (14).

Poem #248—"Why—do they shut Me out of Heaven?" asks: "Why—do they shut Me out of Heaven? / Did I sing—too loud?" (1–2). This would be a very interesting poem to compare to "I reckon—when I count at all." In those first lines, the speaker asks if she is being shut out of heaven for singing too loud; singing is a metaphor for poetry. So, the poem seems to be asking if being a poet is enough to get one shut out of heaven. In the poem's final stanza, the speaker asks: "Oh, if I—were the Gentleman / In the 'White Robe' / And they—were the little Hand—that knocked— / Could—I—forbid?" (9–12). A discussion of this stanza in comparison to "I reckon—when I count at all" would be interesting because in #248, the speaker has imagined herself in the position of God, with the ability to decide who enters the kingdom of heaven.

Sample Topics:

1. **The poet:** How does "I reckon—when I count at all" compare to other Dickinson poems about poets and poetry?

   An essay on this topic might focus on the idea of wealth. Dickinson portrays the poet in "This was a Poet—It is That" as rich. In "I reckon—when I count at all," the poet is able to create anything he desires, even the Sun or a season.

2. **The word:** How does Dickinson's emphasis on the word resemble the biblical treatment of the holy word?

   One approach to a paper on this topic would be to focus on the idea of the immortal. Dickinson writes in "A Word made Flesh is seldom:" "A Word that breathes distinctly / Has not the power to die" (9–10). This might be compared to the summer that is everlasting in "I reckon—when I count at all."

3. **Being godlike:** How does Dickinson compare the poet to God?

If you were to write an essay that discussed Dickinson's predilection for comparing the poet to God, you might focus on the idea of creation. She draws a parallel between the creation of God and the creating that poets do. Sometimes, the parallel favors one above the other. If you were to compare "This is a Blossom of the Brain" with "I reckon—when I count at all," your thesis might be that in the former poem Dickinson suggests that the poet's abilities come from God, while in the latter poem she suggests that the poet's abilities rival those of God. If you wished to compare "It's easy to invent a Life" with "I reckon—when I count at all," you might argue that God's creation is depicted as more capricious than the poet's.

4. **Heaven:** Can a comparison of #248—"Why—do they shut Me out of Heaven?" with "I reckon—when I count at all" help us to understand Dickinson's conflation of religion and poetry?

One possible thesis for comparing these poems would be to argue that the poet often places herself in the role of God. If you wished to contrast the poems, you might say that the idea of heaven and the fear of being excluded from it are more real in "Why—do they shut Me out of Heaven?"

Bibliography and Online Resources

Johnson, Thomas H., ed. *The Poems of Emily Dickinson.* 3 vols. Cambridge, MA: Harvard UP, 1979.

Johnson, Thomas H., and Theodora Ward, eds. *The Letters of Emily Dickinson.* 3 vols. Cambridge, MA: Harvard UP, 1986.

Rosenbaum, S. P., ed. *A Concordance to the Poems of Emily Dickinson.* Ithaca, NY: Cornell UP, 1964.

Sewall, Richard B. *The Life of Emily Dickinson.* Cambridge, MA: Harvard UP, 1974.

#585—"I LIKE TO SEE IT LAP THE MILES"

READING TO WRITE

IN ORDER to write about Dickinson's "I like to see it lap the Miles," you should first understand that the poem is in the form of a riddle. It was not unusual for Dickinson to create poems in this way, as she enjoyed sending children, particularly her young Norcross cousins, poems that were to puzzle and then delight, as they discovered the poems' subject. Two other well-known examples of riddles are #986—"A narrow Fellow in the Grass" and #1463—"A Route of Evanescence." Any essay about a poem like this would likely begin with an explication of what the poem "means." This would be done by line-by-line analysis. In so doing, you will also solve the riddle.

The opening line of the poem introduces a speaker, "I," who is unidentified. The line also introduces a subject, "it," that is unidentified. From the actions of "it," you will ascertain its identity. In line one, it "laps" the miles, a seemingly animalistic thing to do—devouring or drinking the miles. The metaphor continues in the next line, as it will also "lick the Valleys up" (2). At this point, what seems to be suggested is the swift movement of an animal. But in lines three through seven, you see it "stop to feed itself at Tanks—/ And then—prodigious step / Around a Pile of Mountains— / And supercilious peer / In Shanties—by the side of roads." Now it becomes clear that what is being shown is something other than an animal. It is large; its movements not only "lap" and "lick" over vast distances, but it can also "step" around mountains. By now, most of us may be imagining that Dickinson is presenting us with an imaginative view of a train, and the rest of the poem will bear out this reading. As you write, however, you may wish to allow for variant readings.

From the actions of the train, we come to understand that the poem's subject is the "iron horse" of the early railway. In stanza three, the train has pared a quarry "to fit its Ribs" (9), which might be imagined to be its tracks. As it moves between them, the train is "Complaining all the while / In horrid—hooting stanza" (11–12). Here, Dickinson suggests the great noise of the train and its whistle. The poem continues to journey along with the train and speeds up as it nears its final destination. You may wish to discuss how Dickinson's use of the "and then" construction helps to move the poem, and the train, along.

We see the train "chase itself down Hill" (13), an image of its movement and line of cars that follow after each other. The train begins to "neigh like Boanerges— / Then—punctual as a Star / Stop—docile and omnipotent / At its own stable door" (14–17). The image of Boanerges is the most difficult of the poem. As discussed in the "Philosophy and Ideas" section below, Boanerges means "sons of Thunder" and refers to the name Jesus gave to two particularly vocal disciples. You may be able to imagine the train crying like thunder as it comes to its destination. As you write, you will want to consider whether there is any implication in Dickinson's use of the biblical image. You will also want to explain to the best of your understanding a seeming contradiction such as "docile and omnipotent."

TOPICS AND STRATEGIES

This section of the chapter will seek to provide you with various approaches you might take in writing a paper about this poem. These ideas are by no means exhaustive and should be looked at as a starting point for your own investigation.

Themes

"I like to see it lap the Miles" is one of Dickinson's few poems to address a new technology forthrightly. One very obvious theme in the poem is the effect this new technology might have on the landscape, the people, and the animals it will supplant. Another less obvious theme is how the senses can be used to understand something that is entirely new. The

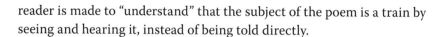

reader is made to "understand" that the subject of the poem is a train by seeing and hearing it, instead of being told directly.

Sample Topics:

1. **Technology:** Much of the discussion of this poem rests upon whether Dickinson is making a statement (pro or con) about technology. In your opinion, how does the speaker feel about the train? Is she more positive or negative?

To create an argument about Dickinson's view of technology in this poem, you must first make a decision based largely upon the images of the poem. Do these images lead you to feel positively or negatively toward the train?

2. **The human element:** There is no human being in the poem other than the speaker of the poem who watches the train. Does this human absence suggest the relative inhumanity of the new technology, even though that speaker does say, "I like to see it"?

A railroad takes people to make it run: conductors, brakemen, track layers, and an assortment of workers. We imagine that the "shanties" the train looks into house someone. Oftentimes, the train is thought of more as a conveyance for people than goods. Write a consideration of the absence of human agency in this poem.

3. **Sensory perception:** The speaker of "I like to see it lap the Miles" comes to understand the train through her senses, as does the reader. The nature of this riddle is that you understand the new technology, the train, without being told about it directly. How does this poem show that poetry is a sensory experience?

Although she could not, perhaps, literally "see" the train move over its entire course, it is likely she could hear a good deal of its movements. She understands and explains in her poem how the train moves, how it will "feed itself," what its "Ribs" look like, and how it sounds. To write an essay on this topic, you would discuss the poem's use of sensory images.

4. **Train v. horse:** Clearly Dickinson is working within a metaphor of the train as horse, not an unfamiliar idea nor one that is specifically Dickinson's. Does the poem lead you to see either the train or the horse as superior?

A paper could be written that argued for the superiority of either one, as depicted in Dickinson's poem. The train was already known as an "iron horse," and in a similar way, we measure the power of our automobiles in "horsepower." Her train does talk "In horrid—hooting stanza" (12). Is this a judgment, or is Dickinson merely attempting to capture the sound of the train? An essay on this topic needs to look at each metaphor applied to the train, and most particularly those that link it to the horse.

History and Context

A possibly productive approach would be to consider this poem in its history and context. The first railroad charter in North America was granted in New Jersey circa 1815 to John Stevens. Rail transport quickly came to represent modernity in the United States. The linking of Connecticut's New London line to western Massachusetts promised to increase travel and commerce between the two states, and Edward Dickinson, Emily Dickinson's father, worked hard to bring the railroad to their hometown of Amherst, Massachusetts. The Amherst and Belchertown Railroad, as it was called, was chartered on May 24, 1851. Its opening was celebrated on June 9, 1853, and Edward Dickinson was honored during the celebration. The railway station abuts the Dickinson property. To this day, the train's whistle is easily heard from the Dickinson Homestead. In 1862, the year Dickinson likely wrote "I like to see it lap the Miles," President Abraham Lincoln signed the Pacific Railway Act, opening up the possibility of a transcontinental railroad. By 1862, there were already more than 30,000 miles of track in the United States.

Sample Topics:

1. **The Amherst and Belchertown Railroad:** The opening of this line was incredibly important to Amherst and the Dickinson family. How could "I like to see it lap the Miles" be considered a celebration of the railroad?

Richard Sewall's biography discusses Edward Dickinson's work to bring the railroad to Amherst and Emily Dickinson's curious behavior at its opening ceremonies (she watched, alone, from the woods). You might look at this and other sources to determine the railroad's importance to the area and to speculate about Emily Dickinson's view of it.

2. **American migration:** The railway allowed the American people ever increasing movement and travel. Is this increased migration seen by the poet as an improvement, or does the poem even take on this question? What is the route that the train takes in "I like to see it lap the Miles"?

Trains were opening up the continent to the American people. Does this poem say anything about these changes? An essay could be written that focuses on the changes the train would bring, and whether this poem begins to accurately depict them.

3. **Biographical context:** Dickinson is known, even by those who know little about her poetry, for staying at home. How can "I like to see it lap the Miles" be read in light of Dickinson's own reclusiveness?

Perhaps the lack of human passengers suggests Dickinson does not see the train as a conveyor of people. Possibly, the way she characterizes the train as animal betrays how foreign this new technology feels to her (though it could be said that depicting the train as a horse attempts to make it familiar). A paper on this topic might look for evidence that the train is threatening or even antihuman.

4. **The American railroad:** By the time of Dickinson's poem, the American railroad had already begun to assume a mythic stature in the works of artists and writers. How can it be argued that "I like to see it lap the Miles" is but one example of a particularly American fascination with the railroad?

American writers of literature and song have viewed the railway with affection. Can you think of other poems, stories, songs, or folk tales that take the railroad as their subject? You might want to look for examples contemporary to Dickinson, or you might want to consider examples that are contemporary to you or that have assumed a place in popular culture so that they are well known to the majority of your audience.

Form and Genre

"I like to see it lap the Miles" is a poem, to some extent, about speed, and its form reflects that. The poem is one long sentence. It consists of three quatrains (the first, second, and fourth stanzas), while the third stanza is five lines long. The rhythms of the poem are mostly iambic, with the stress falling on every second syllable. The meter adheres very closely to the hymn, or common, meter used in more than half of Dickinson's poems. Each stanza in this meter should rhyme at the second and fourth lines so that the rhyme scheme would be *ABAB* or, less often, *ABCB*. The syllable count in hymn, or common, meter alternated between eight and six in each line, and Dickinson's lines here fall closely enough to that pattern, with some deviations, particularly in the third stanza.

The poem rhymes in the second and fourth lines of each stanza with the exception, again, of the third stanza, in which the rhyme is at the third and fifth lines. These, however, are off rhymes, with consonants that are identical but different vowel sounds.

The only mark of punctuation in this poem is the dash. Dickinson used dashes freely, both in her poems and her prose. Here, it feels particularly apt, as the dash seems to convey the movement of the train through space and time. The final dash allows the poem a sense of openendedness, as the train stops, but only temporarily. The reader might also note that none of the stanzas terminate. That is, the concluding line of each stanza is the opening phrase to the next. In stanza one, when we observe the train's "prodigious step" (4), we must continue on to see that it is stepping "around a Pile of Mountains" (5). So in each stanza, the reader is pushed forward with the train.

Sample Topics:

1. **Speed depicted in the form:** How is the form of "I like to see it lap the Miles" particularly suited to its subject?

An essay like this would look at the various elements of Dickinson's poem that cause the reader to read quickly, just as the train moves. You would wish to look at the punctuation, at the repetitions of sounds, and particularly at any deviations from the ballad stanza.

2. **Sound repetition:** The poem contains numerous repetitions of sound. How do these repetitions contribute to the overall effect of the poem? Are the sounds Dickinson depicts meant to echo the sounds the train actually makes?

The poem exhibits a great deal of alliteration, assonance, and consonance. You might consider, for instance, the second stanza's use of assonance, in the repetition of strong vowel sounds; the third stanza's repetition of *h, c,* and *ch* (are these meant to sound like the chugging of a train?); or the alliterative sounds of *l* in the first or *s* in the final stanza. The repetition of the phrase "and then" further moves the poem along.

3. **Solving the riddle:** The form of "I like to see it lap the Miles" helps to reveal the answer to the riddle. How could it be argued that every element of the poem is pointing the reader toward an understanding that a train is being depicted?

An essay such as this would discuss how Dickinson's stylistic choices contribute to the meaning of the poem and allow the reader to "see" a railroad. You would want to consider the poem's diction, its meter, the organization of the stanzas, and the punctuation.

4. **Capitalization:** Dickinson is always unorthodox in her use of capitals. Is there logic behind the capitalization in Dickinson's "I like to see it lap the Miles"?

To write this essay, you would simply look at the capital words. You might want to write them down separately from the poem in an attempt to arrive at a thesis. Basically, you will decide if those words are suggestive of any meaning or importance beyond the poem.

Language, Symbols, and Imagery

The language, symbols, and imagery of "I like to see it lap the Miles" are all possible areas of investigation for essay writers. In Patrick F. O'Connell's essay "Emily Dickinson's Train: Iron Horse or 'Rough Beast'?" he argues that the poem may be read as an "apocalyptic vision" (474) of human subservience to technology. O'Connell details how the poem has more often been read as a playful riddle, too light in tone and content for serious examination. There are at least those two strong interpretations possible. Is the train a playful, though powerful, pony, or is it a "beast," as O'Connell terms it, threatening the people and their quiet lives?

Critics Jane Lowrey and Joseph Mitchell give the poem a more biographical interpretation, linking the poem closely to Dickinson's feelings about her father. Basically, they see the train of "I like to see it lap the Miles" as symbolic of Dickinson's father and therefore expressing her feelings toward him. Edward Dickinson was a strong supporter of rail travel and was instrumental in bringing the railway to Amherst. It might also be possible to interpret the train as a symbol of masculine power.

Some of the imagery in the final stanza is specifically religious, and other images in the final stanza might be read that way. The reference to Boanerges in line 14 comes from Mark 3:17, and if you did not know the word's biblical source, that much of the poem would be mysterious. In the story from the book of Mark, Jesus is speaking to two of his more vocal and passionate disciples, James and John. He gives them the name *Boanerges,* which translates to "sons of thunder." *Boanerges* was also at times applied to conspicuously loud preachers and orators. At its most literal, the reference in Dickinson's poem seems to refer to the noise of the train, though it perhaps causes you to reflect on the nature of that noise. Is it somehow divine? Perhaps the noise can be considered reflective of God's grace or power. In the stanza's next line, the train is described as being "punctual as a Star" (15), and the Christian tradition commonly sees in the star the herald of the birth of Christ. In line 16, the stopped train is described as "docile and omnipotent." *Omnipotent* is a word commonly applied to God as all-powerful. In line 17, the train has stopped, not at its station, for that would give the riddle away, but "At its

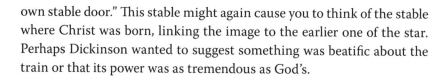

own stable door." This stable might again cause you to think of the stable where Christ was born, linking the image to the earlier one of the star. Perhaps Dickinson wanted to suggest something was beatific about the train or that its power was as tremendous as God's.

Sample Topics:

1. **Religion in the poem:** Is the train meant to be seen as a religious symbol? Your thesis could argue in either direction—that it is or it is not.

   To pursue this topic, you would look particularly at the language and imagery of the fourth stanza to decide whether the religion that is there can be extended to the poem in its entirety.

2. **Personification:** Personification is the giving of human traits to an inanimate object. In "I like to see it lap the Miles" the train, sometimes quite humorously, mimics human and animal behavior. Several topics could come from looking at this personification. Could you argue that Dickinson's personification of the train helps us to "see" the train in a new light?

   Any paper on this topic would look at the ways the train is personified, particularly the imagery and diction used to describe the train and its actions. What sort of personality does the train seem to have? How does Dickinson's use of personification cause you to think about trains in new ways or to better understand, perhaps, how Dickinson views the train?

3. **Train as father:** Do you consider the train in this poem a patriarchal image or an image of male power? An essay could be written that argues with or against the critics who see Edward Dickinson symbolically depicted in "I like to see it lap the Miles."

   In a letter written after her father's death, Emily Dickinson wrote of Edward Dickinson: "His Heart was pure and terrible and I think no other like it exists" (*Letters* 2:538). Her father's strong influence on Emily Dickinson is undeniable, as is his interest in the railroad. An essay that further explored these relationships would look at biographical materials, notably Richard Sewall's biography, to discuss the strong connection between the train and Dickinson's father.

4. **Literal reading:** Sigmund Freud famously remarked that sometimes a cigar is just a cigar. How could you argue that Dickinson's poem could have no other answer than that a train is meant?

Composing this essay will involve discussing the evidence that points to the train as well as the evidence that points away. You might want to consider some of the other contenders critics have brought up, such as Dickinson's father, Christ, or a horse. You would want to successfully argue against these other possible readings.

Compare and Contrast Essays

Dickinson's 1,775 poems allow much opportunity for comparison and contrast among them. For a poem such as "I like to see it lap the Miles," you might find it advantageous to look at some of Dickinson's other riddle poems, for example, "A Route of Evanescence" or "A narrow Fellow in the Grass." These also require the reader to discover their subject in order to answer the riddle. You might find it interesting to look at all of these poems, comparing their similarities and contrasting their differences. Such an exercise might lead some to the thesis that these are poems meant for children or others to claim that these are not among Dickinson's most serious work. A poem such as #1222—"The Riddle we can guess" might provide some illumination in any discussion of Dickinson's riddles.

Sample Topics:

1. **"A Route of Evanescence":** An interesting essay could be written that both compared and contrasted #1463—"A Route of Evanescence," Dickinson's poem about the hummingbird, with "I like to see it lap the Miles." How are these poems similar? How are they different? One possible thesis is that Dickinson,

in these two poems, is masterful at making the reader "see" her subject, without having to "tell" what that subject is.

An essay such as this would look at how the two riddles are constructed. You would likely want to think deeply about #1463's image of "the mail from Tunis" (7) as well as #585's image of Boanerges, the two places in both poems where the language becomes more abstract than concrete. Both poems, it might be noted, try to examine a thing moving too quickly to be seen by the eye.

2. **"A narrow Fellow in the Grass":** This poem was published in the *Springfield Republican* on February 14, 1866, with the title "The Snake." The poem caused Samuel Bowles to remark, "How did that girl ever know that a boggy field wasn't good for corn?" (Bianchi 27). A thesis comparing this poem to "I like to see it lap the Miles" might say, for instance, that while the movement of the snake in #986—"A narrow Fellow in the Grass" is fluid like the train in "I like to see it lap the Miles," it is very clear that the snake is a living, and unpredictable, threat. An interesting essay could also be written that focused on the effect of a poem's having an identifiable speaker, as in "A narrow Fellow in the Grass."

Both poems examine movement, and both are in the form of riddles. What are the other similarities between them? Where are the differences? You might want to discuss the two poems' very different forms. You would certainly want to discuss the "I" of "A narrow Fellow in the Grass," who is, curiously, a male speaker.

3. **"The Riddle we can guess":** In this poem, #1222, Dickinson writes: "The Riddle we can guess / We speedily despise" (1–2). Such a sentiment could provide another topic to address regarding "I like to see it lap the Miles." Is it possible that Dickinson wants the subject of her poem to be apprehended, but not too easily?

A paper on this topic would look at the way the poet both directs the reader toward the answer to her riddle and how she also directs the reader away. You might discuss how the train goes unnamed. You might also want to look at another famous poem by Dickinson about speaking indirectly: #1129—"Tell all the truth but tell it slant."

4. **Poems for children:** Reading other riddle poems by Dickinson could lead you to the conclusion that these poems were primarily meant for children, and an essay could be written that argued that these poems are more suitable for children. Do you think Dickinson meant for some of her poems to be enjoyed only by young people?

An essay intented to make the argument that Dickinson's riddles are meant for a juvenile audience would look at some other examples of her riddle poems, such as #986—"A narrow Fellow in the Grass" or #1463—"A Route of Evanescence." The conclusion that might be drawn by such an essay is that these poems are less "serious" than some of her others.

Bibliography and Online Resources

Banchi, Martha Dickinson. *Emily Dickinson Face to Face.* Boston: Houghton Mifflin, 1932.

Johnson, Thomas H., ed. *The Poems of Emily Dickinson.* 3 vols. Cambridge, MA: Harvard UP, 1979.

Johnson, Thomas H., and Theodora Ward, eds. *The Letters of Emily Dickinson.* 3 vols. Cambridge, MA: Harvard UP, 1986.

Lowrey, R. E. "'Boanerges': An Encomium for Edward Dickinson." *Arizona Quarterly* 26 (1970): 54–58.

Mitchell, Domhnall. "The Train, the Father, His Daughter, and Her Poem: A Reading of Emily Dickinson's 'I like to see it lap the Miles.'" *The Emily Dickinson Journal* 7.1 (1998): 1–26.

O'Connell, Patrick. "Emily Dickinson's Train: Iron Horse or 'Rough Beast'?" *American Literature* 52.3 (Nov. 1980): 469.

Sewall, Richard B. *The Life of Emily Dickinson.* Cambridge, MA: Harvard UP, 1974.

Sielke, Sabine. "Emily Dickinson." *The Greenwood Encyclopedia of American Poets and Poetry.* Ed. Jeffery Gray. Vol. 2. Westport, CT: Greenwood Press, 2006.

#613—
"THEY SHUT ME
UP IN PROSE"

READING TO WRITE

MODERN READERS of Dickinson's "They shut me up in Prose" might be struck by the second's line's "little Girl" even more than the idea of being "shut . . . up in Prose." The idea of being shut up, either literally or figuratively, may be perceived as offensive, as might the reference to being a little girl. Perhaps it is the idea of anyone as willful as the speaker being subjected to another authority that is offputting.

Dickinson's poem compares prose to being put "in the Closet— / Because they liked me 'still'" (3–4). This would be a good point to remind yourself that the speaker of the poem is not necessarily Dickinson herself. There is no evidence that she was ever put into a closet as a child, but the image is a powerful one, as are those that follow. In stanza two, she writes that if they could have "peeped" (5), they would have seen her "Brain—go round" (6). Her brain is not only free but wildly so. The use of the word *peeped* may be in the spirit of a pun, for the full image is of her brain as a bird. Trying to hold her captive, she says, is akin to putting a bird "in a Pound" (8). The image you should get is the comic one of a bird in a fenced enclosure; you should recognize the ridiculousness of anyone believing they could keep a bird in this way. Stanza three makes this clear, as the bird, and the speaker, will themselves away. The prison is nothing to them.

195

TOPICS AND STRATEGIES

This section of the chapter will seek to provide you with various approaches you might take in writing a paper about this poem. These ideas are by no means exhaustive and should be looked at as a starting point for your own investigation.

Themes

One theme that Dickinson returned to again and again was that of being isolated from other people. Although isolation in her poems sometimes carries the negative connotations you might expect, more often, Dickinson depicts isolation as a point of pride. Experiencing isolation seems to mark her speakers as different in the most positive of ways: they are intellectuals, seers, artists, and poets. In this poem, the isolation may be physically real, but the speaker perceives that it is an illusion.

So a reversal takes place in that what others might consider isolation, the speaker finds freedom. It is reminiscent of the well-known story told by her niece Martha Dickinson Bianchi, called Matty, that upon inviting her into her room and then closing the door, Dickinson gestured about and said, "Freedom, Matty" (Bianchi 66). It is as if behind the door Dickinson found the freedom to be herself without constraint. The result of this is her poetry. "They shut me up in Prose" challenges the notion of what freedom is. It suggests that one cannot be held captive as long as the mind is free.

Girlhood is a theme of "They shut me up in Prose." The putting of the child in the closet is described in the past tense. The attempt to put her into "Prose" is in the present. The focus of the poem is the freedom she became aware of while still a girl. Even in a situation meant to be a punishment, the speaker's mind was her own and free. There may be the suggestion that as a woman, she is even more aware of her power than she was before.

Poetry is another theme of "They shut me up in Prose." There is the implicit contrast between poetry and prose, wherein poetry is freedom and prose is captivity. There is the suggestion that the child came to poetry early and then learned that it would ensure her freedom. There is also the suggestion that poetry is something others would keep from her if they could. Much like the child in the closet, Dickinson wrote her work in the confines of her bedroom, and it was a private practice. When others found out how much she had written, they were astonished. It is possible that because she felt no pressure to obtain an audience, she also reveled in the freedom to write as she wished.

Sample Topics:

1. **Isolation:** How does "They shut me up in Prose" depict isolation as a positive thing?

    One possible thesis is that the speaker's perception, or will, determines reality. This undermines any power others might believe they have over her. But if she were not isolated, perhaps she would not realize the extent of her own power.

2. **Freedom:** How does "They shut me up in Prose" show another type of freedom?

    If you were to write on this topic you might focus on the idea of the secret. The speaker knows a freedom that others cannot imagine. You could also focus on the metaphor of the bird, a familiar symbol of freedom.

3. **Girlhood:** Is there a focus on the idea of girlhood in this poem?

    For instance, does the speaker mention gender because attempting to shut up a child is more likely to happen to a girl than to a boy? Does the gender matter? Is this a feminist poem? Do you think some people would be surprised (particularly in 19th-century America) at a woman's mind that moved as the speaker's seems to?

4. **Poetry:** How does this poem draw a distinction between poetry and prose?

    There are many ways to approach an essay on this topic, and some are discussed above. You could focus on Dickinson's disinclination toward publishing and argue that this assured her an independence that allowed her to become such a distinctive writer. You could argue that Dickinson discovered that being a poet allowed her a freedom not afforded to other women of her time.

Language, Symbols, and Imagery

Prose in this poem becomes synonymous with a host of negative images. It could be interpreted as mundane or everyday, but it is also like a prison. You might consider that every literate person can write prose, but few can write poetry. In that sense, poetry is another mark of the exceptional. Prose might also be linked to being "still," or silence.

She compares prose to a closet, maybe less captivity than a confinement. Many people consider verse to be too ordered by rules to master. Yet, in this poem, to the poet, prose is too confining. The other type of confinement here is the difference between physical confinement and mental freedom. The child is confined in the closet, but the mind is free. Dickinson's ability to turn prose into poetry might be witnessed in her letters. Her prose keeps threatening to fly from the page.

The bird is a familiar avatar for the poet. Usually, the comparison comes in terms of song. The job of the bird and the poet is to sing. Here, the idea of flight is added. As the bird can always escape into flight, the poet has verse to escape into. That this particular bird can behave like "a Star" (10) perhaps gives some suggestion of the height of its flight. This bird can also "laugh" (12) at those who would attempt to cage it.

Of course, that laugh is in part a show of power. Power is another theme of this poem, and you might wish to investigate power as an image in "They shut me up in Prose." A great deal of the poem is about questions of power. "They" who would shut the girl in the closet seem to possess it. The girl knows otherwise. Like those who would attempt to fence a bird, "they" are slightly ridiculous. The final line is an outright dismissal of those people and what they represent, as she says, "No more have I" (12).

Sample Topics:

1. **Prose:** How does "Prose" function in this poem?

There are many ways to approach an essay on this topic. One would be to discuss the idea of prose as captivity versus poetry as freedom. Another would be to explore the idea that prose is a form of silence to the poet. Still another would be that prose is the province of "little girls," while poetry attracts rarer beings.

2. **Confinement:** How does the speaker of this poem defy her confinement?

A possible thesis for an essay on this topic would be that the poet defies captivity by intellectual will. You might also approach this topic by contrasting a girl with a woman. Whereas a girl might be put into a closet for punishment, it is a far less likely option for an "unruly" woman.

3. **Bird:** How does the image of the bird function in "They shut me up in Prose"?

To write an essay on this topic you would likely want to spend some time considering the connotations and the images that come to mind when you think of birds. You might think of freedom, flight, height, solitude, independence, divinity, song, and a host of other things. This bird is distinctive. It has a personality and a sense of humor.

4. **Power:** Who holds the power in "They shut me up in Prose"?

If you were to write on this topic, you might argue that the poem is about power. You might even argue that the poem's message is that poetry is power. To do so, you would focus on images of power in the poem. As in many Dickinson poems, this one subverts the reader's expectations. When you come to the first line or stanza, you might expect the speaker to be a victim; as the poem concludes, you find that the speaker is anything but.

Compare and Contrast Essays

An obvious poem to compare to "They shut me up in Prose" is #657—"I dwell in Possibility." Both contrast poetry and prose, with prose being portrayed negatively. Both give the sense that poetry is a private or secret vocation. The image of the sky, its height and its stars, is present in both poems. There are so many similarities that it may be the differences you choose to discuss.

The wild freedom depicted as belonging to the poet in "They shut me up in Prose" is another of Dickinson's attempts to "place" the poet. The poet is, in a word, exceptional. The poet's power is mystical or supernatural. It defies description. There are a number of Dickinson poems about poets, but two that might be of help to you in writing an essay on "They shut me up in Prose" are #448—"This was a Poet—It is That" and #569—"I reckon—when I count at all." In all three poems, you see Dickinson depicting the poet as having an almost godlike power.

The image of flight is so compelling in "They shut me up in Prose" that you might be interested in finding other Dickinson poems that have similar images. One that could be interesting to contrast with "They shut me up in Prose" is #956—"What shall I do when the Summer troubles." This could make a particularly interesting essay because the latter poem has not been much discussed. In it, Dickinson talks about the summer as a disturbing season, because of its beauty and abundance and also because the one she would like to share it with is far away. A great deal of the summer's beauty is in its birds and their song. She asks, What should "I do when the Skies a' chirrup / Drop a Tune on me" (5–6)? The question almost seems to suggest that though everything about her is moving her to write a poem, the absence of the beloved prevents her. The final stanza is particularly illuminating in reference to "They shut me up in Prose." Poem #956 concludes: "'Twouldn't afflict a Robin— / All His Goods have Wings— / I—do not fly, so wherefore / My Perennial Things?" (13–16).

The image of a child put into the closet is disturbing. This is not the only disturbing image of childhood in Dickinson's work. You might want to contrast or compare "They shut me up in Prose" with some of her other poems that touch on this time, such as #486—"I was the slightest in the house" or #612—"It would have starved a Gnat." "I was the slightest in the house" has almost the atmosphere of a fairy tale. The smallest in the house takes the "smallest Room" and her meager possessions. She is largely silent and entirely unobtrusive. She says: "I could not bear to live—aloud / The Racket shamed me so— / And if it had not been so far— / And any one I knew / Were going—I had often thought / How noteless—I could die" (11–16). "It would have starved a Gnat" begins very much like "I was the slightest in the house," with a child who subsists on little. As in "They shut me up in Prose" the metaphor for freedom is flight. The speaker in "It would have starved a Gnat" has not "the Art" (13) to fly, but the desire is strong.

Sample Topics:

1. **Poetry vs. prose:** How do #657—"I dwell in Possibility" and "They shut me up in Prose" compare?

   If writing about these two poems, it will be easy for you to discuss their many similarities. One is the metaphor of poetry and prose as houses, or places to dwell. The theme of freedom is apparent in both. Your thesis might focus on poetry as freedom and prose as confinement.

2. **The place of the poet:** What does Dickinson feel is the place of the poet?

   One possible thesis is that the poet in Dickinson's poems is a source of endless admiration. Whether the poet flies like a bird, is rich beyond reason, or can create like a god, the poet's abilities defy description.

3. **Flight:** What is the meaning of flight in Dickinson's "They shut me up in Prose" and "What shall I do when the Summer troubles"?

   You might argue that in Dickinson, flight is synonymous with poetry. You might also argue that these are both synonymous with freedom. There is a strong contrast between the poem where flight is easy for the speaker and the other where flight is impossible. Perhaps there are some events one cannot escape, not even with poetry.

4. **Childhood:** How do Dickinson's poems depict childhood?

An essay that contrasted "They shut me up in Prose" with "I was the slightest in the House" might argue that the latter poem depicts a speaker who has not found her voice. You might focus on images of silence and song in the two poems. If you were to contrast "It would have starved a Gnat" with "They shut me up in Prose," you would have to dismiss the idea that the child in Dickinson is undergoing real captivity or starvation. Your thesis might be, rather, that in these two poems, the absence of poetry is depicted as a cruelty akin to the abuse of a child.

Bibliography and Online Resources

Bennett, Paula. *Emily Dickinson: Woman Poet.* Iowa: U of Iowa P, 1991.

Bianchi, Martha Dickinson. *Emily Dickinson Face to Face: Unpublished Letters with Notes and Reminiscences by Her Niece.* Boston: Houghton Mifflin, 1932.

Cushman, Stephen. *Fictions of Form in American Poetry.* Princeton, NJ: Princeton UP, 1993.

Galvin, Mary C. *Queer Poetics: Five Modernist Women Writers.* Westport, CT: Praeger, 1999.

Johnson, Thomas H., ed. *The Poems of Emily Dickinson.* 3 vols. Cambridge, MA: Harvard UP, 1979.

Johnson, Thomas H., and Theodora Ward, eds. *The Letters of Emily Dickinson.* 3 vols. Cambridge, MA: Harvard UP, 1986.

"On 613—'They shut me up in Prose.'" Modern American Poetry. 17 Oct. 2006. <http://www.english.uiuc.edu/maps/poets/a_f/dickinson/613.htm>.

Sewall, Richard B. *The Life of Emily Dickinson.* Cambridge, MA: Harvard UP, 1974.

#657—"I DWELL IN POSSIBILITY"

READING TO WRITE

IN THIS poem, Dickinson writes: "I dwell in Possibility— / A fairer House than Prose" (1–2). Christopher Benfey, author of *Emily Dickinson and the Problem of Others*, says of "I dwell in Possibility": "As in many Dickinson poems, it is the first one or two lines that are most memorable" (33). As you read this poem and consider how to write about it, you may want to pay close attention to those first two lines. Not only are they the most memorable, as Benfey says, but they also set up the conceit (a metaphor that is extended for the duration of the poem) upon which the poem is built. These two lines set up the comparison between poetry and "Prose," along with the idea that poetry is "Possibility." They also introduce the idea that poetry is a "House," a place where one can "dwell," or live.

As Suzanne Juhasz writes in "'I Dwell in Possibility': Emily Dickinson in the Subjunctive Mood," "This is one of many poems in which Dickinson describes the space in which she lived her richest life" (106). One way to approach writing about this poem would be simply to work out the conceit by explaining what sort of space Dickinson describes. Dickinson claims that possibility is "a fairer House than Prose." She goes on to enumerate how it is fairer, and behind every reason is a meaning greater than what seems evident on the surface. While the advantages of being "numerous of Windows" (3) may seem evident, you will want to consider what this might mean in the conceit that the poet is building. Windows allow for looking out and for looking in. They allow in light, and again, you would want to consider what light so often stands for: understanding, hope, happiness, and ease, to name but a few. Also, you would want to remember how important the idea of seeing was for Dickinson. Windows allow someone who is inside to be an observer. Similar to the "Doors" of line four, access and denial of access are both implied.

The poem ends in a seeming contradiction. Although the poet has described a house so large as to encompass the trees and the sky, it is still possible for the speaker to grasp it in her "narrow Hands" (11). As you write, consider how this is possible, as well as other questions the poem may raise. For instance, who would be the "Visitors" (9) to "Possibility"?

TOPICS AND STRATEGIES

This section of the chapter will seek to provide you with various approaches you might take in writing a paper about this poem. These ideas are by no means exhaustive and should be looked at as a starting point for your own investigation.

Themes

One theme present in this poem is the enormous possibility of poetry. As she enumerates the ways the "House" of "Possibility" is fairer than "Prose," you will want to consider how each of the images presented adds to its fairness. Why would a poet like Dickinson value, for instance, "Chambers" that were "Impregnable of Eye" (6)? Remember that as Dickinson constructs this particular house of poetry, she is its creator, and what she emphasizes is likely what is important to her.

Another theme you might want to write about is the idea of isolation or privacy being central to the creative process. As Benfey says, "This poem . . . says something about privacy, as though privacy is tied in some necessary way to what Dickinson calls 'possibility.' . . . Prose would then correspond to the public realm" (28). If you wished, it would then be possible to talk about this poem in terms of Dickinson's reluctance to publish. Perhaps you would want to look at poem #709, which begins, "Publication—is the Auction / Of the Mind of Man" (1–2). That Dickinson perhaps saw her poems as being for an elect few would underscore the idea in "I dwell in Possibility" that her house has only "the fairest"(9) of visitors. As Julia M. Walker writes in "ED's Poetic of Private Liberation," "In this poem Dickinson uses poetry as the definition of the place in which she lives. It is a house of infinite proportions—numerous windows for gazing out, a superior number of doors for going out and coming back in, as many chambers as the trees in the forest. It is a house which protects but does not confine" (21).

Seeing, and all the connotations attached to the idea of sight, are a common thematic concern for Dickinson. In this poem, there are the windows, "more numerous" than in "Prose." Elsewhere, for instance in "I heard a fly buzz—when I Died," Dickinson explicitly equates windows with eyes. The sense in "I dwell in Possibility" is that the speaker can look out, but that others cannot look in. The chambers of her house are "Impregnable of Eye."

Sample Topics:

1. **Poetry vs. prose:** Why does poetry, according to this poem, hold more possibility than prose? Does the poet suggest that poetry is a superior literary form?

   An essay on this topic might explore the ways "I dwell in Possibility" compares poetry and prose. A possible thesis would be that Dickinson's poem proves that poetry is superior to prose by showing that poetry eludes definition.

2. **Privacy and isolation:** How does "I dwell in Possibility" create a space for the speaker to dwell alone?

   An essay on this topic might touch on various aspects of Dickinson's biography, although this would not be necessary. It would be enough to consider why poetry should be a place to live alone. The poem shows "Visitors" being admitted. Why would a poet fantasize about a space such as the one created in this poem?

3. **Seeing:** How much is Dickinson's poetry about seeing?

   Many of Dickinson's poems focus on sensory experience as an important aspect of writing. In this poem, "Windows" are part of what makes poetry an admirable home. It is the first characteristic she names. But why would poetry allow us to see better or more than prose?

4. **Being seen:** Why would Dickinson's poems reveal a reluctance to be seen?

Impregnable seems an unusual choice of words. It carries some connotation of being sexually inviolable. Considering what you know about Dickinson, you might write an essay that reflects why the poet would consider uninvited stares a violation. You could concentrate on her reluctance to publish. You could also shape your essay around Dickinson's reclusive habits, if you wished to take an autobiographical approach.

Philosophy and Ideas

In the final stanza of "I dwell in Possibility," Dickinson writes that in possibility her "Occupation" (10) is "This— / The spreading wide my narrow Hands / To gather Paradise" (10–12). The use of the word *paradise* has led some readers to see this poem as a statement of Christian belief, where Christianity is "Possibility." The "Everlasting Roof" of line seven would be analogous to a heavenly home. The fair "Visitors" of line nine could be other believers, those who have already died and entered paradise, or angels.

It might also be said that Dickinson is offering poetry as an alternative to conventional religion in "I dwell in Possibility." This would mean that any religious imagery in the poem is somewhat blasphemous or at least used unorthodoxly. When she speaks of "Paradise," she would be saying that she (the speaker of the poem) is able "To gather Paradise" in her own hands. God is not necessary to her idea of paradise.

Virginia Woolf's classic essay *A Room of One's Own* (1928) resonates when reading the work of Dickinson. Woolf writes: "A woman must have money and a room of her own if she is going to write" (1). Dickinson, of course, had those requirements and made full use of them. The autonomy she gained from never marrying, remaining childless, and staying within the confines of her father's house gave her the space to write. In any number of poems, she extols the freedom she finds in her own small room. Perhaps one idea present in "I dwell in Possibility" is the possibility the poet carries with her, the freedom of the mind. As Woolf writes in her essay, "There is no gate, no lock, no bolt that you can set upon the freedom of the mind" (Ch 4).

One possible idea in the poem can be surmised from a letter Dickinson wrote to her brother, Austin, on December 15, 1851. In it, she laments the sobriety of the Homestead in his absence: "We do not have much poetry, father having made up his mind that its [sic] pretty much all *real life*. Fathers [sic] real life and *mine* sometimes come into collision, but as yet, escape unhurt!" (*Letters* 161). Just preceding these lines, she writes of an absence of jokes and laughter, so that "poetry" seems to stand for fun and imagination and fancy. It stands in stark contrast to her father's idea of "real life," which he would have govern their household. But when she writes that her father's real life sometimes collides with her own, she also allows that poetry is her "real life." The quotidian, represented by her father, Edward Dickinson, would then be like prose.

Sample Topics:

1. **Christianity:** Is "I dwell in Possibility" a poem of Christian belief?

   An essay that argued that this poem is about Christianity would state that Dickinson is describing a particularly Christian view of paradise. As stated in the book of John, "In My Father's house are many mansions" (14:2). The prose mentioned in line two might be contrasted with the Bible's poetry.

2. **Poetry as religion:** How does this poem support the idea that Dickinson's religion was poetry?

   An essay on this topic might answer the above question with a statement such as this: "I dwell in Possibility" shows the poet creating her own version of "Paradise." Evidence to support the argument might detail how the poet begins by building a place to live, but that place becomes more than any house, it becomes a place where the poet can live forever. Poetry becomes a way of ensuring immortality, and all it takes are her "narrow Hands" to create it.

3. **Personal freedom:** Is the "Possibility" Dickinson describes a form of personal freedom?

If you wished to argue that "I dwell in Possibility" celebrates personal freedom, you might want to read Woolf's *A Room of One's Own,* but it would not be necessary. The poem offers evidence in the imaginary space created by its speaker. She wields complete control over her vision and who has access to it. It is her own "narrow Hands" that hold "Paradise."

4. **Poetry as real life:** How does Dickinson's letter to Austin hint at yet another level of meaning for "I dwell in Possibility"?

When Dickinson writes of the "House" of "Prose," prose might also be read as prosaic: mundane, dull, or uninteresting. Her letter to Austin supports this idea. Poetry then becomes its opposite. A paper on this topic might look for other evidence that Dickinson considered the world of her mind and of her making more "real" than the daily life of her household.

Language, Symbols, and Imagery

Dickinson's "I dwell in Possibility" is a poem rich in imagery. Nearly any word in it, particularly those she chose to capitalize, could be analyzed for its meaning within the poem. What are the possible meanings and connotations of *possibility?* It could be meant literally, that it is possibility without limitation and all the freedom this implies. Because of the juxtaposition of the word with *prose,* however, most readers have taken *possibility* to be a synonym for poetry. Juhasz calls it "the idea of imagination itself" (105). Others have seen it as having a Christian perspective, linking it to the final line's "Paradise."

The house and its windows and doors all hold symbolic meaning. Juhasz suggests that it is a house of language (20). Benfey writes that "the suggestion of openness to experience, in the number of windows and doors, is belied by the 'impregnable chambers.' The doors, in retrospect, seem as much for exclusion as for admission—only the 'fairest visitors' are admitted. ('Inference,' one might say, dwells more in the house of prose.)" (28). Domhnall Mitchell in "Emily Dickinson and Class" sees the large number of windows as a signal of the wealth of the people inside. One could consider this idea of wealth either literally or figuratively. The windows also suggest light and the ability to see, both powerful metaphors in Dickinson's work.

The house created in this poem has many chambers, which she writes are "Impregnable of Eye." For all the many windows, it is a house that no one can see into. Benfey suggests this allows the poet the privacy necessary for her work. The choice of the word *impregnable* also creates an image of violation, as if to look into her house uninvited would be akin to physical transgression.

In the penultimate line of the poem is the image of the speaker's "narrow Hands." Although she spreads them "wide" (11), their span is still narrow, but in them she can gather all of paradise. What do her hands represent? Hands are sometimes a synecdoche for work, as when we ask someone to lend us a hand. For the poet, the hands could symbolize the agency of creation.

Sample Topics:

1. **Possibility:** What does *possibility* signify in "I dwell in Possibility"?

Although a number of critics have answered this question for themselves, there is still room for more consideration of *possibility*. What does it mean, for instance, to "dwell" in it? A paper on this topic might argue that the poet's ability to dwell in possibility is a sign of her unlimited power.

2. **The house:** In this poem, Dickinson constructs a house. What do you think the significance of this house is?

A paper on this topic would spend some time describing the house for its audience. Such a description would benefit from an explanation of the possible symbolism of the elements of the house: What are the doors? What are the windows? You might wish to consider the importance of home to Dickinson.

3. **Impregnable chambers:** What does it mean to have "Chambers" that are "Impregnable of Eye"?

This is such a curious image that it warrants further consideration. An essay that examined this image might wish to talk about "seeing" and "eyes" in Dickinson's work. She creates, after all, a house from which she can see out but others cannot necessarily see into. What are those chambers? Are they aspects of the mind? What are the rooms like in the house of possibility?

4. **Her hands:** What is the significance of the "narrow Hands"?

The poem moves outward, describing a universe of unlimited space and possibilities. In line 11, the focus moves to the speaker's "narrow Hands." It is like the rapid movement of a camera from a panorama to a close-up view. All that has been described, the speaker suggests, is contained in her hands.

Compare and Contrast Essays

Dickinson's #613—"They shut me up in Prose" is a poem that bears comparison to "I dwell in Possibility." In #613, prose has a stifling effect; it is like being shut in a "Closet" (3). The speaker compares herself to a bird. Through the workings of her brain, she is able to release herself from "Captivity" (11) at an instant. The idea of being shut up takes on a double meaning. In prose, she is not only confined, but she is also silenced.

There are a number of poems that might lead you to conclude that Dickinson considered her poetry a secret, and sacred, gift. In #486—"I was the slightest in the House," the speaker tells of a time when she "never spoke—unless addressed— / And then, 'twas brief and low— / I could not bear to live—aloud— / The Racket shamed me so" (10–13). The poem concludes with the idea that she could have easily died in that silence. By contrast, in #454—"It was given to me by the Gods," the speaker is given a present by the gods when she is very small. She keeps it, secretly, in her hand. She says that when she heard the word *rich* it moved her to smile: "Rich! 'Twas Myself—was rich— / To take the name of Gold— / And Gold to own—in solid Bars— / The Difference—made me bold" (13–16).

A theme that runs throughout Dickinson's work is the power of the poet and the power of poetry. Like the little girl with the ability to mint her own gold bars in "It was given to me by the Gods," the poet in #448—"This was a Poet—It is That" is rich beyond measure. A comparison of "This was a Poet—It is That" with "I dwell in Possibility" could help prove that Dickinson was again writing of the poet in the latter poem. Dickinson's #1263—"There is no Frigate like a Book" presents the book and the poem as conduits to a sort of paradise. She also employs a familiar metaphor by saying that poetry and books are available to even "the poorest" (5) and that they may travel with them "Without oppress of Toll" (6). If you were to compare #1263 with "I dwell in Possibility," you would likely concentrate on how Dickinson considers words the passageway to imaginary realms.

Sample Topics:

1. **Poetry and prose:** How could a comparison of # 613—"They shut me up in Prose" and "I dwell in Possibility" result in a greater understanding of Dickinson's views on poetry and prose?

    These poems are very similar. In each, the poet manages to escape her everyday existence. One possible thesis is that these poems show that Dickinson viewed poetry as a means of escape.

2. **Poetry as a secret gift:** How can poems such as #486—"I was the slightest in the House" and #454—"It was given to me by the Gods," when compared to "I dwell in Possibility," lead you to conclude that Dickinson considered poetry her secret and a gift?

    A paper on this topic might argue that Dickinson viewed poetry as a power that she owned. In "I dwell in Possibility," there is the description of tremendous power combined with the idea that it can be seen only by those visitors the poet chooses to admit. "It was given to me by the Gods" shows a child with the ability to turn a word into reality. When she invokes the word *gold*, it comes to her in "solid Bars." But this is a secret she holds in her hands.

3. **The power of the poet:** How does Dickinson characterize the power of the poet?

In Dickinson's work, you see her belief in the absolute power of the poet. Comparing #448—"This was a Poet—It is That" to "I dwell in Possibility" proves the likelihood that the latter poem is also about poetry. To show this power, she sometimes uses words related to material wealth, such as *riches* or *poverty*. At other times, as in "I dwell in Possibility," her descriptions are purely fanciful.

4. **The power of the poem:** What do Dickinson's #1263—"There is no Frigate like a Book" and #657—"I dwell in Possibility" suggest about poetry and the imagination?

An essay on this topic would perhaps state that in these poems, Dickinson suggests that poetry has the power to create worlds in the imagination. The essay would go on to discuss how the two poems compare. Does #1263 somehow amplify #657? It seems that "There is no Frigate like a Book" enlarges upon the idea of "Possibility." One difference between the poems is that "I dwell in Possibility" creates a world available to only "the Fairest." "There is no Frigate like a Book" suggests that anyone can travel there.

Bibliography and Online Resources

Aviram, Amittai. *Telling Rhythm: Body and Meaning in Poetry*. Ann Arbor: U of Michigan P, 1994.

Benfey, Christopher. *Emily Dickinson and the Problem of Others*. Amherst: U of Massachusetts P, 1984.

Campbell, Donna. "Emily Dickinson." *Washington State University*. 30 Oct. 2006. 10 Aug. 2006. <http://www.wsu.edu/~campbelld/amlit/dickinson.htm>.

Dickinson Electronic Archives. 1994. Martha Nell Smith. 10 Aug. 2006. <http://www.emilydickinson.org/writings_menu.html>.

Johnson, Thomas H., ed. *The Poems of Emily Dickinson*. 3 vols. Cambridge, MA: Harvard UP, 1979.

Johnson, Thomas H., and Theodora Ward, eds. *The Letters of Emily Dickinson.* 3 vols. Cambridge, MA: Harvard UP, 1986.

Juhasz, Suzanne. "'I Dwell in Possibility': Emily Dickinson in the Subjunctive Mood." *Emily Dickinson Bulletin* 32 (Jun. 1977): 105–109.

———. *The Undiscovered Continent: Emily Dickinson and the Space of Mind.* Bloomington: Indiana UP, 1983.

Mitchell, Domhnall. "Emily Dickinson and Class." *The Cambridge Companion to Emily Dickinson.* Ed. Wendy Martin. Cambridge: Cambridge UP, 2002. 191–214.

New, Elisa. "Difficult Writing, Difficult God: Emily Dickinson's Poems Beyond Circumference." *Religion and Literature* 18 (Fall 1986): 1–27.

Sewall, Richard B. *The Life of Emily Dickinson.* Cambridge, MA: Harvard UP, 1974.

Walker, Julia M. "ED's Poetic of Private Liberation." *Dickinson Studies* 45 (1983): 17–22.

Weisbuch, Robert. *Emily Dickinson's Poetry.* Chicago: U of Chicago P, 1975.

Woolf, Virginia. "A Room of One's Own." *University of Adelaide Library.* 15 Mar. 2006. 10 Aug. 2006. <http://etext.library.adelaide.edu.au/w/woolf/virginia/w91r/index.html>.

#712—
"BECAUSE I COULD
NOT STOP FOR DEATH"

READING TO WRITE

DICKINSON'S POEM #712—"Because I could not stop for Death" has been called by Allen Tate "one of the perfect poems in English" (13). You may also encounter this poem with the title "The Chariot," given it by Thomas W. Higginson and Mabel Loomis Todd in their edition of Dickinson's works. Like #465—"I heard a Fly buzz—when I died," the speaker of this poem is someone who has already died.

One reason this poem has been so much discussed is the sheer volume of ideas that it contains. The highly imaginative scenario, the carriage ride with death, provokes a consideration of what it means to live and to die; each word seems laden with meaning. The speaker begins: "Because I could not stop for Death— / He kindly stopped for me" (1–2). Death is personified as male and is often read as a suitor, since the carriage ride was a common part of courtship. "Immortality" (4), then, would be the chaperone. But you need not read the carriage ride, necessarily, as an erotic or flirtatious interlude. It is enough to recognize, in order to write an essay, that there are three in the carriage. The rest of the poem is devoted to the journey.

The second stanza begins: "We slowly drove" (4). Death, being outside time, has no reason to hurry. The speaker, now riding alongside Death, has become, in her attitudes, more like him. She has put away the concerns of the living. As you write about this poem, you might pause to consider whether the entire poem is about the slow departure from life.

The third stanza might be representative of the seasons of life. You might notice that the word *passed* is repeated three times, and note, too, that the dead are often spoken of as having "passed away." Here, the carriage passes, first, the school and the children at their play. The carriage next passes the fields of "Gazing Grain" (11), which could be equated with the work of adulthood, the fruit of labor, and also the height of the day. Finally, it passes the "Setting Sun" (12), and the day, and the life, draws to its close.

At this point, the speaker corrects herself, and this type of self-correction is a notable characteristic of Dickinson's verse. You might want to consider what this sort of reversal means here, or what effect it has on you as a reader. Does it make the poem more accessible? Perhaps it leads you to trust or identify more with the speaker. In line 13, the speaker says: "Or rather—He passed Us." The Sun is personified as yet another masculine presence in the poem; his passing seems almost cruel when she considers how she is dressed. The speaker becomes aware that her dress will not protect her from the cold. The reader may think of the way the dead are generally laid to rest, in finery unfit for burial in the earth.

The fifth stanza is a metaphor: The grave is a house. This is where the ride "paused" (17), but it is not necessarily where the ride ended. What do you think of this metaphor? Is it comforting to think of the grave as a house, or is it frightening? You could enlarge upon your feelings about this metaphor to talk about the poem as a whole. Does the poem offer any comfort regarding the end of life, or is the carriage ride horrific?

TOPICS AND STRATEGIES

This section of the chapter will seek to provide you with various approaches you might take in writing a paper about this poem. These ideas are by no means exhaustive and should be looked at as a starting point for your own investigation.

Themes

The theme of exclusion or isolation is prevalent in Dickinson's poetry. Oftentimes, the act of isolating oneself confers a superior status on the individual, as if the ability to be alone signals an enviable independence or power. You might think of a poem such as "The soul selects her own

Society." In "Because I could not stop for Death," the speaker's isolation grows as the carriage ride progresses.

And what is the status of the speaker here? It has been suggested that all of Dickinson's speakers from beyond the grave have an authority that a living speaker could not possess. Often in Dickinson's poems, the status of the speaker is the theme. By marriage, by death, by creating a poem, or by some other experience unavailable to the general population, a person becomes unlike anyone else.

But death comes to all people, not just to a chosen few. Perhaps one of the only ways to differentiate oneself in death is by one's behavior. One theme present in this poem might be expressed as the importance of meeting death with dignity. The protagonist of the poem does not forget who she is when confronted with her end. She maintains her composure; she behaves as a "lady." Some might be tempted to see her as overly passive. Does she allow herself to be taken away, or has she met with a force that cannot be resisted?

In stanza three, the carriage passes children, fields, and finally, "the Setting Sun." This progression might be interpreted as a move from childhood, to adulthood, and into old age, and one theme present in the poem is that life passes by in what can feel like a day. The carriage ride encompasses the day, the seasons, and time. There are many ways you might approach this poem thematically to talk about time as it is depicted here. You might wish to say that life is a journey toward the grave, or that the life on Earth is short compared to the life in the grave.

Sample Topics:

1. **Exclusion:** The poem seems to enact the process of dying as a gradual exclusion from life and life's concerns. Are the dead special because they are alone or because they possess knowledge that the living cannot?

   There are several ways you might approach the theme of exclusion in "Because I could not stop for Death." You might argue that exclusion confers a status on the speaker, that death is a form of exclusivity. It might be equally as valid to read the exclusion described in the poem as being left out of what is really important—living.

2. **Status:** Does the speaker's ability to speak from beyond the grave make her special? Is her social status important to understanding the poem?

The dead are often accorded more respect than the living. You might want to argue that this is the case here. Or you might feel that even though the speaker has died, she is still uncertain about what has happened to her. Perhaps the meaning of her death, if it had any, eludes her. Another approach might be to argue that this is an overly clean, overly civil death. After all, the carriage ride is not a bullet. Is it significant that the speaker seems to be a lady of means?

3. **How to meet death:** Does the poem have anything to teach us about dying? Is there a lesson meant about how to meet death?

One possible theme is that there is a proper way to meet death. Unlike some characters in folklore and literature, Dickinson's speaker does not attempt to run from Death when he comes for her. You might want to argue that this civilized depiction of death is a model. Conversely, you might argue that this model is unrealistic.

4. **The passing of time:** How is time depicted in this poem? How does the speaker's view of time change as she moves through the stages of death?

There are many ways to approach the thematic concerns with time in the poem. The speaker seems, in the first line, to have been too busy to be concerned with death; she "could not stop." Look at the words that indicate time in the poem: *immortality, eternity, centuries, day, slowly, paused, passed,* and *haste.* It could be argued that time is the subject of "Because I could not stop for Death."

Character

Unlike many of Dickinson's poems, this one is rich in characters. Thomas H. Johnson called Death in this poem "one of the great characters of literature" (*Interpretive Biography* 222). The speaker describes his "Civility" (8) and the way he "kindly" (2) stopped for her. From this small bit of evidence, many have assumed Death to be a gentleman. Others have believed him to be a more menacing character, again upon scant evidence.

You may want to consider why the character of Death is so evocative, and why he has been read by so many as the speaker's lover. Admittedly, the speaker and Death could be engaged in the common courtship ritual of the carriage ride, chaperoned by Immortality. But their ride could be still more innocent. The equating of sex with death is an undeniable part of literature. Do you detect eroticism in the poem? Does Death seduce or does he abduct? If he is her lover, what sort of lover do you believe him to be?

Immortality is another character in the poem, and if you are reading the carriage ride as a play between a man and a woman, then Immortality would be their chaperone. For a man and a woman to ride together without a chaperone would have carried a hint of scandal among those of Dickinson's station. Immortality is with them but is not described at all. At the fifth stanza, those on the ride pause before the grave. A question you might want to answer for yourself is whether the ride continues. By the end of "Because I could not stop for Death," has the speaker been abandoned by her companions? Immortality was a central concern of Dickinson's. In a letter to Higginson on June 9, 1866, she writes: "You mention Immortality. That is the Flood subject" (*Letters* 454).

The Sun might be discussed as another character in the poem, but the speaker is the last major character and the last of the three participants in the ride. She is identifiably female and of a certain class; she could be said to be a gentlewoman (you can infer this from her language, her dress, and her actions). What more might be said about her? One of the wonders of this poem seems to be that Dickinson created so deftly, and with very little description, a drama with characters that readers believe they recognize.

Sample Topics:

1. **Death:** What qualities does Dickinson attribute to Death? Do you see him as kind and polite? Do you see him as a seducer? Is Death really cruel?

A paper might be written that argued the figure of Death is as kind as the speaker says he is. You might, on the other hand, wish to argue that his kindness is a deception, and the speaker is naive in her perceptions. There is evidence in the poem for both readings.

2. **Death as lover:** Death in this poem has often been read by critics to be the dying woman's suitor. What evidence exists in the poem for such a reading?

Do you see the poem as an erotic exchange? Does the ride suggest flirtation, engagement, or marriage? Many have argued that this element is present, but there is still more that could be said on this topic. You might wish to write a paper that discussed the nature of this courtship. Does Death abandon her to "Eternity" (24), for instance, or to the grave?

3. **Immortality:** If Death is the woman's suitor, then Immortality would be their silent chaperone. Is Immortality in league with Death and meaning to trick her into taking this ride? Is Immortality what is offered to each of us to make us trust or welcome Death?

A paper that wished to argue that Immortality is Death's accomplice in his deception would likely want to explore why Immortality is silent. Immortality is not described by the speaker; perhaps this is an indication of how little Immortality can be known, even by one who is dead. You might want to discuss the difference between immortality and eternity.

4. **Woman:** You know a good deal about the woman who is the "I" of "Because I could not stop for Death." As the poem's speaker, her perceptions and her voice form the poem. What can you say about her as a character?

A paper could be written to argue that the woman is hopelessly unaware. If she is unaware and naive, then all that she perceives can be called into question. This opens the poem up to variant readings: for instance, what she perceives as a civil drive could be an abduction. The grave could be more ground than house, and eternity might be an unreachable destination.

Philosophy and Ideas

What this poem has to say about death is one obvious question to ask while reading it. The answer is not clear. While some might accept the speaker's perception of death as a kindly presence, others have doubted the speaker's ability to know or to understand. After the concrete imagery of the first five stanzas, the final stanza is largely abstract. It is as if, now that her journey has brought her to the grave, she knows less than she did before. She uses the curious word *surmise* in line 23 to describe what she believes about her destination. Of course, to surmise is not to know and betrays her uncertainty.

The poem closes with the word *eternity*, and another weighty idea is introduced. The carriage held Death and Immortality. How is eternity different from immortality? She has now realized that the "Horses' Heads / Were toward Eternity" (23–24), but has eternity been reached? If it has not been reached, then how can we be sure of its existence? How can a reader, in fact, accept what the speaker has surmised? The final stanza is also in the present tense, while the poem up until this point is in the past. This switch from past to present may be only to show that this is where the speaker is now, or it may suggest that in eternity she is always in the present.

Any poems about death, immortality, or eternity will likely touch on questions of religious belief as well. Dickinson did not openly profess her faith in Christianity, though her poems often have religious content. In a letter to her friend Abiah Root in May 1849, she wrote that she felt pressured to "give up and become a Christian. It is not now too late, so my friends tell me, so my offended conscience whispers, but is hard for me to give up the world." It is hard to miss the repetition of the phrase "give up" to describe both becoming a Christian and giving up the world. "Because I could not stop for Death" seems to have a similar view, that death (and with it Christianity and thoughts of immortality and eternity) steals one from life and that this is implicitly cruel. There is no mention of God in the poem, and the absence seems almost conspicuous.

Returning to Dickinson's letter to Root and the idea of giving up the world, you might want to look at the progression of the carriage. Like Dickinson's "I heard a Fly buzz—when I died," this poem depicts the process of dying as a slow relinquishing of the things of life, shown as a diminishment of sight. Looking in particular at stanza three, you will notice that what the speaker sees changes. In the poem's final stanza, the horses are reduced to only "Horses' Heads," and it is as if all she can see at this point are those heads, nothing else, and all that is left of her life is this focus and movement toward eternity.

Sample Topics:

1. **The nature of death:** What does this poem say about the nature of death? Is death to be welcomed or feared?

   An essay could be written to argue this question from either perspective. From a Christian viewpoint, the movement toward eternity and the giving up of "labor" and "leisure" (7) is surely positive. From a more worldly perspective, those scenes "passed" in stanza three might be too wonderful to be forgotten entirely, even in the grave.

2. **The nature of eternity:** Does "Because I could not stop for Death" draw a distinction between eternity and immortality?

   Would you argue that such a distinction has been made? If so, then what is the difference? Does immortality hold a promise of the Christian afterlife that eternity does not? One possible thesis for a paper addressing these questions might be the following: The final line of Dickinson's "Because I could not stop for Death" shows eternity as a perhaps unreachable goal.

3. **Religious belief:** "Because I could not stop for Death" does not have a conventional view of the afterlife. What sort of afterlife is depicted here?

   A paper discussing religious belief in this poem might mention such things as the absence of God in the poem, as a character or as a promise. It might focus on stanza five and the depiction of the grave as a home, perhaps implying that this resting place is truly final.

4. **Seeing:** Dickinson's poems suggest a belief that life is experience. Seeing is often a metaphor for living. How does this poem express that idea?

A paper examining this idea would likely focus on stanzas three and six. In stanza three, the speaker of the poem tells us what she is seeing as she rides, and her sight is unique. While schoolchildren are a common enough sight, what is one to make of the "Gazing Grain" or the curious idea of passing the "Setting Sun" (which she then corrects in stanza four)? By stanza six, her sight has been reduced to just those "Horses' Heads."

Form and Genre

In form and genre, "Because I could not stop for Death" could almost be said to fall between the lyric and the narrative. It is written in common, or hymn, meter: four lines per stanza, with a pattern of four beats in the first and third lines of each stanza and three beats in the second and fourth lines. This form is reflective of the traditional ballad, with four lines per stanza and four beats in every line. In a traditional ballad, the ending would be tragic. Usually, someone would die. Perhaps there would be a ghost or some otherworldly presence. A hymn, meanwhile, would end triumphantly, often with a vision of the Christian afterlife in paradise. You can see how, in form and content, "Because I could not stop for Death" seems to straddle the two genres.

"Because I could not stop for Death" can also be read as an allegory, wherein each element of the poem also has a literal interpretation. The fanciful idea of a carriage ride with Death could be interpreted as a literal journey to death: an illness, the process of dying, or the process of living. Some critics, such as William Galperin, see the poem as an allegory for marriage. In that reading, a suitor is like Death, and the home becomes a grave to the naive young woman who agrees to accompany him. She literally gives up her life to become his wife. The thin clothing she describes in stanza four could be perceived as wedding attire. A Christian reading might see, on the other hand, the speaker becoming the bride of Christ.

When "Because I could not stop for Death" was first published, in 1890, editors Higginson and Todd chose not to include the final stanza. The poem was not published in its entirety until 1955. Without the final four lines and all they contain, particularly the switch into the present tense, "Because I could not stop for Death" is a very different poem. The final stanza allows the speaker to continue from or beyond the grave, while the fifth stanza pauses and ends with the metaphor of the grave as house. A paper might be written contrasting the two different forms in which this poem appeared.

Sample Topics:

1. **Ballad:** How is "Because I could not stop for Death" like a traditional ballad?

   A paper on this topic would look closely at the ballad form and what it traditionally has been. A good case could be made that this poem carefully mimics an orally transmitted ballad. You might find it helpful to listen to one of the several musical arrangements of this poem that are widely available.

2. **Hymn:** Listening to this poem as a song might also lead you to thoughts of it as a hymn. What are the distinguishing features of a hymn, and how does "Because I could not stop for Death" compare?

   You may wish to argue that this poem is more hymn than ballad. In order to do so, you might also wish to answer the question of whether the speaker's death is a positive or a negative experience. A paper on this topic might also discuss Christian views of the afterlife.

3. **Allegory:** The poem presents a literal death as an allegorical carriage ride. Are there other allegorical readings possible?

One common reading of this poem is that it is an allegory of marriage, an institution that Dickinson herself never entered. During the 19th century, a woman or girl usually passed directly from her father's house to her husband's; in every way, marriage represented a shift from one life to another. Does the poem have evidence that supports reading it as an allegory of marriage? If so, what is Dickinson saying about the lives of the women who were her contemporaries? A paper on this topic would attempt to demonstrate that many of the poem's images reflect courtship and an eventual marriage.

4. **Importance of the final stanza:** How does the presence of the final stanza alter your reading of the poem?

The term *stanza* comes from the Italian word for "room." Every stanza should be a progression, like moving through distinct rooms in a house. Therefore, every stanza should be important and essential. Is stanza six essential? A paper on this topic would argue that stanza six represents a true conclusion to the poem.

Language, Symbols, and Imagery

The drive in "Because I could not stop for Death" symbolizes the movement through life and into death. In stanza three, the carriage passes from childhood, past the "Gazing Grain," which in its ripeness might be seen as representative of maturity, and finally past the "Setting Sun," symbolic of endings. When the Sun has set, and the air grows cool (and, by implication, the physical body), death is near and so is the grave. An essay that explicitly examined this ride and attempted to explain each occurrence would delve deeply into the symbolism of Dickinson's poem.

Home was incredibly important to Dickinson. Her letters and her poems attest to this, as does her self-imposed relative isolation in the Dickinson Homestead. She wrote: "Home—is the definition of God" (Sewall 270). In "Because I could not stop for Death," Dickinson uses the metaphor of the grave as a "House" (17). It is a house that is, all but its roof, under the ground. This might be considered an attempt on the poet's part to reduce death to the knowable: a suitor, a ride, a house. Or does it have the opposite effect? Perhaps these homelike metaphors only add to the terror.

If the figure of Death in the poem is understood to be a suitor, then it would be reasonable to conclude that the poem culminates in a marriage of sorts. Perhaps the metaphor is that death itself is a marriage, though some have seen in the poem a commentary on the institution of marriage. The reverse would be that marriage is death. Either interpretation would involve reading the poem as an extended metaphor of marriage. The first three stanzas would then be a courtship. The fourth stanza would describe the bridal dress and the speaker's sense that she is unprepared for what will follow. Finally, the poem reaches the grave or house, the image of a prison to which the woman finds herself confined. The woman has lost her life, whether you read this literally or metaphorically.

"Because I could not stop for Death" is rich in repetition. An essay could be written that argues that the poem's power rests in those repetitions. For instance, the word *stop* appears twice in the first two lines of the poem. The word *pass* in various forms appears four times. The word *paused* in line 17 echoes both. Another form of repetition is alliteration, the repetition of the initial sounds of words. Some examples are *labor* and *leisure* in line seven, *recess* and *ring* in line 10, and *gazing grain* and *setting sun* at the conclusion of the third stanza. In stanza five, the word *ground* is used twice, to end the second and fourth lines.

Sample Topics:

1. **The drive as life:** If the drive is a metaphor for life, what does life consist of?

   A paper could be written that argues that the drive the speaker takes with Death is a metaphor for life. If so, then Dickinson highlights various aspects of life, excluding, perhaps, some you might think are important. By discussing the drive, the stops, the pauses, what is seen, and certainly its conclusion, you might be able to make some claims for what the poem is saying about life. One possible thesis is that life is a slow moving toward death.

2. **Death as home:** What should a reader make of the idea of the grave as a home? Does Dickinson mean for this image to be comforting or frightening?

You might want to read Sigmund Freud's essay "The Uncanny" for his discussion of the definition of *unheimlich.* Loosely translated from the German, this word would point toward a fear of the "un-home-like." Freud argues that fear arises from those things that are first homelike, or *heimlich.* If you used this essay, you might argue that Dickinson's attempts to represent death by the knowable (a suitor, a carriage ride, a house) only emphasize how unknowable and strange it is.

3. **Death as marriage, or vice versa:** Is the poem an extended metaphor about marriage? Does it suggest that death will be like a marriage, or that marriage is like death?

This is really two possible topics. Taking the first, you would argue that the poem is about death, but that Dickinson views death like a marriage: a courtship, a commitment, a pact. A feminist reading might state that marriage, as it is represented in the poem, resembles death. The speaker, who is at first too busy with living to give up her pursuits, is "stopped" by her suitor. In such a reading, it is a literal house that becomes her grave.

4. **Repetition:** Does "Because I could not stop for Death" depend upon repetition to make it more haunting or memorable?

An essay on this topic would isolate the many repetitions in the poem, both those mentioned above and any others you find. Alliteration often seems to move the tone of a poem toward the lighter end of the spectrum. Does it have that effect here? What about the repetition (four times) of "passed" before the carriage "paused"? The use of the word *ground* to terminate both lines 18 and 20 seems to emphasize that the speaker is in the ground.

Compare and Contrast Essays

"Because I could not stop for Death" is essential Dickinson, and so it is a relatively easy poem to turn to for comparing or contrasting with other Dickinson poems. To write a paper on Dickinson's depiction of deathbed scenes, you might turn to poems such as #187—"How many times these low feet staggered," #465—"I heard a Fly buzz—when I died," or #280—"I felt a Funeral, in my Brain." Although there are many areas in which to compare or contrast these poems and others like them, one thing Dickinson does is to describe things the reader is familiar with, such as funerals, housekeeping, carriage rides, and flies, in order to get at what is unknowable: the experience of death.

A powerful image in "Because I could not stop for Death" is that of the grave as a house. There are other Dickinson poems that attempt to describe the grave or the loss of a loved one into the ground. You might want to look at #49—"I never lost as much but twice," #1743—"The grave my little cottage is," or #449—"I died for Beauty—but was scarce."

Perhaps the carriage ride in "Because I could not stop for Death" is a funeral procession. Immortality then might be an undertaker. The speaker's light clothes might be typical funeral dress. Dickinson has a number of poems about funeral processions, wherein the procession is another way to talk about the death. Some of these are #98—"One dignity delays for all," #389—"There's been a Death, in the Opposite House," #445—"'Twas just this time, last year, I died," and #457—"Sweet—safe—Houses."

Poem #1445—"Death is the supple suitor" is an ideal poem to pair with "Because I could not stop for Death." It is a much later poem that seems to compress the ideas of "Because I could not stop for Death" into a more straightforward statement. An essay on these poems would have much to say about how they compare. Looking at even a few of the poems listed above might lead to the conclusion that Dickinson often returned to the themes of "Because I could not stop for Death" throughout her work.

Sample Topics:

1. **Deathbed poems:** How does Dickinson call upon what is familiar, such as a carriage ride or a fly, to represent the mystery of death?

One possible thesis on this topic is that Dickinson's deathbed poems depict death as a gradual diminishment of the senses. Sight and other means of perception are slowly lost so that the dead finally reside in a place that they are powerless to understand. "Because I could not stop for Death" and "I heard a Fly buzz—when I died" would be ideal poems for a discussion of this type.

2. **Grave poems:** Does a comparison of Dickinson's grave poems help to illuminate the imagery of "Because I could not stop for Death"?

In poem #1743—"The grave my little cottage is," Dickinson again uses the metaphor of the grave as house. To compare this poem with "Because I could not stop for Death" might provide a greater understanding of the earlier poem. One possible thesis is that in again depicting the grave as a house, Dickinson is revealing an anticipation of a life after death.

3. **Funeral poems:** Dickinson's poems often depict funerals, from the mundane to the frightening. Does reading another of Dickinson's poems about funerals help you to understand "Because I could not stop for Death"?

The poem "'Twas just this time, last year, I died" compares in many ways to "Because I could not stop for Death." Both contain funeral processions, for instance, and a speaker who is speaking from the grave. One possible thesis is that both poems emphasize how difficult it is for the dead to leave behind the things of the world.

4. **Death, the suitor:** The idea of death as a suitor is a powerful one, and to compare poems in which Dickinson depicted death in this way could produce a strong essay. How does Dickinson treat Death, the suitor?

In "Death is the supple suitor," Dickinson returns to the ideas of the earlier "Because I could not stop for Death." In most every detail of the narrative, the later poem coincides with the earlier, but it only has 12 short lines and contains little imagery. A paper comparing these poems might arrive at an argument stating that the earlier poem is the more effective.

Bibliography and Online Resources

Anderson, John Q. "The Funeral Procession in Dickinson's Poetry." *Emerson Society Quarterly* 44 (Fall 1966): 8–12.

Aviram, Amittai. *Telling Rhythm: Body and Meaning in Poetry.* Ann Arbor: U of Michigan P, 1994.

Cameron, Sharon. *Lyric Time: Dickinson and the Limits of Genre.* Baltimore: Johns Hopkins UP, 1979.

Freud, Sigmund. "The Uncanny." *San Diego State University.* 27 Jul. 2006. <http://www-rohan.sdsu.edu/~amtower/uncanny.html>.

Galperin, William. "A Posthumanist Approach to Teaching Emily Dickinson." *Approaches to Teaching Dickinson's Poetry.* Ed. Robin Riley Fast and Christine Mack Gordon. New York: MLA, 1989. 113–117.

Higginson, T. W., and Mabel Loomis Todd, eds. *Poems by Emily Dickinson.* Boston: Roberts Brothers, 1890.

Johnson, Thomas H. *Emily Dickinson: An Interpretive Biography.* Cambridge, MA: Belknap Press of Harvard University, 1955.

——, ed. *The Poems of Emily Dickinson.* 3 vols. Cambridge, MA: Harvard UP, 1979.

Johnson, Thomas H., and Theodora Ward, eds. *The Letters of Emily Dickinson.* 3 vols. Cambridge, MA: Harvard UP, 1986.

"On 712 ('Because I could not stop for Death')." *Modern American Poetry.* 18 Jul. 2006. <http://www.english.uiuc.edu/maps/poets/a_f/dickinson/712.htm>.

Sewall, Richard B. *The Life of Emily Dickinson.* Cambridge, MA: Harvard UP, 1974.

Tate, Allen. *Reactionary Essays on Poetry and Ideas.* New York: Scribner's Sons, 1936.

Wolff, Cynthia Griffin. *Emily Dickinson.* New York: Knopf, 1993.

#754—
"MY LIFE HAD STOOD—
A LOADED GUN"

READING TO WRITE

CHRISTOPHER BENFEY writes that "[Adrienne] Rich's excavation of Dickinson's life and work, and her focus on such heretofore neglected poems as 'My Life had stood—a Loaded Gun,' set the agenda for feminist criticism of Dickinson's life and work" ("Emily Dickinson and the American South" 44). Dickinson's "My Life had stood—a Loaded Gun" is one of her more violent and least understood poems. Sometimes read as a feminist statement, other times as a love poem, either secular or religious, it may also be read as a declaration of poetic intent and a paean to poetic power. In the first line, the loaded gun is identified as her life. The owner of that life is not herself, but some other who recognizes her. In the second stanza, the owner and she roam together, and where they roam is an exalted type of wood. Curiously, they hunt the doe together. As William Faulkner wrote, it is wrong to kill a doe. And this line in particular has excited some controversy. Perhaps the female the two of them hunt is also Dickinson. Her master and she are out looking, in the words of the cliché, for herself. The "Him" of line seven is again the owner. She, the loaded gun, "speaks" for the owner, and the natural world attends to her sound. Her sound is, of course, as mighty as a shotgun blast, and in the daylight it casts its light upon the valley, and the fire is "Vesuvian" (11), which brings to mind other of Dickinson's lyrics. Eventually, however, their "good" (13) day is done. The night holds other pleasures. Dickinson always draws a distinction between the duties of the day and the plea-sures to be had at night, those activities that she largely hid, such as her writing. At night, the poet says, she guards her "Master's head," and it is a supreme luxury to couch with him. It is better than rest.

The penultimate stanza contains the poem's threat. Her master's enemy is her own as well, and to that enemy she claims to be deadly. With her eye or her hand, she can freeze that enemy. As she says, "None stir the second time" (18). The final stanza of the poem is very difficult indeed. It reads: "Though I than He—may longer live— / He longer must—than I—/ For I have but the power to kill, / Without—the power to die—" (21–24). If one accepts the premise that poetry is her master, a fit-ting paraphrase would be, I may outlive my poetic gift, but I pray it is not so; I have the power now to arrest the world with my speech (that is, to kill), but I have not the power to die. And to live without the gift, as most poets would agree, is not to live at all. It is the poem that does not have "the power to die," a testament to Dickinson's belief in the immortality of the word. But the poetic gun does have "the power to kill" others.

TOPICS AND STRATEGIES

This section of the chapter will seek to provide you with various approaches you might take in writing a paper about this poem. These ideas are by no means exhaustive and should be looked at as a starting point for your own investigation.

Themes

One possible theme apparent here is the power of poetry. In the Dick-inson canon, there are many poems that offer supporting evidence for this reading. In poem #358, for example, Dickinson writes, "When the Ball enters, enters Silence— / Dying—annuls the power to kill" (7–8). These lines are a bit clearer than the final stanza of "My Life had stood—a Loaded Gun." Still, the conceit is the same: The ball is death. Death equals silence. Therefore, the adverse is that life equals speech. Since death deprives one of the ability to speak, and it also "annuls the power to kill," death is also the end of speech, and for as long as one is speaking, one can be assured of life. As she writes in poem #1651, "A Word that breathes distinctly / Has not the power to die." In her correspondence,

Dickinson returns to this metaphor even more explicitly. She says of letters that "an earnest letter is or should be life-warrant or death-warrant, for what is each instant but a gun, harmless because 'unloaded,' but that touched 'goes off'?" (*Letters* 656).

Another theme present in "My Life had stood—a Loaded Gun" is the power of rage. The speaker compares her life to the loaded gun and apparently feels pleasure at her ability to kill. She says: "And do I smile, such cordial light / Upon the Valley glow— / It is as a Vesuvian face / Had let its pleasure through" (9–12). Some find the idea of a woman possessing such rage unusual, even frightening. Others have found it inspiring. The poem shows another facet of Dickinson. The idea that the person who wrote this was frail and shy to the point of neuroses seems unlikely.

The poem has often been read as a feminist statement: the woman making a claim to a great and lethal power. Certainly, one theme running through the poem is the dynamic between men and women, or masculine and feminine principles. This requires that the gun be female, although this is nowhere specified in the poem. By the second stanza of the poem, the gun and its owner are identified as a "We" (5). It is the gun who will "speak for Him" (7). It is said specifically that they "hunt the Doe" (6), and one might wonder why they hunt only the female of the species.

A common theme in literature is the link between sex and death. In stanza four, the "Master" sleeps, and the gun guards him. She says guarding him is "better than the Eider-Duck's / Deep Pillow—to have shared" (15–16). For some readers, this suggests a sexual reticence on the part of the speaker. Would she rather kill for him than lie beside him? She is proud of her ability to protect and to speak. The questions remain about what sort of couple they are. She is waiting until he identifies and possesses her, but to what extent is she possessed?

Sample Topics:

1. **The power of poetry:** What sort of statement does "My Life had stood—a Loaded Gun" make about the power of poetry?

   A thesis for a paper on this topic might state the true subject of "My Life had stood—a Loaded Gun" is that words can be as powerful as bullets. Such a paper would reflect on what Dickinson believes her "Life" to have been and who she believes to be her "Owner." It would discuss images of speaking and of explosion and would try to reach some conclusion about the meaning of the poem's difficult final stanza.

2. **Rage:** Given what you know about Dickinson, does an expression of rage come as a tremendous surprise?

A paper that wished to discuss rage in "My Life had stood—a Loaded Gun" would perhaps focus on traditional representations of Dickinson. The vision of Dickinson that exists in the movie *The Belle of Amherst* or in the tendency of scholars and teachers to refer to her as "Miss Dickinson" does not account for the violence she displays in this poem. You might argue that such anger was likely part of the makeup of any woman artist in 19th-century America. You could also argue that traditional representations of Dickinson as a frail flower should be adjusted to accommodate the anger shown in a poem such as this one.

3. **Masculine and feminine dynamics:** Is this a poem about the way men and women relate to each other, at least as they did a century ago?

Would it be unusual for a woman to consider herself inert or inanimate until "owned" by a man? A paper on this topic might argue that while the poem in some ways replicates the traditional male and female roles, it also subverts them. After all, it is the woman, or the gun, who is the man's protector.

4. **Sex and death:** Can the poem be read as an exploration of the boundary between sex and death?

A paper on this topic would focus on the sexual imagery in the poem. Guns are often thought to be phallic symbols. Is that the way the gun operates here? The idea of possession carries sexual connotations. Why do they hunt "the Doe"? One possible thesis would be that violence is described in terms of sexual pleasure in "My Life had stood—a Loaded Gun."

Language, Symbols, and Imagery

The entire poem is based on the metaphor of the life being a "Loaded Gun." Part of its difficulty is untangling that metaphor and the metaphors that develop the poem's initial conceit. The idea of life as loaded gun (not just a gun, but a loaded one) is a powerful one.

The poem is also built on paradoxes, particularly the final stanza. What does it mean to have "the power to kill, / Without—the power to die" (23–24)? The most obvious interpretation is that the gun is an inanimate object, possessing only the power to kill. But the gun is also a metaphor for life, so you must ask how the life of the speaker cannot die.

Albert Gelpi, in "Emily Dickinson and the Deerslayer: The Dilemma of the Woman Poet in America," rejects a strictly autobiographical reading of "My Life had stood—a Loaded Gun." However, if you read Dickinson's letters to "Master" (compiled by R. W. Franklin), it will be tempting to imagine that the anonymous beloved addressed in the letters may be the same "Owner" and "Master" she alludes to in the poem. Reading the letters will certainly provide you with a different picture of Dickinson. As Gelpi characterizes them, they are "three draft-'letters' from the late 1850s and early 1860s, confessing in overwrought language her passionate love for the 'Master' and her pain at his rejection" (122). It is uncertain whether Dickinson ever sent the letters, and the identity of Master is unknown. She used *Master* as a title for others at times, such as T. W. Higginson, so she did not reserve this word only for her beloved. However, it is tempting to imagine that the beloved is meant when the word *Master* is encountered in the poems.

The central image and metaphor in the poem is the loaded gun. What does it mean to have a life that is a loaded gun? A paper that focused on this image and attempted an analysis of it would nearly always be of interest. Although many critics have responded to the idea of the loaded gun, its symbolic weight has not been exhausted. The poet Adrienne Rich, in her seminal essay entitled "Vesuvius at Home: The Power of Emily Dickinson," wrote that this is "a poem about possession by the daemon, about the dangers and risks of such possession if you are a woman, about the knowledge that power in a woman can seem destructive, and that you cannot live without the daemon once it has possessed you. . . . But this woman poet also perceives herself as a lethal weapon" (87).

Sample Topics:

1. **Metaphor:** What are some of the metaphors in "My Life had stood—a Loaded Gun"? Why have they proven to be so powerful?

A paper on this topic might simply analyze how the metaphor of the loaded gun works throughout the poem in a line-by-line reading. One possible thesis is that a life that is a loaded gun is a life of contained energy. Another is that the poem is a veiled discussion of sexual awakening. Still another is that this poem reveals Dickinson's awakening into the life of poetry.

2. **Paradox:** How can you explain the paradoxes present in the final stanza of "My Life had stood—a Loaded Gun"?

The paradoxes of the final stanza are a little like the riddles of other Dickinson poems. Using evidence from "My Life had stood—a Loaded Gun," arrive at an answer for what this paradox is saying. One possible thesis is that "My life had stood—a Loaded Gun" is a poem about the power of poetry. With Dickinson as poet, her "Master" is the poetry, which must live longer than she.

3. **Master:** How can reading R. W. Franklin's *The Master Letters of Emily Dickinson* change or enlarge your understanding of "My Life had stood—a Loaded Gun"?

Reading Dickinson's Master Letters, as they have come to be called, will certainly give you greater perspective on her life. In addition, it will perhaps move you to believe that many of her poems are about "Master." One possible thesis for an essay on this topic would be that "My Life had stood—a Loaded Gun" is a poem about her love for Master, using details from the letters and from the text of the poem as supporting evidence.

4. **The loaded gun:** Do you think the metaphor of the loaded gun would have interested so many readers and critics if the poem were written by a man?

The idea of a woman's life as a loaded gun seems particularly powerful. Is it the sexual idea of possession and ownership by the man, is it the violence of the gun, or is it something else that makes this metaphor so surprising and apt? Although the idea of service to and protection of the master is there, so is the willingness to kill. The possible subservience in this sort of life is tinged with lethal power.

Compare and Contrast Essays

There are poems in the Dickinson canon that resemble "My Life had stood—a Loaded Gun" but have received very little, if any, critical attention. One of these is #488—"Myself was formed—a Carpenter." Here is that poem's first stanza:

> Myself was formed—a Carpenter—
> An unpretending time
> My plane—and I, together wrought
> Before a builder came (1–4).

Like "My Life had stood—a Loaded Gun," this poem is based upon a metaphor. Here the speaker is a "Carpenter." Eventually a "builder" comes with the intent to perhaps hire her, depending on her skills. The poem's final line attests to her skills, as she sees them: "We—Temples build—I said" (12).

In #506—"He touched me, so I live to know," the speaker is transformed by the touch of an unidentified "He." Putting this poem alongside "My Life had stood—a Loaded Gun" gives credence to the idea that the latter is a love poem. In both poems, male possession changes the speaker's life from one of potential to one of perhaps immortal power.

Rich took the title of her essay, "Vesuvius at Home: The Power of Emily Dickinson," from the final line of Dickinson's "Volcanoes be in Sicily." The image of the volcano is reminiscent of the moment in "My Life had stood—a Loaded Gun" where Dickinson writes that when the gun smiles, "It is as a Vesuvian face / Had let its pleasure through" (9–10). Rich takes the volcano to be a metaphor for Dickinson's power as a poet.

Dickinson's "A Word made Flesh is seldom" contains the following lines reminiscent of the conclusion of "My Life had stood—a Loaded

Gun": "A Word that breathes distinctly / Has not the power to die" (9–10). Both poems share imagery of sexuality and religion. Comparing the two may give you further insight into "My Life had stood—a Loaded Gun."

Sample Topics:

1. **Life as a metaphor:** Although there are a number of similarities between #488—"Myself was formed—a Carpenter" and "My Life had stood—a Loaded Gun," the latter has received much critical attention, whereas the former poem has not received any. Why do you think this might be the case?

A possible thesis might say something to the effect that although Dickinson often used various metaphors to characterize her life, "My Life had stood—a Loaded Gun" speaks to modern-day feminist concerns and so has received more attention than a poem like "Myself was formed—a Carpenter." You might then go on to focus on the lack of conflict and violence in that poem.

2. **The transformative moment:** One of the constant themes in Dickinson's work is the transformative moment, when a person is changed utterly from what she or he was. How does Dickinson depict this moment?

There are many poems that depict such a change. Dickinson's #506—"He touched me, so I live to know" would be an interesting one to compare to "My Life had stood—a Loaded Gun." In "My Life had stood—a Loaded Gun," the speaker is touched and becomes a lethal weapon. In "He touched me, so I live to know," the touch transforms her into a queen.

3. **The volcano:** How can comparing "My Life had stood—a Loaded Gun" to #1705—"Volcanoes be in Sicily" or #601—"A still—Volcano—Life" reveal yet another way of looking at Dickinson the poet?

One possible thesis is that the image of the volcano, silent until it explodes, is a metaphor for Dickinson herself. In a letter to Higginson, Dickinson tells him that whenever she tries to contain herself, her "little force explodes" (*Letters* 414). You might consult a concordance of Dickinson's work to find other instances of *volcano, volcanic, explosion,* or similar words.

4. **The power to die:** In #1651—"A Word made Flesh is seldom," Dickinson again speaks of the power not to die. Does this reveal an answer to the final, paradoxical stanza of "My Life had stood—a Loaded Gun"?

Comparing the two poems might help you arrive at some answer for yourself about that final stanza. The lines from #1651 about "A Word that breathes distinctly" not having "the power to die" perhaps open up only more questions, but that is not the worst way to approach a paper. These lines could suggest an equation like this: life = gun = words = Jesus. This, in turn, could perhaps lead you to a thesis such as this: Dickinson wrote that her "Life had stood—a Loaded Gun"; the owner who picks her up and makes full use of her power is God, when he reveals to her the power of words and her own poetic gifts.

Bibliography and Online Resources

The Belle of Amherst. Dir. Charles S. Dubin. Perf. Julie Harris. 1976. Kino Video, 2004.

Benfey, Christopher. "Emily Dickinson and the American South." *The Cambridge Companion to Emily Dickinson.* Ed. Wendy Martin. Cambridge: Cambridge UP, 2002. 30–50.

———. *Emily Dickinson: Lives of a Poet.* New York: George Braziller, 1986.

Bennett, Paula. *My Life a Loaded Gun: Dickinson, Plath, Rich, and Female Creativity.* Chicago: U of Illinois P, 1990.

Cameron, Sharon. *Lyric Time: Dickinson and the Limits of Genre.* Baltimore: Johns Hopkins UP, 1979.

Cody, John. *After Great Pain: The Inner Life of Emily Dickinson.* Cambridge, MA: Harvard UP, 1971.

———. "Emily Dickinson's Vesuvian Face." *American Imago* 24 (Fall 1967): 161–180.

Franklin, R. W. *The Master Letters of Emily Dickinson.* Amherst, MA: Amherst College Press, 1986.

Gelpi, Albert. "Emily Dickinson and the Deerslayer: The Dilemma of the Woman Poet in America." *Shakespeare's Sisters: Feminist Essays on Women Poets.* Ed. Sandra M. Gilbert and Susan Gubar. Bloomington: Indiana UP, 1981. 122—134.

Johnson, Thomas H., ed. *The Poems of Emily Dickinson.* 3 vols. Cambridge, MA: Harvard UP, 1979.

Johnson, Thomas H., and Theodora Ward, eds. *The Letters of Emily Dickinson.* 3 vols. Cambridge, MA: Harvard UP, 1986.

Rich, Adrienne. "Vesuvius at Home: The Power of Emily Dickinson." *On Lies, Secrets, and Silence.* New York: W. W. Norton, 1995. 157–184.

Rosenbaum, S. P. *A Concordance to the Poems of Emily Dickinson.* Ithaca, NY: Cornell UP, 1964.

Sewall, Richard B. *The Life of Emily Dickinson.* Cambridge, MA: Harvard UP, 1974.

#1129—
"TELL ALL THE TRUTH
BUT TELL IT SLANT"

READING TO WRITE

"TELL ALL the Truth but tell it slant / Success in Circuit lies" (1–2). So begins the Dickinson poem that has been taken by many as instruction on how to write poetry. Her biographer, Richard Sewall, finds "Tell all the Truth but tell it slant" to be a poem key to understanding Dickinson herself. Sewall writes of Dickinson: "She avoided specifics, dodged direct confrontations, reserved commitments. She told the truth, or an approximation of it, so metaphorically that nearly a hundred years after her death and after much painstaking research, scholars still grope for certainties" (3). An example of Dickinson's famous compression, this poem's eight lines touch on larger truths and have sent critics scrambling to point out the exact truth she might be disclosing. In language such as "the Truth must dazzle gradually / Or every man be blind" (7–8), some feel there is evidence that Dickinson is pointing at a particular religious truth. As you read the poem, you may wish to consider what truths are best approached obliquely. Did Dickinson likely have any one truth in mind? Is this poem a statement of poetic philosophy? How can one tell "all the Truth" while telling "it slant"?

TOPICS AND STRATEGIES

This section of the chapter will suggest various approaches you might take in writing a paper about this poem. These ideas are by no means exhaustive and should be looked at as a starting point for your own investigation.

Themes

The idea of coming at a thing "slant" is a primary theme in poem #1129. The truth is important and should be known, but it is also so majestic as to be damaging if we come upon it abruptly. The poem begins with this statement and then essentially reiterates and expands upon the idea until the poem's conclusion.

"Tell all the Truth but tell it slant" also returns to a common theme of Dickinson's: the contrast between seeing and blindness. She uses this metaphor in line three, where she describes the truth as "too bright for our infirm Delight." The "Lightning" (5) that must be explained to children is another example. It is as if looking into the lightning directly, like staring too long at the Sun, will harm the children. At the poem's conclusion, she states that all are like children when faced with the truth, and if the truth does not come gradually then "every man be blind" (8).

The poem asks the reader to think about the nature of truth. Some students begin by believing that "Tell all the Truth but tell it slant" is a poem about "white" lies. Careful reading shows it to be about more than this. It is concerned with not only one truth but *the* truth, and all of it. So an even greater question arises. How does one tell *all* the truth?

Circumference is an important word in the Dickinson canon. In "Tell all the Truth but tell it slant," Dickinson writes that "Success in Circuit lies" (2), and *circuit* becomes synonymous with circumference. If *circumference* is defined as the boundary encompassing an area or object (or in this case, truth), then *circuit* is the course traveled around that boundary. In a letter to T. W. Higginson dated July 2, 1862, Dickinson famously wrote: "My Business is Circumference" (*Letters* 412). In a later letter, Dickinson states, "The Bible dealt with the Center, not with the Circumference" (*Letters* 850), and you get a better idea of how she uses the word. The Bible deals with an ultimate truth; Dickinson tries to come nearer to it by circling around it.

Sample Topics:

1. **Slantness:** What does it mean to tell something "slant"?

An essay on this topic would seek to explain what Dickinson means by this word. One possible thesis is that when Dickinson uses the word *slant*, she lets us know the ultimate truth is unavailable to us; we can only attempt to approach it.

2. **Seeing and blindness:** In the context of this poem, what does it mean to "see"?

Dickinson is always concerned with seeing and not seeing. In this poem, the lightning that is the truth will blind if not got at gradually. You might say that Dickinson is using "seeing" here as a metaphor for understanding. Another possible thesis is that it is impossible for mortal eyes to "see" the truth. Perhaps you can only know it with the heart or on some other level of perception. Perhaps you can only know it after death.

3. **Truth:** What does Dickinson mean when she talks about truth? Are all truths equally dazzling?

An essay could be written attempting to explore the idea of truth in this poem. What does the poem have to say about honesty? A possible thesis on this topic could be that Dickinson's "Tell all the Truth but tell it slant" causes the reader to consider the nature of truth. Those things that are particularly "true," such as love, faith, and death, must be approached gradually and with great respect.

4. **Circumference:** What is Dickinson getting at when she writes, "Success in Circuit lies"?

An essay on this topic would look at Dickinson's diction and her choice of the word *circuit*. The essay would also discuss Dickinson's frequent references to *circumference*. As a thesis, you might say something to the effect that for Dickinson, any topic or pursuit that was worthwhile deserved to be approached with trepidation.

Philosophy and Ideas

An idea that seems to be at the heart of "Tell all the Truth but tell it slant" is the old idea that the truths of God, if experienced directly, would blind humankind. Here is a passage from Exodus on that subject: "And it came to pass on the third day in the morning, that there were thunders and lightenings [*sic*] and a thick cloud upon the mount. . . . And the Lord said unto Moses, Go down, charge the people, lest they break through unto the Lord to gaze, and many of them perish" (9:16–21). God says to Moses that he must keep the people at a distance, for if they see God, they will die. God and his wisdom are often synonymous with the truth.

Another biblical convention is that since humankind is not prepared to know the truth directly it must be taught in parables. As Jesus said to his disciples, who were special among men, "Unto you it is given to know the mystery of the kingdom of God: but unto them that are without, all these things are done in parables" (Mark 4:11). This would be similar to Dickinson's message, except she knows no one is prepared to learn the truth directly.

"Tell all the Truth but tell it slant" has been embraced by a number of communities outside the literary. It routinely finds a place on the syllabus of courses in psychology, philosophy, and medicine. Curiously, this poem has been taken by the medical community as a directive for how to communicate with patients. At one time, it was considered best to keep a negative diagnosis from the patient. Now it is recommended that the truth be told, if told "slant."

The community that has most taken this poem as gospel is the community of poetry writers. The message that has been taken away is that this poem is a prescription for how to write a poem. It would seem that Dickinson followed this course, whether she specifically wrote this poem about poetry writing or not. One common criticism of poetry by those who do not care for it is the difficulty it presents because it does not often state directly what it means.

Sample Topics:

1. **Religion:** How can "Tell all the Truth but tell it slant" be said to be about faith?

The message of Dickinson's poem falls in line with Christian teaching. If you were to write about this in an essay you might bring in knowledge you have about the Bible or Christianity or other religions.

2. **Circuit/parables:** Why would the roundabout way be considered the best way for getting at the truth?

One way to approach an essay on this topic would be to argue that Dickinson's poem is applicable in any discussion of truth. Other than the example of Jesus' teachings, what other parables or stories are used in an attempt to explain what may be unexplainable? You might think about stories that are told to children to explain natural phenomena or the mythology of the Greeks. Without being factually true, these stories sometimes move people to a greater understanding of themselves and their world.

3. **Medicine:** In what other areas of thought or life would "Tell all the Truth but tell it slant" seem to apply?

A paper on this topic might argue that "Tell all the Truth but tell it slant" has implications for people beyond those who are interested in poetry. If you wished to focus your essay on the medical community, you might conjecture about what it means to deliver the truth "slant" if you are a physician, and why this would be preferable to a more direct approach.

4. **Poetry:** Why has this poem been embraced by writers of poetry?

One possible thesis is that Dickinson's poem is reflective of the practice of poetry. Poets believe that multiple meanings can be imparted by the same poem (or image or line, etc.). Rather like the example of Jesus and the parables, the reader's responsibility for discovering meaning, or learning it only slowly, is what gives the message personal importance.

Language, Symbols, and Imagery

This poem begins with a proverb: "Tell all the Truth but tell it slant / Success in Circuit lies." Dickinson often begins in this way, and the rest of a poem is an explication or amplification of the first two lines. The statement seems to admit no argument. And yet the poem is built on contradictions that begin in the first line. The reader is told to tell "all" the truth, but is then told to "tell it slant." The poem does not make clear how this is done (and by its own prescription, perhaps, should not). In line two, Dickinson writes that "Success in Circuit lies." Although the meaning of the word *lies* seems quite clear in context, its presence here may cause you to think about lying. Is to tell the truth slant akin to lying? Other images that are oddly paired are the "infirm Delight" and the idea that the truth "must dazzle gradually."

Dickinson was fascinated with the idea of seeing. In this poem, the images reflect that interest. Light is often synonymous with truth. Here, light becomes the principal image the poem is built upon. The word *slant* might be considered a part of this imagery, as *slant* is often used to describe a way of looking at something. Certainly, by line three, you notice the emphasis on words such as *bright, delight, lightning, dazzle,* and *blind.*

Part of the artistry in "Tell all the Truth but tell it slant" is in the use of alliteration. An essay could be made that traced the alliteration throughout the poem. The major repeated sounds are the "t" and the "s." Carefully tracing the repeated sounds can help you to understand how Dickinson created her poem.

Sample Topics:

1. **The proverb:** How does it affect your reading when a poem begins in this way?

   One reaction you might have to the proverb is a tendency to accept the authority of the poet right away. The poet seems certain of her message. How would you question her?

2. **Contradictions:** What are the contradictions in "Tell all the Truth but tell it slant" about?

The poem begins with a contradictory idea. If you were to write an essay discussing this and the other contradictions, you might say that this poem does what it says. "Tell all the Truth but tell it slant" attempts to get at the truth, but the reader must first resolve its contradictions.

3. **Light:** How is the image of light used in "Tell all the Truth but tell it slant"?

Consider the images of light in the poem. One possible thesis might be that Dickinson uses light as a synonym for truth. To write on this topic, you would use the images, already discussed above, as the basis for your discussion. Light can blind. Lightning can kill. And yet the connotations of light tend to be overwhelmingly positive.

4. **Alliteration:** How does Dickinson's use of alliteration in "Tell all the Truth but tell it slant" create a sense of coherence?

A little bit of alliteration can go a long way, but Dickinson repeats sounds to great effect in this poem. The repeated "s" and "t" sounds of the first stanza are less evident in the second. One possible thesis is that the words *truth* and *circuit* are the basis for the poem. All other words follow from these and in some way echo them.

Compare and Contrast Essays

Gary Lee Stonum in *The Dickinson Sublime* argues that "Tell all the Truth but tell it slant" is less about the poet than about her audience. Further, he argues that this is true of many of Dickinson's poems that have been taken up by poets as expressions of how to do their work or how to live (62–63). You might want to consider if this is true of such poems as #441—"This is my letter to the World," #448—"This was a Poet—It is That," or #569—"I reckon—when I count at all."

Dickinson's poem #365—"Dare you see a Soul *at the White Heat?*" is a curious poem that bears some resemblance to "Tell all the Truth but tell it slant." In both poems, there is the threat of looking too closely at what is real. "Dare you see a Soul *at the White Heat?*" creates a metaphor of the anvil and the forge to describe the soul that is on fire. It also dares its audience to look. As in #1129, light becomes a repeated image.

In #1651—"A Word made Flesh," Dickinson writes, "Each one of us has tasted / With ecstasies of stealth / The very food debated / To our specific strength" (5–8). The poem also says that when the "Word made Flesh" is taken, it is "Nor then perhaps reported" (3). Comparing this poem to "Tell all the Truth but tell it slant" would certainly bolster any reading of the latter as a religious poem. Like the truth in "Tell all the Truth but tell it slant," the "Word made Flesh" is best delivered by an intermediary. In this poem, the intermediary is specifically Jesus. As in other Dickinson poems, the connection between language and religion is explored.

Another poem that has light as a central image is #883—"The Poets light but Lamps," cited as follows in its entirety:

> The Poets light but Lamps
> Themselves—go out—
> The Wicks they stimulate—
> If vital Light
>
> Inhere as do the Suns—
> Each Age a Lens
> Disseminating their
> Circumference—

Here you see not only the idea that poets help to disseminate the light but also the idea of circumference. These two images, so central to "Tell all the Truth but tell it slant," are here aligned with the poet.

Sample Topics:

1. **Her audience:** Are Dickinson's poems about poetry really about her audience?

   A comparison of one or more of the poems discussed above with "Tell all the Truth but tell it slant" may lead you to a thesis such as although Dickinson declined to publish, her poems show a tremendous concern for her audience.

2. **Looking:** How does #365—"Dare you see a Soul *at the White Heat?*" share with "Tell all the Truth but tell it slant" a fascination with looking?

A comparison of these two poems would likely yield some interesting observations. You could trace the image of light throughout both or discuss what it means to see. Why should the reader be afraid of the soul on fire? An answer to this question might lead you to discuss power in both of the poems, or religion, or something else that you see.

3. **Truth and the word:** Why does Dickinson place an intermediary between truth and the word?

This topic would cause you to consider the conventional religious belief that an intermediary is needed between humankind and God. You might be able to arrive at some interesting conclusions by also considering Dickinson's beliefs about language as gleaned from these two poems. One possible thesis might be that these show that Dickinson considered language the equivalent of religion.

4. **Circumference and light:** How do these images compare in "Tell all the Truth but tell it slant" and "The Poets light but Lamps"?

One possible thesis on this topic is that reading "The Poets light but Lamps" makes it clear that "Tell all the Truth but tell it slant" is a poem about poetry. The two poems seem closely aligned. For evidence, you might discuss the emphasis on light and circumference in both works. You might also want to look at "A Word made Flesh" to see how Dickinson considered the endurance of the word to be akin to transubstantiation. The poet may die, but the true word cannot.

Bibliography and Online Resources

Barnes, Daniel R. "Telling It Slant: Emily Dickinson and the Proverb." *Genre* 12 (1979): 219–241.

Gross, John J. "Tell All the Truth but—." *Ball State University Form* 10 (Winter 1969): 71–77.

Hecht, Anthony. "The Riddles of Emily Dickinson." *Obbligati: Essays in Criticism*. New York: Atheneum, 1986.

Johnson, Thomas H., ed. *The Poems of Emily Dickinson*. 3 vols. Cambridge, MA: Harvard UP, 1979.

Johnson, Thomas H., and Theodora Ward, eds. *The Letters of Emily Dickinson*. 3 vols. Cambridge, MA: Harvard UP, 1986.

Pridmore, Jan. "Emily Dickinson (1830–1886): A Guide to Literary Criticism on the Internet for Emily Dickinson." *Literary History*. 27 Apr. 2006. <http://www.literaryhistory.com/19thC/DICKINSON_E.HTM>.

Sewall, Richard B. *The Life of Emily Dickinson*. Cambridge, MA: Harvard UP, 1974.

Stonum, Gary Lee. *The Dickinson Sublime*. Madison: U of Wisconsin P, 1990.

#1732—"MY LIFE CLOSED TWICE BEFORE ITS CLOSE"

READING TO WRITE

THIS POEM was given the title "Parting" in *Poems by Emily Dickinson* (1896). While this might seem an apt title, with the word taken from line seven, you will want to consider as you read whether the poem is about any parting or if it is about the parting that only comes with death. The date of the poem's composition is unknown, but it is often linked to the deaths of two of Dickinson's friends from her early youth: Leonard Humphrey and Benjamin Newton. But we do not know exactly what caused her life to close "twice before its close" (1). Whatever the events were, they affected the speaker as if they were her own death.

Since she is still alive, it is possible that there is more suffering and loss in her future. This is the feared "third event" (4) that may come. The tone suggests that she expects such suffering, unless she herself dies first. The word *unveil* in line three alludes to being shown or seeing, an idea Dickinson often returns to. But the idea that "Immortality" (3) can unveil this suffering also suggests how thin the line is between the living and the dead.

The final two lines are memorable and haunting: "Parting is all we know of heaven, / And all we need of hell" (7–8). The separation that death brings from those we love is a hell to those who are left behind. All we know of heaven is that it parts us from those we love. All we know of either heaven or hell is that it separates us. It is a paradox that contains an essential truth.

Whatever two events befell Dickinson, if you read the poem autobiographically, the lesson she learned from them applies to us all.

TOPICS AND STRATEGIES

This section of the chapter will seek to provide you with various approaches you might take in writing a paper about this poem. These ideas are by no means exhaustive and should be looked at as a starting point for your own investigation.

Themes

Parting is so much a theme of this poem that it was taken as its title. One reason the final lines are relevant and universal is that everyone has some experience of parting, if not with death. Like death, parting is impossible to explain or understand. As she writes in lines five and six, she has experienced nothing "So huge, so hopeless to conceive / As these that twice befell."

In eight short lines, this poem seems to sum up as much as can be said about death by the living. To lose those we love is like dying ourselves. Yet, as long as we live, we live under the threat of such loss. We know nothing of the world beyond except that it separates us. And to be parted is everything. The poem does seem to express doubt about the existence of the biblical heaven and hell, as our knowledge of heaven seems less than our ability to approximate the torments of hell.

This brings up another theme of the poem, which is the theme of knowing. As she writes, "Parting is all we know of heaven, / And all we need of hell." There are some things that are impossible to know with certainty. These things, as she writes in line five, are "hopeless to conceive." Perhaps they do exist, but are veiled by "Immortality." Perhaps it is only the living who are shut out of knowing.

Sample Topics:

1. **Parting:** What does "My life closed twice before its close" tell us about parting?

   If you wished to argue that "My life closed twice before its close" is a love poem, you would not be alone. One possible thesis is that to part from someone you love, Dickinson tells us, is the only way to know what it is like to die.

2. **Death:** What does "My life closed twice before its close" tell us about death?

You might argue that this poem shows that the death of those we love is the worst hell we can experience in this life. You could also argue that the poem seems to accurately show the tragedy that death is to those who are left behind. Another possible thesis is that every death we experience lessens us and brings us closer to the mysteries of the hereafter.

3. **Heaven and hell:** How are heaven and hell depicted in "My life closed twice before its close"?

We do not know, Dickinson says, anything of the biblical heaven and hell. Parting from those we love approximates them emotionally. These two poles of our imagination, heaven and hell, can also be internal states. Heaven is more accessible for believers.

4. **Knowing:** What does Dickinson seem to be saying about knowing?

One possible thesis is that only when we die will we know the secrets of immortality. The deaths of those close to us give us a glimpse. Dickinson's poems show that she was very interested in the question of what we can know.

Compare and Contrast Essays

The losing of someone beloved to death was a subject Dickinson often revisited, so you will find no shortage of poems to compare or contrast to "My life closed twice before its close." On the subject of loss, you might look at #88—"As by the dead we love to sit" or #104—"Where I have lost, I softer tread." In these relatively early poems, Dickinson's take on the subject of loss is a bit less specific than in "My life closed twice before its close." Both poems are set in the graveyard. In "As by the dead we love to sit," the poem discusses how loss makes the dead seem more precious, perhaps, than those we love who are here with us. In "Where I have lost, I softer tread," the poem's speaker shows how she behaves when someone she loves has died. The final stanza makes it clear that she does not know why she has lost; only the angels do.

You will find no shortage of poems on the separation that death brings. Among those you might wish to discuss or read are #1731—"Love can do all but raise the Dead," #1741—"That it will never come again," and #1742—"The distance that the dead have gone." All of these poems are undated, but you will notice from their numbers that Thomas H. Johnson believed them to be composed around the same time as "My life closed twice before its close." Thematically, it is easy to see why. In "Love can do all but raise the Dead," Dickinson makes that first statement and then steps back from it. If love were less human, if it did not need to sleep and eat, if it were more vigilant, maybe it could raise the dead. In "That it will never come again," she writes: "That it will never come again / Is what makes life so sweet" (1–2). This poem seems to argue that the likelihood that there is no hereafter makes us love life all the more. "The distance that the dead have gone" shows a speaker looking so longingly after the dead and hoping for their return that she no longer dwells entirely with the living. She wonders if perhaps she is dead, too. A really tragic vision of separation by death can be found in #1612—"The Auctioneer of Parting." There, God is an auctioneer, calling out, "Going, going, gone" (2). When he "brings his Hammer down" (4) he sells us only "Wilderness" (5) and "Despair" (6). A poem that very much resembles "My life closed twice before its close" in its depiction of parting is #1739—"Some say good-night—at night." The end of this poem has a paradox quite similar to the end of "My life closed twice before its close," though the subject here is not death so much as the simple good-bye. In that final stanza, Dickinson explains that she always says goodnight when others say good-bye: "For parting, that is night, / And presence, simply dawn— / Itself, the purple on the height / Denominated morn" (5–8).

The poem from Dickinson's canon that most resembles "My life closed twice before its close" is #49—"I never lost as much but twice." Johnson dates "I never lost as much but twice" as the earlier poem. It alludes to what would seem to be the same double loss but also suggests that a third loss has taken place. The great difference between them is the attitude of the speaker. If you were to write about these two poems, you might focus on the last stanza of "I never lost as much but twice." There, Dickinson writes that after her two earlier losses, "Angels—twice descending / Reimbursed my store— / Burglar! Banker—Father! / I am poor once more!" (5–8).

If you wanted to talk about Dickinson's portrayal of the prospect of meeting the dead again, you might return to #1741—"That it will never come again" or #1742—"The distance that the dead have gone." "That it will never come again" seems to betray no hope. "The distance that the dead have gone" perhaps holds out a little. In #1760—"Elysium is as far as to" and other of her poems, you will find a bit more hope.

Sample Topics:

1. **Loss:** How do Dickinson's poems depict the pain of loss?

   One thesis you might arrive at by comparing or contrasting "Where I have lost, I softer tread" or "As by the dead we love to sit" with "My life closed twice before its close" is that Dickinson was continually wrestling with the pain of losing those she loved. You might also argue that poetry was her way of grappling with this loss.

2. **Separation:** How does Dickinson depict separation in her poems?

   She never shows separation to be a good thing, even if it is only a good-bye. The threat of death is too closely present ever to be sure that a separation will be temporary. The poem or poems you choose to write about will dictate what you have to say. However, if you were to compare "Some say goodnight—at night" with "My life closed twice before its close," you might write that such a comparison makes clear that the separation in the latter poem is death.

3. **Losing twice:** What does comparing "I never lost as much but twice" and "My life closed twice before its close" tell you about the two events that Dickinson may have experienced?

If you were to write on these two poems you might argue that the speaker of "I never lost as much but twice" is far more in control than the speaker of "My life closed twice before its close." Critics have focused on the demands of the speaker in the former poem. How can she address God so angrily and so decisively? She expects him to reimburse her; she also accepts that such a thing might be possible.

4. **Meeting again:** Do Dickinson's poems hold out a hope of meeting again those we have lost?

Depending on the poem or poems you choose to talk about in reference to "My life closed twice before its close," you might find more or less hope of that future meeting. That would, of course, influence the wording of your thesis. If you compare "Elysium is as far to" with "My life closed twice before its close," you might focus on the idea of the nearness of death to life. Death is separated from life by only a veil or a wall between rooms.

Bibliography and Online Resources

Higginson, T. W., and Mabel Loomis Todd, eds. *Poems by Emily Dickinson, Third Series.* Boston: Roberts Brothers, 1896.

Johnson, Thomas H., ed. *The Poems of Emily Dickinson.* 3 vols. Cambridge, MA: Harvard UP, 1979.

Johnson, Thomas H., and Theodora Ward, eds. *The Letters of Emily Dickinson.* 3 vols. Cambridge, MA: Harvard UP, 1986.

Sewall, Richard B. *The Life of Emily Dickinson.* Cambridge, MA: Harvard UP, 1974.

INDEX

abduction ix
"After great pain, a formal feeling comes" 100, 127–138
afterlife 164, 165, 168–170, 221–222
allegory x, 222–224
alliterations 225, 226, 245, 246
American migration 187
Amherst and Belchertown Railroad 186–187
anonymity 104, 105
apartness 119
audience 247–248
awareness 93

"Bacchus" (Emerson) 76
ballad 222, 223
battlefield 67, 70–71
"Because I could not stop for Death" viii–x, 174–175, 214–229
belief 221–222
Bianchi, Martha Dickinson 45
Bingham, Millicent Todd 45
biographical reading 49, 133, 187
birds 54, 55, 195, 198, 199
Blake, William vi–vii
blindness 242
bobolink 125
body 127–128
body paragraphs 19–23
bog 104–105, 106, 107

Calvinism 166, 167
capitalization 170, 171, 189–190

character 2–4, 217–220
childhood 201–202
children's poems 194
Christianity 65–66, 114, 115, 166, 206, 207. See also religion
church vs. home 123
circuit 54, 244
circumference 54, 55–56, 241, 242, 248
citations 27–36, 32, 33–34
Civil War 49, 50, 66, 94, 95–96, 131, 132, 165–167
clustering 10
coherent paragraphs 20–23
compare and contrast 8–9, 56–57
  of "Because I could not stop for Death" 227–229
  of "I dwell in Possibility" 210–212
  of "I felt a Funeral in my Brain" 100–102
  of "I heard a Fly buzz—when I died" 174–176
  of "I like to see it lap the Miles" 192–194
  of "I'm Nobody! Who are you?" 107–110
  of "I reckon—when I count at all" 180–182
  of "I taste a liquor never brewed" 75–77
  of "Much Madness is divinest Sense" 142–144
  of "My life closed twice before its close" 252–255

of "My Life had stood—a Loaded
    Gun" 236–238
of "Some keep the Sabbath going to
    Church" 124–126
of "The Soul selects her own Society"
    117–119
of "Success is counted sweetest"
    69–71
of "Tell all the Truth but tell it slant"
    246–248
of "There's a certain Slant of light"
    86–88
of "They shut me up in Prose" 199–
    202
of "This is my letter to the World"
    152–155
of "This was a Poet—It is That"
    159–161
compression 116–117, 136, 157, 158, 240
conclusion (essay) 25–27
conclusion (poem) 116, 117
confinement 198, 199
conformity 140, 141
context. See history and context
contradictions 150, 151, 245–246

dashes 46, 135–136
day 230–231
dead, voices of 174–175
death 47–48
    boundary with life 163–165
    characteristics of 217–219
    as home 224–225, 226
    as knowledge 96, 97
    life after (See afterlife)
    as lover ix, 214, 218, 219, 228–229
    as marriage 225, 226
    meeting 216, 217
    nature of 220, 221
    in 19th century 166, 167
    "obsession" with 45–46
    of others 251, 252
    pain vs. 133, 134–135
    as psychological crisis metaphor 90
    reaction to 130
    sex and 232, 233
    views of 174, 175
deathbed 174, 175–176, 227–228

decay 168, 169
definition poems 177
definitions 70
desire 61–62, 64
despair 79, 80, 81
Dickinson, Edward 190
Dickinson, Emily
    biography of 41–44
    correspondence of 43–44, 46–47, 235
    influences on 45–46
    myth of 148, 149
    publication of 44–45
    speaker in poems vs. 41
    writing about vii, 41–60
Dickinson, Susan Gilbert 43, 44
diction 68, 84, 145
didacticism 56–57
divinity 114, 115, 140, 141, 144
doe 230
drive as life 224, 225
"Dulce et decorum est" (Owen) 5
dying, power of 231, 238

editing 44–45, 94, 95, 223
Emerson, Ralph Waldo 142, 160, 161
essays. See writing
essence 157, 158
eternity 220, 221
excess 73, 74
exclusion 112–113, 215–216
exterior 79, 80, 81, 86–87, 96–97

failure 63–64
faith 51, 178, 179
fascicles 44, 53
father, train as 191–192
feminism 51, 230, 232
fidelity 114–116
figurative images 5
first person 12
flat characters 3
flight 201
fly 172
"Fog" (Sandburg) 5–6
formal outline 13, 17–18
form and genre 4–5, 52–53, 135–137,
    170–172, 188–190, 222–224
format 27–36

freedom 196, 197, 206–207, 208
frog 106–107, 109
funerals 94, 95, 128, 228

garden 122, 123
genre. *See* form and genre
gift, poetry as 211
Gilbert, Susan. *See* Dickinson, Susan
  Gilbert
girlhood 54, 55, 195, 196, 197
God 119, 177, 180–182, 243
grave 228
gun 234, 235–236

hands 150–152, 209, 210
Hawthorne, Nathaniel 6, 9
heart 128
heaven 126, 181, 182, 250, 252
hell 250, 252
history and context 7–8, 49–50, 94–96,
  131–133, 148–150, 165–168, 186–188
home 47, 48, 74, 75, 121–122, 123, 224–
  225, 226
horse, *vs.* train 186
house 116, 117, 203–204, 208, 209
humanity 165, 185
humility 146–148
hunting 230
hurt 130
hymn 170, 171, 222, 223

ideas. *See* philosophy and ideas
"I dwell in Possibility" 199–200, 203–213
"I felt a Funeral in my Brain" 90–102, 227
"I heard a Fly buzz—when I died" 100,
  162–176, 227
"I like to *see* it lap the Miles" 183–194
imagery 5, 82, 83, 87, 172, 173. *See also*
  language, symbols, and imagery
immortality ix, 146, 147, 159, 160, 214,
  218, 219
"I'm Nobody! Who are you?" 103–110,
  142, 152
impregnable chambers 209, 210
imprisonment 143
independence 146, 147
inebriation 73–75
informal outline 13, 15–17
inner life 134

interior 79, 80, 81, 86–87, 88, 96–97
interiority 134
introductions 23–25
invention 10
"I reckon—when I count at all" 177–182,
  200
irony ix–x
irreverence 167–168
isolation 47, 48, 91–92, 93, 196, 197,
  204–205
"I taste a liquor never brewed" 72–78

Johnson, Thomas H. 45

Keats, John 152–153, 154
king 173
knowledge 96, 97, 251, 252

landscapes 81
language, symbols, and imagery 5–6,
  54–56
  in "Because I could not stop for
    Death" 224–226
  in "I dwell in Possibility" 208–210
  in "I felt a Funeral in my Brain"
    98–100
  in "I heard a Fly buzz—when I died"
    172–173
  in "I like to *see* it lap the Miles"
    190–192
  in "I'm Nobody! Who are you?"
    106–107
  in "My Life had stood—a Loaded
    Gun" 234–236
  in "The Soul selects her own Society"
    116–117
  in "Success is counted sweetest"
    66–69
  in "Tell all the Truth but tell it slant"
    245–246
  in "There's a certain Slant of light"
    83–86
  in "They shut me up in Prose" 198–
    199
  in "This is my letter to the World"
    150–152
  in "This was a Poet—It is That" 156
letters 43–44, 46–47, 131, 133, 148–149,
  234, 235

life 77, 163–165, 168, 169, 224, 225, 237.
 See also afterlife
light 54, 55, 84, 86, 245, 246, 248
liquid 77
lists 9
literal images 5
literal reading 192
little girl 54, 55, 195, 196, 197
loaded gun 234, 235–236
looking 248
losing twice 254–255
loss 47, 48, 254–255
love 70, 112, 113
lover, death as ix, 214, 218, 219, 228–229
lyric 52–53

madness 90, 92, 93, 140, 141
majority 108–109, 139–140, 143–144
mapping 10
marriage, death as 225, 226
masculinity 66, 232, 233
Master Letters 44, 131, 133, 234, 235
medicine 243, 244
meeting again 255
men 232
messages 152, 153
metaphor 5, 68, 84, 98, 99, 164, 165, 234, 235, 237
meter 53, 135, 136–137, 170, 171, 188
migration, American 187
minority 108–109, 139–140, 143–144
MLA Handbook for Writers of Research 31
MLA (Modern Language Association) style 31–32
Mount Holyoke Female Seminary 42
mourning 80, 81–82
"Much Madness is divinest Sense" 107–108, 139–144
"My life closed twice before its close" 250–255
"My Life had stood—a Loaded Gun" 230–239
myth, of Dickinson 148, 149

name 3–4, 106, 107, 109–110
narrator. *See* speakers
"narrow Fellow in the Grass, A" 193
nature 51–52, 72, 73, 74, 76–77, 146, 147, 178–180

nectar 67
nerves 127–128
New England 131, 132
night 230–231
19th century 49–50, 166, 167
nobody 103, 106, 107, 109
notes 10
numbness 130

Online Writing Lab (OWL) 31–32
outline 13–18
Owen, Wilfred 5

pain 87–88, 101–102, 127–129, 133
parables 243, 244
paradise 122–124
paradox 61, 71, 234, 235
paragraphs 19–23
paralysis 101, 133, 135
parenthetical citations 32, 33–34
parting 250–252
passing 215, 216
perception 140–142, 168, 169, 185
personal freedom 206–207, 208
personal religion 123, 124
personification 191
philosophy and ideas 8, 50–52
 in "After great pain, a formal feeling comes" 133–135
 in "Because I could not stop for Death" 220–222
 in "I dwell in Possibility" 206–208
 in "I felt a Funeral in my Brain" 96–97
 in "I heard a Fly buzz—when I died" 168–170
 in "The Soul selects her own Society" 114–116
 in "Success is counted sweetest" 64–66
 in "Tell all the Truth but tell it slant" 243–244
 in "There's a certain Slant of light" 82–83
plagiarism 34–36
plank 98, 99–100
poems and poetry 51, 52, 56
 Bible as 126
 for children 194

importance of 159, 160, 178, 179
as metaphor 206, 207, 208, 211
possibility of 204, 205
power of 212, 231–233
practice of 243, 244
vs. prose 196–198, 201, 205, 211
poet 147, 156, 157, 158, 159, 160, 177–178, 180–182, 201, 212
"Poet, The" (Emerson) 160, 161
"Poets light but Lamps, The" 247
popularity, of "This is my letter to the World" 148, 149
possessions 168, 169
possibility 208, 209
power 198, 199, 212, 231–233, 238
prayer 125–126
primary sources 27–32
privacy 204–205
pronouns 21
prose 196–199, 201, 205, 211
proverb 245
publication 44–45, 94, 95, 148, 149–150, 223
"Publication—is the Auction," essay on
body paragraphs for 19–23
citations for 27–36
conclusion for 25–27
introduction for 23–25
outline for 13–18
sample 36–40
thesis statement for 11–13
punctuation 31, 46, 53, 136, 170, 171, 188
Puritanism 114, 115

questions, as thesis statement 11
quotations, using 27–36

rage 232, 233
railroad 186, 187–188
reading 1–2, 10
"After great pain, a formal feeling comes" 127–129
"Because I could not stop for Death" 214–215
"I dwell in Possibility" 203–204
"I felt a Funeral in my Brain" 90–91
"I heard a Fly buzz—when I died" 162–163
"I like to *see* it lap the Miles" 183–184

"I'm Nobody! Who are you?" 103–104
"I reckon—when I count at all" 177–178
"I taste a liquor never brewed" 72–73
"Much Madness is divinest Sense" 139–140
"My life closed twice before its close" 250–251
"My Life had stood—a Loaded Gun" 230–231
"Some keep the Sabbath going to Church" 121–122
"The Soul selects her own Society" 111–112
"Success is counted sweetest" 61–62
"Tell all the Truth but tell it slant" 240
"There's a certain Slant of light" 79
"They shut me up in Prose" 195
"This is my letter to the World" 145–146
"This was a Poet—It is That" 156
real life, poetry as 207, 208
reason 102
recognition 104–106
religion 50–51, 65–66, 123, 124, 168–170, 190–191, 206, 207, 220, 221–222, 243–244. *See also* Christianity
religious imagery 82, 83, 87, 172, 173
repetition 21–22, 67, 91, 98, 99, 150, 151, 189, 225, 226
repression 91, 92, 93
rhyme scheme 137, 170–172, 188
riches 156, 157, 158
riddle 183–184, 189
"Riddle we can guess, The" 193–194
round characters 3
"Route of Evanescence, A" 192–193

sample essay 36–40
Sandburg, Carl 5–6
Scarlet Letter, The (Hawthorne) 6
seasons 87, 88
secondary sources 32–34
secrets 152, 154
seeing 54, 84, 164, 165, 205–206, 221, 222, 241, 242, 248
seen, being 206
self-portrait 56

self-reliance 113–114, 143
senses 5, 67–68, 69, 96, 97, 163, 164, 168, 185
sentence order 20–23
separation 254
Sewall, Richard 35–36
sex, death and 232, 233
Shakespeare, William vi–viii
similes 5
society 112, 113
"Some keep the Sabbath going to Church" 121–126
Song of Myself (Whitman) 103–104, 154–155
soul 111–112, 114, 115, 116, 117, 118–119
"Soul selects her own Society, The" 107–108, 111–120, 142
sound repetition 67, 91, 98, 99, 150, 151, 189, 225, 226
sources 27–36
speakers 3, 41, 72, 174–175, 218, 219–220
speed 188–189
spiritual paralysis 101
stanza 94, 223, 224
status 216, 217
Stearns, Frazer 94, 95–96
stone 116, 117
success 61, 63
"Success is counted sweetest" 61–67
suffering 61, 64–65, 82, 83, 86
suitor, death as ix, 214, 218, 219, 228–229
summer 178–179, 180
survival 129
symbols 6. *See also* language, symbols, and imagery
synesthesia 83–84, 85, 172, 173
syntax 84, 85, 128

technology 184–185
"Tell all the Truth but tell it slant" 240–249
tense 98, 99
themes 2, 47–49
  in "After great pain, a formal feeling comes" 129–130
  in "Because I could not stop for Death" 215–217
  in "I dwell in Possibility" 204–206
  in "I felt a Funeral in my Brain" 91–93

in "I heard a Fly buzz—when I died" 163–165
in "I like to *see* it lap the Miles" 184–186
in "I'm Nobody! Who are you?" 104–106
in "I reckon—when I count at all" 178–180
in "I taste a liquor never brewed" 73–75
in "Much Madness is divinest Sense" 140–142
in "My life closed twice before its close" 251–252
in "My Life had stood—a Loaded Gun" 231–233
in "Some keep the Sabbath going to Church" 122–124
in "The Soul selects her own Society" 112–114
in "Success is counted sweetest" 62–64
in "Tell all the Truth but tell it slant" 241–242
in "There's a certain Slant of light" 80–82
in "They shut me up in Prose" 196–198
in "This is my letter to the World" 146–148
in "This was a Poet—It is That" 157–158
"There's a certain Slant of light" 79–89
thesis statement 10–13
"They shut me up in Prose" 142, 195–202
this 145
"This is my letter to the World" 145–155
"This Living Hand" (Keats) 152–153, 154
"This was a Poet—It is That" 156–161, 180, 200, 211
time ix, 79, 96, 133, 134, 216, 217
Todd, Mabel Loomis 44
tone 150, 151, 162–163
topics and strategies 10, 47–57
  for "After great pain, a formal feeling comes" 129–137
  for "Because I could not stop for Death" 215–229
  for "I dwell in Possibility" 204–212
  for "I felt a Funeral in my Brain" 91–102

for "I heard a Fly buzz—when I died"
    163–176
for "I like to *see* it lap the Miles"
    184–194
for "I'm Nobody! Who are you?"
    104–110
for "I reckon—when I count at all"
    178–182
for "I taste a liquor never brewed"
    73–77
for "Much Madness is divinest Sense"
    140–144
for "My life closed twice before its
    close" 251–255
for "My Life had stood—a Loaded
    Gun" 231–238
for "Some keep the Sabbath going to
    Church" 122–126
for "The Soul selects her own Society"
    112–119
for "Success is counted sweetest"
    62–71
for "Tell all the Truth but tell it slant"
    240–248
for "There's a certain Slant of light"
    80–88
for "They shut me up in Prose"
    196–202
for "This is my letter to the World"
    146–155
for "This was a Poet—It is That"
    157–161
topic sentences 19
train 186, 191–192
transformative moment 237
transitions, in paragraphs 21, 22–23
truth 241, 242, 243, 248
20th century 49, 50

unconsciousness 101
understanding 96, 97, 168
unified paragraphs 19–20

universality 132–133
us *vs.* them 104, 105

value, of desired 61–62
victor *vs.* vanquished 62–63, 64
visual arts 82–83
voice 104, 105
volcano 237–238

war 65, 66, 68
weight 85–86
white 54
Whitman, Walt vii, 103–104, 154–155
women 51, 52, 233
words 146, 147, 159, 160, 181, 248. See
    also diction
works cited pages 32, 34
world, *vs.* paradise 122–124
writers, other 57
writing 1–40
    about character 2–4
    about Dickinson vii, 41–60
    about form and genre 4–5
    about history and context 7–8
    about language, symbols, and imagery
        5–6
    about philosophy and ideas 8
    about themes 2
    with citations 27–36
    comparison and contrast 8–9
    conclusions 25–27
    format 27–36
    introductions 23–25
    outline 13–18
    paragraphs 19–23
    plagiarism and 34–36
    preparing for 9–40
    with primary sources 27–32
    reading in 10
    sample essay 36–40
    with secondary sources 32–34
    thesis statement 10–13